Social Contracts
and
Economic Markets

Social Contracts
and
Economic Markets

Judith R. Blau

University of North Carolina at Chapel Hill
Chapel Hill, North Carolina

Plenum Press • New York and London

Library of Congress Cataloging-in-Publication Data

Blau, Judith R., 1942-
    Social contracts and economic markets / Judith R. Blau.
        p.   cm.
    Includes bibliographical references and index.
    ISBN 0-306-44391-0
    1. Sociology--Philosophy. 2. Social contract. 3. Social
    exchange. 4. Social structure. 5. Markets.   I. Title.
    HM24.B553   1993
    301'.01--dc20   93-13915
                                                                                            CIP

ISBN 0-306-44391-0

© 1993 Plenum Press, New York
A Division of Plenum Publishing Corporation
233 Spring Street, New York, N.Y. 10013

Printed in the United States of America

To REVA,
for her impatient, dogged questions and
for her increasingly sophisticated ones

Preface

The thesis of this book is that people enter into social contracts because they are different from one another and have incentives to cooperate. In economic life, people have identical interests—namely, their own self-interests—so they have an incentive to compete. The social worlds that we create, or map, and those that are already mapped for us are increasingly complex, and thus the tracking of rationality is not so straightforward, although it is everywhere evident.

In a sense, this book grew out of two questions: Why hasn't the United States had a second revolution? Or is the revolution yet to come? Many have discussed the current crises that confront contemporary society, such as great economic inequalities, poverty, the declining quality of jobs, the growing power of corporate elites, and racial antagonisms. I attempt to understand these problems in terms of the radical restructuring of social life by economic and spatial forces. My speculative thesis is that social organizations must reinforce social contracts and nurture the opportunities for them to be forged. However, contemporary organizations, particularly economic ones, have internalized the principles of economic markets, thereby inducing competition and easing out cooperation. In defining social contracts, I draw from Rousseau and also from Marx and his analysis of use value. One hopes that new organizational forms based on principles of democracy and community will evolve. In a diverse, multicultural society, this requires great mutual understanding and cooperation and the recognition of differences. Another concern I have is to distinguish between postmodern, a set of historical conditions, and postmodernism, an emerging intellectual and cultural orientation. My position is that postmodernism—with its emphasis on ambiguity, the attempt to recognize and reconcile group differences, and an interest in recapturing and reliving collective experiences—may be a palliative opposition to stark economic and political realities.

In another sense, this book grew out of some of my concerns with social theory, namely, the premises of exchange theory and rational choice theory. Enjoined in a long social contract with the author of a book on exchange theory, I had an opportunity and an obligation to question some of its premises. I also attempt to sort out some of the "middle-range" implications of reconciling agency theory with structural theory. At the level on which I engage these problems, I do not consider them to be contradictory.

The premises laid out in the early analysis (Chapters 1 through 5) deal with contracts and markets, structure and agency, competition and cooperation. Specifically, after positioning my arguments about the problem of reflexivity in the social sciences in Chapter 1, I consider issues of social contracts and economic markets (Chapter 2), cooperation and competition (Chapter 3), civility (Chapter 4), and sources of opportunities (Chapter 5). Whereas the substantive discussions in Chapters 3 through 5 deal mostly with individuals, those in Chapters 6 through 9 pertain to issues on a broader scale: spatial arrangements (Chapter 6), the historical trajectory of social-class composition in the United States (Chapter 7), economic organizations (Chapter 8), and leisure (Chapter 9). In the final two chapters, I grapple with ways in which sociologists might distinguish morals from ethics. This in turn informs my analysis of how ethics, grounded in a recognition of social, political, and economic interdependencies, can be relevant for thinking about the provision of public goods and the preservation of individual rights.

Acknowledgments

The support of the National Science Foundation (SES-8907665 and SES-9144781) for historical studies of cultural organizations has allowed me to work on these related theoretical problems, and my collaborator, Kenneth C. Land, has been patient as I have tried to coordinate the research with writing this book. Other support has been provided by the University of North Carolina's Institute for Research in Social Science, the University of North Carolina's Institute for the Arts and Humanities, and the Program on Non-Profit Organizations of Yale University. For the seclusion to develop the initial conception for this project, I am grateful for the opportunity to have spent a summer residency at the Bellagio Conference Center with support from the Rockefeller Foundation. The intellectual environment of my department at the University of North Carolina is challenging, exciting, and supportive. I thank my colleagues and the graduate students there for contributing to this environment.

Robert K. Merton gave me an initial push to write this book, and I thank him for his continued support and for detailed comments on portions of the early manuscript. Also, very special thanks are due to Ivar Berg, whose encouragement, comments, and prodding mean a great deal to me. Ivar, as well as Rekha Mirchandani and Peter Blau, read the entire last draft and provided insightful comments on my arguments and challenged me on many points. Not all their criticisms have been satisfactorily resolved, but I hope I have addressed their criticisms of logic so that remaining differences are matters of interpretation. I also acknowledge comments by Melanie Archer, Herbert Gans, Richard Hall, and Arne Kalleberg, each of whom provided detailed comments on sections of the manuscript for this book. Ken

Land confronted me with counterevidence and helped to make things more challenging at every turn.

Social debts are as often forgotten as intellectual ones. For their encouragement and interest, I want to thank Sally Massengale, Linda Nathanson, and T. N. Stephenson. And, most especially, I thank a great friend and special colleague, Rachel Rosenfeld. During the many months I was secluded in my study, writing this book, Rachel sent me cheery news from the outside world on e-mail. Her articles on stratification were tremendously helpful in my thinking. I wish I had half her toughness and courage. Although Peter Blau and I have not discussed his earlier book, *Exchange and Power in Social Life*, for a very long time, our continuing conversations—arguments and agreements—about national and international politics, the arts, and sociology, and also our fact-finding discussions (such as "where does autosave save a document?") are everywhere evident in this book. When agreeing and when disagreeing, it is a pleasure to have a colleague-spouse who engages intellectual puzzles with such gusto.

All of us who teach engage in soul searching: How can we attempt to answer students' questions about that which we ourselves have so much uncertainty? How can we help them come up with better or alternative formulations? I wrote this book with this foremost in my mind. Challenged by a student of comparative literature, I was prodded to consider the relevance of ethics and intellectual currents in the humanities for the social sciences. And I hope I have convinced her that economics and sociology might be relevant in the humanities. I am so pleased to dedicate this book to her.

Contents

1

Reflexivity and Social Science

. . . recognizing the social origin of ideas of justice does not commit us to refraining from judging between systems. . . .
—MARY DOUGLAS, *How Institutions Think*

In social life rationality must be—and generally is—finely tuned to deal with differences in order to make the best of them so that we can achieve individual and collective goals. Some people prefer to speak French, some English; a few people are pianists, but there are many more who like to listen to piano music; some individuals are very good at fixing cars, and enjoy doing it for a living, whereas others have trouble finding the oil reservoir. We map our activities in terms of such differences. In economic realms, in contrast, we have identity of interests—the pursuit of our own particular well-being. The complementarity of social interests helps to limit exploitation and cheating (free-riding) in economic life. But not entirely. This is the analytical problem I pursue in this book.

It is important for the analysis I undertake—the distinction between social contracts and economic markets—to consider how Jean-Jacques Rousseau defined "the social contract" and how Karl Marx defined "use value," for they both maintained that in social arrangements people quite naturally monitor cooperation. Otherwise, outside of these social arrangements, in political and economic institutions, cooperation is immensely problematic.

1

SOCIAL SCIENCE AND ITS WINDOW PROBLEM

As social "scientists," most of us are eager to find sufficient regularities in the world to pose accounts as to why things happen the way they do (to find general principles that appear to account for, say, changes in fertility, crime, or poverty rates, or why workers are happy or unhappy in their jobs, or when tolerance increases and when it decreases). Our dreams, hopes, and reflections about the human condition are sanitized, however, by the inherent nature of empirical research; and any temptation to draw grandiloquent, or even spirited, conclusions is squelched by the rules we have made for ourselves. We look at facts through the opaque windows of paradigms, useful theoretical constructions.[1]

For example, Laqueur makes the point that the evidence from DNA research does not sustain a vision of sexual dimorphism, thus challenging both contemporary biological theory and commonsense views.[2]

Yet, social scientists are still by and large obliged to treat "gender" as a "variable" because, if nothing else, it accounts for quite a bit of the explained variance in, say, wages, and assortative mating. Institutions—cultural frameworks, organizations, social groups—also make and apply labels ("women," "men," "children," "window washer," "stockbroker") and confer identities.[3] When social scientists abandon a paradigm—say, a paradigm of gender—they do so with some risk, by flaunting conventional understandings and accumulated empirical generalizations.

It is no wonder that our colleagues in the humanities, who work and write by different rules—imagination, empathy, suspense, and confrontation—believe social scientists to be a boring lot. However, I contend here that there is an important meeting ground: namely, axioms, simple (but hardly simplistic) premises that social scientists pilfer from elsewhere—notably from philosophy and the humanities. Axioms are beyond proof; for another thing, they are too general and vague to be logically confirmed. Here are some examples: people are more or less rational; people are ruled by their unconscious; the existing social order reproduces itself; human societies move in some direction; human societies veer from one extreme to another; reforms are mutually supportive; and reforms undo themselves.[4]

My assumption (axiom) is that people reason things out and act rationally when they have the opportunities to do so. This is not the kind of rationality that assures us of the truth or of attaining wisdom. As Ernest Gellner points out, calculating rationality did not need to be invented; all that was needed was for the chains of traditions to be struck away.[5]

There is, however, an abiding contradiction in rationality. Specifically, there is a difference between economic rationality and social rationality. In our economic lives, we all have identical self-interests, namely, to rationally pursue our own ends or to maximize our welfare. We participate in economic exchange on the basis of identity of interest. In contrast, in our social lives, our rationality is inexorably bound up in relationships, in others' interests, and in collective ends. Our social rationality is thus based on differences, and unless we cooperate, we cannot achieve social objectives.[6]

There is no strong assumption of individualism here, with respect neither to economic nor to social rationality. In a myriad of situations we are ignorant about the implications of various strategies, means, and ends, and in these situations we seek out experts.[7]

If I think that my car is using too much gasoline, I first take some estimates of the mileage I am getting, and then I consult an expert. Or, however much I trust my husband's judgment on most matters, I might evaluate his proposal for a holiday at the North Pole with some skepticism. What is there really to see there? I have terrible circulation; will my toes freeze? I have the forboding sense that I am in for a long excursion without the slightest possibility of having a single hot shower. I consult experts. My willingness to cooperate in this venture presumes I value his company, but before I agree, I reason the whole thing through.

HISTORICAL RUPTURES AND 'ISMS

Both contemporary and retrospective views tend these days to focus on major reversals, catastrophes, disjunctures, and breakdowns. This is not a denial of continuity but a recognition that the world order is in the midst of cataclysmic changes that are difficult to understand. In many academic disciplines there is an interest in trying to discover how new social forms emerge, the inherent weaknesses in prevailing institutions and emerging strengths of alternative ones, and likely sources of change and transformation.[8]

It is argued that a major change occurred in the West around, say, 1970, which involved a reversal of economic and social currents and a process that is still unfolding. *Postmodern* is what Gallie would term an "essentially contested concept"—that is, a concept used aggressively, spiritedly, and with thinly veiled partisan intent.[9] I shall distinguish the historical divide and process, *postmodern*, from its accompanying (or antecedent) intellectual currents, which, for convenience, I shall term *postmodernism* (or poststructuralism).

Because I spell out this historical process in considerable detail in Chapters 5, 6, and 7, I shall only briefly provide the outline here. For some, the postmodern epoch can be dated quite precisely, although the dates vary. Some will fix its beginning with the termination of the Bretton Woods agreement on August 15, 1971, which abandoned the policy of fixed international exchange rates.[10] For others, the post-modern period began with the recognition of the disillusionment with modernist buildings, which is claimed to have fallen on July 15, 1972, the day that a modernist-style, low-income St. Louis public housing development, Pruitt-Igoe, was dynamited because it was unhabitable.[11] Still historically, but with less precision, it began with the 1973 oil embargo and international recession,[12] or, alternatively, the year of the virtual bankruptcy of New York City, specifically, 1975.[13]

Whatever the date, the consequences and the concomitant features have included the downward spiral in the economic well-being of average Americans, increasing economic inequalities, increasing global interdependencies, new waves of American militarism, varieties of expressions of nationalism, the ever-increasing power of multinational corporations, the depersonalization of sources of information, and er-ratic, but generally increasing, political contention over individual rights.

Accompanying these historical conditions are a variety of social responses: a growing awareness and concern about global interdepen-dence; a disenchantment with the notion of historical inevitability; less pretension about high culture; and growing uncertainties about the legitimacy of any particular economic and political system. In cultural and literary terms, this has entailed the dissolution of form and content, subjectivity, and an attempt to subvert the structure of language.[14]

The earlier promise of linguistic structuralism (early Barthes,[15] Saussure[16]) was that language, text, indeed culture, was juxtaposed to a social order that it could reproduce or critique. For some, more recent postmodernists, a prime concern is deconstruction of cultural products, and, more generally, a denial of dialectical juxtapositions. As a turning point, Barthes, chucking the enterprise of critic (i.e., a structured "work" versus an objective critic), proclaimed in 1973 that "all theory, ideology, determinate meaning, social commitment have become inher-ently terroristic."[17] No structure. No critic. No objectivity.

From this point all boundaries and oppositions collapsed for many postmodernists. For example, as "nomad philosophers," Deleuze and Guattari take the deconstructionist project to its greatest extreme, denying the division between representation, subject, concept, and being.[18] Explicitly aligning themselves with the romantic currents of the nineteenth century, Deleuze and Guattari argue that among Lucretius, Hume, Spinoza, Nietzsche, and Bergson (ponderous romantics all) there exists a "secret link constituted by the critique of negativity, the cultivation of joy, the hatred of interiority, the exteriority of forces and relations, the denunciation of power."[19]

All that is left is discourse. In describing the "pure event," the collapse of the origin of a thing with its end, Baudrillard thus expresses the connection between the past and the present:

> Today every event is virtually without consequences, it is open to all possible interpretations, none of which can fix meaning: the equi-probability of every cause and of every consequence—a multiple and aleatory ascription.[20]

Notwithstanding this "too-strong programme"[21] in postmodern-ism and poststructuralism, I nevertheless contend that sociologists should listen. For one thing, the European intellectual traditions have fostered among Americans a growing interest in understanding the local and particular, which often means, the "other," the less privileged. Postmodernism has shown how we are afflicted by all sorts of mystifica-tions (perhaps by its own mode of mystification). For example, it might be said we have paid a high price for our ideology of relativism; we have been content to tell others that their lives and conditions are opaque to us, which also serves the purpose of concealing ourselves from them. In an interesting way, the literature of the postmodernists shows that there are diversities of discourse, that none is especially privileged, and that none is more mystifying than the others. This, I will argue, is the emphasis on pluralism, not cultural and social relativism.

At the same time, when the subject (text) becomes indistinguish-able from the interpretation (critic), dissolved in language, the her-meneutic circle precludes criticism and reflectivity. It is our obligation, Raymond Williams maintains, to engage in

> the steady discovery of genuine forms and social locations, with all the properly cultural evidence of identification and presentation, local stance and organization, intention and interrelation with others, moving as evidently in one direction as in the other [to provide a] specific response to the society.[22]

My objective is not to trace the currents of postmodernist theory but rather to describe some of the ways we might be reflexive about the sociological enterprise under the conditions of the postmodern. I also stress that somewhere between historical events (very big and very small) and cultural currents are the ways that people lead their ordinary lives.

NOTES

1. See Thomas Kuhn, *The Structure of Scientific Revolutions*. Chicago: University of Chicago Press, 1962.
2. Thomas Laqueur, *Making Sex: Body and Gender from the Greeks to Freud*. Cambridge: Harvard University Press, 1990.
3. See Mary Douglas, *How Institutions Think*. Syracuse, NY: Syracuse University Press, 1986.
4. Some of these examples are from Albert O. Hirschman, *The Rhetoric of Reaction*. Cambridge: Harvard University Press, 1991.
5. Ernest Gellner, *Plough, Sword, and Book*. London: Collins Harvil, 1988, p. 175.
6. This is emphasizing a distinction that is generally not made in sociology. For example, Peter M. Blau posits that people seek to adjust conditions and means to achieve ends in social relations and in economic spheres. See his *Exchange and Power in Social Life*. New York: John Wiley, 1964.
7. See Harold I. Brown, *Rationality*. London: Routledge, 1988.
8. For various statements on periodization and discontinuities in history, see Michael Kammen, *A Season of Youth*. Ithaca: Cornell University Press, 1978; Siegfried Kracauer, *History: The Last Things before the Last*. New York: Oxford University Press, 1969; Fernand Braudel, *On History*. Trans. Sarah Matthews. Chicago: University of Chicago Press, 1980; Charles Tilly, Louise Tilly, and Richard Tilly, *The Rebellious Century*. Cambridge: Harvard University Press, 1975; Marshall D. Sahlins and Elman R. Service (eds.), *Evolution and Culture*. Ann Arbor: University of Michigan Press, 1988.
9. W. B. Gallie, *Philosophy and the Historical Understanding*. 2nd ed. New York: Schocken, 1968.
10. Henry Bretton, *The Power of Money*. Albany: State University of New York Press, 1980, p. 161.
11. Arguably, architecture critic Charles Jencks was the first to use the concept *postmodern*; see his discussion of the failure of modernist codes in "The Architectural Sign," pp. 233–242 in Geoffrey Broadbent, Richard Bunt, and Charles Jencks (eds.), *Signs, Symbols, and Architecture*. Chichester: John Wiley, 1980. In this piece he draws on arguments from his *Modern Movements in Architecture*. Garden City, NY: Doubleday, 1973.

12. Bennett Harrison and Barry Bluestone, *The Great U-Turn: Corporate Restructuring and the Polarizing of America*. New York: Basic Books, 1988.
13. For a general discussion, see David Harvey, *The Condition of Postmodernity*. Oxford: Basil Blackwood, 1989, pp. 327–335.
14. See Edith Kurzweil, *The Age of Structuralism*. New York: Columbia University Press, 1980.
15. Roland Barthes, *Elements of Semiology*. New York: Hill and Wang, 1968 [1964]
16. Ferdinand de Saussure, *Course in General Linguistics*. Edited by Charles Bally and Albert Sechehaye. Trans. Wade Baskin. New York: McGraw-Hill, 1966 [1959].
17. Roland Barthes, *The Pleasures of the Text*. New York: Hill and Wang, 1975 [1973], p. 36.
18. Giles Deleuze and Felix Guattari, *A Thousand Plateaus: Capitalism and Schizophrenia*. Trans. and Foreword by Brian Massumi. Minneapolis: University of Minnesota Press, 1987.
19. Ibid., p. x.
20. Jean Baudrillard, "Fatal Strategies," pp. 185–206 in *Selected Writings*. Ed. and Introduction by Mark Poster. Stanford, CA: Stanford University Press, 1988, p. 193.
21. I quote David Bloor here. He argues for a "strong programme" of objectivity in sociology that includes values. See his *Knowledge and Social Imagery*. 2nd ed. Chicago: University of Chicago Press, 1991.
22. Raymond Williams, *The Politics of Modernism*. Ed. and Introduction by Tony Pinkney. London: Verso, 1989, p. 175.

2

Tumbling toward
Two Thousand

Pangloss taught meta-physico-theologo-cosmolonigology. He proved admirably that there is no effect without a cause and that in this best of all possible worlds . . . things cannot be otherwise; for since everything is made for an end, everything is necessarily for the best end. One day when Cunegonde was walking near the castle, in a little wood which was called The Park, she observed Doctor Pangloss in the bushes, giving a lesson in experimental physics to her mother's waiting maid. . . . Mademoiselle Cunegonde had a great inclination for science and she watched breathlessly the reiterated experiments she witnessed; [observing] sufficient reason, the effects and the causes.
—François-Marie Arouet de Voltaire

Our story starts with Voltaire, who lived and wrote in the midst of scientific progress, intellectual optimism, and the increasing momentum of economic production.[1] The century of the Enlightenment would end with the French Revolution, Napoleon's fanatical wars, increasingly strong economic ties among European states, and the advent of the bourgeoisie. Voltaire, it can be said, was a transitional figure in the Enlightenment. Though ever hopeful about the future, he was also earnestly ironic about his utopian and excessively optimistic and good-natured Enlightenment comrades.

Throughout much of the post-Enlightenment period, during the nineteenth century, metaphysicians were devoted to burying the notion of reason and chided the eighteenth-century philosophers for their stubborn cheeriness. But Voltaire is not completely innocent. On the matter of French industriousness, he wrote (from the haven of England), "in matters of importance, the French are just a lot of whipped cream,"[2] and, not chancing progress to nature's providential laws, he admonished his compatriots, "you had better get off your duffs" (more precisely, "*il faut cultiver notre jardin*").[3] *Candide* is a biting satire on optimism.

The premises and logic of Enlightenment thinking have not altogether disappeared in the popular mind. We cherish them still as they rest on principles of progress and goodwill; the affirmation of religious tolerance; the discrediting of torture and slavery; the recognition of the rule of law and the condemnation of arbitrary state power; the idea that the purpose of government is the greatest happiness of the greatest number; and the value of reason and science for the improvement of the human condition.

Still, they rest uneasy in postmodern society, with its indeterminacies, and its big "absences"—that is, absences of mastery, purpose, paradigm, progress, and design. The Eurocenteredness of eighteenth-century thought is also unsettling, as it found fierce expression in colonialism, and cooperation among European nation-states to carve up the rest of the world for domination and economic exploitation.

The argument that follows in this chapter is, unfortunately, based on a superficial analysis of rather complex issues pertaining to the Enlightenment and critical analyses of subsequent nineteenth-century social thought. Some will find it annoying that I have ignored particular contributions (such as Hobbes's and Locke's work on social contracts), but the purpose is to lay out those issues that I believe are of special relevance in contemporary debates rather than an exposition of a long tradition. Besides, in this chapter I lay the groundwork for substantive arguments in later chapters.

SOCIOLOGY: STUCK IN THE ENLIGHTENMENT

Whereas the Enlightenment project provided an overarching ethical framework in the eighteenth century, as the foundations for art, philosophy, literature, and, equally significant, as the guidelines for Realpolitik, the project was considered quite dead in the nineteenth century. All kinds of romanticisms took its stead—nihilism, transcendentalism, idealism, classicism, and hedonism. Never mind that the captains of industry and the heads of state were still rolling on old notions from the eighteenth century, nineteenth-century philosophers were more introspective and looked elsewhere for an anchorage. The romantic movement in philosophy, arts, and literature (the Pre-Raphaelites, Wagner, Thoreau, Victor Hugo, Dostoevsky) sustained a powerful momentum. Voltaire's savoir-faire, both in satire and in earnest, unleashed irrationality of various kinds and admixtures of escapism, romanticism, gloom/doom, and utopian traditions.

Science, on the other hand, veered off into the direction of reason and a belief in clear-headed thinking, for the most part ignoring the ponderous worlds of metaphysics, art, and literature. Likewise in the social sciences there was a sustained attempt to maintain the promise of the Enlightenment project—that is, through a collective commitment to objectivity, reason, the reformability of society—and to analyze social arrangements in terms of the principles of natural laws.

The nineteenth-century precursors of the social sciences in large measure avoided the escapist and romantic traditions of the Enlightenment backlash. For example, while Nietzsche pondered over the inevitability of catastrophe and advocated nihilism, Marx was proclaiming the social and economic rights of citizens and political freedom. While Croce was brooding over how to fit everything under one rubric ("spirit") and to get rid of "cause," Max Weber wrote about rationality and the new economic order and also about the necessity of power holders to obtain social consent and govern on the basis of legitimacy.

As Goethe was drawing the line between what ought and ought not to be explored, Émile Durkheim argued that science could explain morals just as easily as it could explain society, the natural outcomes of reasonable people's extent of mutual interdependence. Even Freud, rather the connoisseur when it came to matters of passions and the nonrational, disclosed the way in which individuals could not only tame their passions, but by understanding their origins as well, could achieve reason and deep fulfillment.

A main point is that throughout the nineteenth century, there was a curious distance between escapism/pessimism/irrationalism in letters, arts, and philosophy and coherence/optimism/rationalism in social thought. This distance only recently has narrowed as the controversies of postmodernism have spilled over into all of the social sciences. The nineteenth-century social philosophers whom we take as the precursors of contemporary mainstream sociology largely ignored their own contemporaries who revealed (or concealed) truth in obscure philosophies that bounced from romanticism to disenchantment, from hyperrational to irrational. Another point is that, with the major exception of Marx and Engels, nineteenth-century social philosophers were also most comfortable with explanations that were compatible with the status quo. They were preoccupied with understanding mechanisms that maintained the social order, the nature of social evolution, and the legitimacy of authority. They were, we might say, a very contented group of men.

Still ignoring Voltaire's sarcasm, twentieth-century sociology sought understanding through systematic inquiry and wiggishly championed the pursuits of cause and effect, historical inevitability, progress and progression, and individual improvement. "Education," Durkheim had said. "More education," echoed Parsons. Both were optimistic. It was as if society operated by a capillary principle, according to which expanding qualifications only need be in sync with ever-expanding opportunities.

Structural-functionalism mistook Voltaire's witticisms as guidelines: "'Tis demonstrated," Voltaire wrote, "that things cannot be otherwise; for since everything is made for an end, everything is necessary for the best end, in this best of all possible worlds."[4] The rally of the twentieth-century structural-functionalist (to exaggerate only a trifle) was that the purpose of it all, as science and reason would disclose, was the proper fit between means and ends. If wisdom teeth, the appendix, the little toe, status differences, prostitution, deviance, low wages, and wealthy elites are with us now, that only goes to show you that they must serve some good purpose.

In this chapter, I attempt to reconstruct a fairly simple explanation of why sociologists—liberal men and women of good will—broke ranks with the philosophical romantic currents of the nineteenth century but now raise cain that we did. Why did we maintain an alliance with the Enlightenment? But, why now, question that we did? My two sources on the Enlightenment project are Alvin Gouldner, American sociologist and critic of the Enlightenment project, and Alfred Cobban, a French historian and ambivalent apologist of the Enlightenment project. Their writings have considerable bearing on how I interpret the relevance of Marx and Rousseau in coming to grips with the difference between economic and social life and the role that culture plays in mediating these two realms.

CRITICS OF THE SOCIOLOGICAL ENTERPRISE

The ultimate death knell to the Enlightenment and its flawed preachments, according to Alfred Cobban, was its embeddedness in

European thought and traditions. What obscured its otherwise human-itarian credo was a fierce nationalism. While European powers unified their own nation-states, they ignored cherished ethical tenets when it came to their client states. Thus, Cobban focuses on the political and economic consequences of Enlightenment Eurocentered thought, the subordination of science and the social sciences to politics, and the abdication of ethical responsibility all around.[5]

As for the romantic movement of the nineteenth century, Cobban argues that it was a consequence of disillusionment with the optimism of the eighteenth century: "Primitivism and subjectivism of the roman-tic movement led almost irresistibly away from reason and faith in human nature."[6] However innocent or not, some members of the scientific community aligned themselves with imperialistic objectives, and others were just ethically indifferent. For the humanist, Cobban, sociology went off its tracks as Comte denounced equality as a source of anarchy and promoted the study of the laws of social evolution as a way of understanding social order. As Comte put it, "If there are (as I doubt not there are) political evils which, like some personal sufferings, cannot be remedied by science, science at least proves to us they are incurable."[7]

Alvin W. Gouldner's book *The Coming Crisis of Western Sociology* was an unrelenting attack on structural-functionalism that held sway in sociology through the 1950s and 1960s, everywhere distancing itself from social and economic crises, as offering great optimism for a world in which the minor imperfections of capitalism had all but to be worked out.[8]

Gouldner's thesis is that the Enlightenment project was abandoned by two significant groups—first by the philosophers-romanticists, and second by the economists-utilitarians. Sociology, instead, went its own way, and steered an altogether different—and largely retrograde—course, adapting Positivism (an heir of Enlightenment traditions, and, thus, aligning itself with the natural sciences), and strongly rejecting the notion of individual utility in favor of collective solidarity and group utility, a vestige of French Enlightenment thinking. In a sense, soci-ology was "stuck" in the eighteenth century.

Gouldner himself was highly critical of the philosophical roots of individual utilitarianism (the hobbyhorse of economists), yet believed that collective utilitarianism adopted by Durkheim and Weber, among others, was an egregiously flawed concept. For one thing, it substituted the imperative of individual gain with utilitarian culture (accumulation, materialism, and the replacement of wants with needs). For another, it reified a social order at the cost of understanding problems of economic domination and economic injustices:

> [Sociology]'s response to counterbalance the operating code of the new utilitarian economy, which, being concerned with the efficient use and production of utilities for private gain, stressed unrestricted individual competition, stripped men of group involvements—to be used when useful and discarded when not. . . . In fine, the newly emerging sociology did not reject the utilitarian premises of the new middle-class culture, but rather sought to broaden and extend them. *It became concerned with collective utility in contrast to individual utility, with the needs of society for stability and progress, and with what was useful for this. In particular it stressed the importance of other, "social utilities, as opposed to an exclusive focus on economic utilities.*[9]

In retrospect, another way of positioning Gouldner's criticisms is that by replacing economic utilitarianism by social utilitarianism, social philosophers ignored economics altogether. Karl Marx and Friedrich Engels would be the only exceptions. Indeed, the macroeconomic and political economy issues that Marx and Engels tackled were ignored by mainstream American sociology, except in more or less veiled ways (let us say less in the late work of the Lynds, Mannheim, and C. Wright Mills, and let us say more in the works of Robert Blauner and Seymour Martin Lipset).

Another reason, according to Gouldner, why sociology clung to Enlightenment traditions is that sociology proclaimed its identity as a science. As science, Gouldner wrote, sociology adopted "acute sentiments of detachment [and] Positivism transformed this detachment into an ideology and morality."[10] There is no question that Gouldner himself was an empiricist, as his other works, such as *Patterns of Industrial Bureaucracy*[11] and *Studies in Leadership*,[12] clearly illustrate. Positivism was the faith of theorists: "a search for the meaning of the personally real, that which is already assumed to be known through personal experience."[13] In contrast, empirical facts were in the domain of the honest falsifier: "valid-reliable bits of information about the social world."[14]

In *The Coming Crisis*, the crisis of subjectivity was rooted in theory, not so much in facts. In *Enter Plato*,[15] the crisis of subjectivity was rooted in both. Theory, by totalizing human experiences, according to Gouldner, denies the autonomy of "facts," that is, the subjectivity of individuals. Social theory, he argued, is like a Platonic assertion that there is no difference between the world and the ideal (Plato's continuum from becoming, being, forms, to good), or between the visible, mere appearances and a hidden, truer reality. Theory thus removes reality from life as it is experienced, on the Platonic assumption that the reality of the forms (concepts) maintains the distinction between appearance and reality only by removing reality from life as people experience it. The reification of forms, or concepts, is thus a denial of passion, emotion, feelings on the one hand, and a failure to recognize that theory is an ideological enterprise on the other.[16] *Enter Plato* is not an easy book, for it is a metaphor of the sociological enterprise, not a head-on critique. But when it is combined with *The Coming Crisis*, there are, I believe, two points here.

The first point is that functionalist social theory floundered owing to sociologists' failure to recognize that their ideological biases were clouded by their claims of scientific objectivity. The second one is that even "facts" (appearances, the visible) lose their ontological independence, as theory abstracts them from participants and holds them out as unknowable to participants. By abstracting the reality of experiential life, social theory runs the risk of confusing the interpreter and the interpreted, thus polemicizing the autonomy of those we study because we have "explained" them.

And this is arguably correct. To paraphrase Tom Bottomore, we tended to view society as one without major faults, to see the general course of development as determined by a relatively harmonious process of economic growth, and to view as legitimate the dominance of technical elites.[17] The second point is different in that it addresses the domain and style of inquiry. Are facts things like human passion and emotion, for which intersubjectivity is important? Or are facts things like the distribution of income, gender, and a person's wages (the kind of facts that engaged Marx, and, indeed, the grist of much of Gouldner's own mill). I take this point up again later; Clifford Geertz is helpful on the matter of thinking about facts that require intersubjectivity.

When surveying the range of Gouldner's writings, Geertz appears to have advocated a three-pronged approach: reflexivity, subjectivity, and criticism. The latter—criticism—is clear enough, and I take up the problem of subjectivity throughout this chapter. The first is problematic. For Gouldner, reflexivity appears to mean self-criticism: "the ingrained *habit* of viewing our own beliefs as we now view those held by others."[18] Although it is now recognized that this statement is remarkably precocious in light of current poststructuralist views of interpretation, at the time his position confused his contemporaries. Even his admirers maintained that critical analysis and reflexivity ("navel contemplation") were incompatible.[19] Other Marxists, Raymond Williams

and Henri Lefebvre, make Gouldner's position more tenable, whereas
Anthony Giddens and Jeffrey Alexander obfuscate the difficulties even
further.

Raymond Williams, sometime sociologist and sometime culture
critic, puts the matter about subjectivism more bluntly than Gouldner:
Marx and Engels failed to ground their metatheory in "the ordinary
structure of feeling," and social scientists, in Williams's view, continue
to do so at their peril.[20] Similarly, Lefebvre suggests, had Marx and
Engels paid less attention to undoing the pathology of utilitarianism,
"the science of the more," and paid more attention to romantic traditions
(Brontë, Pushkin, and Byron [my examples]), they would have done a
better job in plumbing man's soul.[21] In other words, according to
Williams and Lefebvre, interpretive frameworks, including self-reflection,
and immersion in subjective feeling do not preclude critical analysis.

Ruminations by non-Marxist contemporary theorists, such as
Jeffrey Alexander and Anthony Giddens, reflect even less ambivalence
about the role of the subjective in both social theory and empirical
research but are elusive on the matter of criticism. Theory, according to
Giddens, cannot be kept wholly separate from the world that is being
studied—universes of meaning and social action—and thus there is a
"double hermenuetic," involving the theorist and the world, the acting
agent and the world. Though there is still the presumption for Giddens
that empirical research draws on "facts" that are used in qualitative or
quantitative empirical research, these, too, are not especially in the
realm of objective reality. Facts provide an "index of a phenomenon: and
exemplify the processes of social life, but facts too are implicated in the
double hermeneutic, as actors can also get to know the facts, which in
turn, alter their perceptions and actions."[22] Objective and subjective are
not that problematic in other words, as they fold into each other and are
inseparable. Reflexivity is parceled up as a result, owing to the necessity of recognizing the plurality of interpretive frameworks.[23]

My answer to this debate is incomplete, perhaps, but I find it
useful. Much of the theoretical enterprise must be sufficiently autonomous and independent of existing social conditions so that reflexive
critical assessments of those social conditions are possible. In that
regard, honesty with respect to logic, inferences, and observations
(facts) are consistent with a critical enterprise. More generally, to deny
that our quest for understanding is free from ethical and policy considerations would be foolish. For this reason alone, reflexivity about our
own vested interests and values appears fairly important.[24] However, as
Archer warns, whether the issue at stake is subjective awareness or

understanding objective conditions, reflexivity must rely on the simple-mindedness of a knowing subject.[25] Theory, for her, cannot be such a muddle of frameworks that it denies the distinction between a "knower" and what is to be known.

Not all facts are equal. What we learn in studies of prisoners or of the homeless, and in interviews with the superrich or with migrant farmers, requires empathy and subjectivism. Working with facts like the incarceration rate, estimating the numbers of homeless, and studying the interlocks of the superrich does not load so heavily on the subjective frameworks of the sociologist.

Both fieldwork and analyses of secondary data, however, require assumptions, axioms, that must be dredged up from somewhere, and that somewhere is often beyond the domain of science. It may ultimately be settled by science, for example, whether men and women think in different ways or not, and how specific social influences bear on aggressive and nonaggressive behaviors. But that is not now the case. In the meantime, we work on certain reasonable premises, which are just as much subjective and intuitive hunches as they are based on accumulated knowledge and understanding. In short, the problem of subjectivity in science will not go away so easily. Moreover, our most basic axioms that are derived from what we consider to be problematic about the human condition—cooperation, competition, power, freedom, equality, rights—come not from science, in my opinion, but from a big kettle of ideas to which philosophers, theologians, writers, and historians have undoubtedly contributed the most.

THE SOCIAL CONTRACT

These, then, are the considerations that led me back to a virtually forgotten concept in sociology and a highly contested one in philosophy, *The Social Contract*.[26] Rousseau's book was the doctrine of popular sovereignty. Although portions of Rousseau's writing have been criticized for contending that the state has a will of its own, and, thus, provided a rationale for authoritarian elites,[27] his main emphasis is on freedom and equalitarianism: "Man is born free, and yet we see him everywhere in chains."[28] In 1791 he denounced slavery; if not advocating revolution, he himself was a dissenter (and a refugee for many years after *The Social Contract* was censored by the Swiss authorities for its revolutionary objectives). He contended that governments are not permanent but must be subordinate to the public will:

> The body politic . . . begins to die from its birth, and bears within
> itself the causes of its destruction . . . it depends on [human
> beings] to give the longest possible existence to a State, by giving
> it the best possible constitution.[29]

The state is legitimate only when it expresses the public will. Social
arrangements, according to Rousseau, were the products of human
choice, and people must bear the moral responsibility for the kind of
society they construct or accept.

As a political and social theorist, Rousseau virtually ignored problems of the economy. How would people get along with scarcity? Would
people abide by economic equality?

Would there be no self-interest? Marx is extremely helpful here.
However, instead of turning to Marx's theoretical constructions, I turn
to "use value," the axiom on which exchange value and, in turn, his
entire theory of political economy ultimately depend. However, let us
first be clear about Rousseau's axiom: "Sentiments of sociability" would
ensure the making of the social contract.[30] (This created subsequent
problems for Rousseau, as I shall explain.) The point to be made here is
that Rousseau recognized a *focal point of cooperation that would insure
association and sociability that would transcend self-interest.*

Use Value

Marx distinguished between use value and exchange value in the
first few pages of *Capital*,[31] building on earlier arguments from the
Economic and Philosophical Manuscripts. Use value is a form of exchange,
namely,

> Exchange of human activity within production itself and also of
> human products with each other is equivalent to species-activity
> and species enjoyment whose real, conscious, and true being is
> social activity and social enjoyment.[32]

In other words, it is the significant value of work that is embedded
in social relations, is concrete, and bears an immediate relation to work
and to social cooperation. The axiom of use value rests on the notion of
free and unforced exchange. Thus, Marx does not refer to common
subjectivities, as Rousseau does, but instead grounds his axiom in *social
exchange, work, and cooperation*. Instead of dawdling on the problems of
feelings and sentiments, Marx immediately sets to work on the abstrac-
tions, notably exchange value.

As capitalism introduces exchange value, use value is subsumed under markets and contaminated by price. Work, cooperation, and exchange lose their intrinsic value when artificial rules are introduced to translate one commodity into another—that is, labor can be translated into profits, capital into corn or oil, land into machinery. According to David Harvey, Marx could have started his theory of value with the particularities and specificity of use value, or he could have started—as he did—with an abstract theory and a material investigation of society, as a means to dissect the inner workings of capitalism. Marx took the latter route.[33] That is, Marx took use value as a priori, immediately abstracted exchange from use value, and, thereby, ignored the particularities of cooperation, sentiments, and sociability. Another way of putting this is that Marx suppressed the diverse and heterogeneous in favor of explaining the universal condition of people.[34]

However, I contend, that by refocusing attention on the localism of work, "new history" has helped to fill in the gaps left by Marx. Historians, notably E. P. Thompson, Eric Foner, and Herbert Gutman, attended to the details of workers' lives by highlighting the importance of culture and daily practices. And much of new history was an exploration of the intricate relations within culture, daily experiences, and workers' relations with one another. As Gutman notes, the aim was to show how aspirations and expectations interpret experience and thereby help shape workers' lives.[35]

Alternative Readings of Rousseau

I have argued that Rousseau ignored *why* it is that people have sentiments of sociability that are powerful enough to override self-interest. However, Marx's concept of use value helps to clarify this hiatus in Rousseau's conception of the social contract. Namely people cooperate because production requires exchange and cooperation is intrinsically gratifying. Here we can conclude that Rousseau's "sentiments of sociability" are quite compatible with this expanded definition of the social contract.[36] However, as far as Rousseau is concerned, we are not out of the woods yet. On what does he ground subjectivity? And what is the antithesis of sociability? For the late Rousseau (in *Confessions*), the issues hung on problems of self, writing, frailty, and the absence of love. Just the sort of thing that deconstructionist literary critics like to chew on, and chew him up they did. Although this is exceptionally complex, the general line of criticism taken by de Man and Derrida is instructive, and in the end, helps to ferret out issues that literary theory and the social sciences have in common.

Perhaps owing to his waffling over history and what comes first—
love or selfhood—Rousseau, it is argued, believed that everything
begins from zero, that is, history was created from nothingness. For de
Man, Rousseau's state of nature is a fiction without diachronic possibilities. Having been created, history and literature mix with allegory.
In allegorical analysis, there is no solution, but varieties of solutions,
which sends us back to the text itself. Thus, reflexivity has no independence of the text, and the text is the proliferation of the particular.[37]

In his deconstruction of Rousseau's *Confessions*, Derrida contends
that Rousseau creates contradictions between writing and cathexis, and
thereby concludes "that there is nothing outside of the text."[38] De Man's
criticism is more political in the sense that he considers Rousseau's
autobiography and philosophy as equally fictitious. While denying the
capacity of the reader to correct error, de Man suppresses language of
categories, indeed, of self-consciousness.[39]

Readers at this point, may say, so what? Literary theory is not
sociology. But, on the point of Rousseau, the matter is important for
it has bearing on the earlier discussion of the axiom and the role of
subjectivity in social theory. It is a literary theorist, Fredric Jameson,
who helps us in this regard. He argues that the dialectic in *The Social
Contract* emerges from the contrast between the "social contract" and the
artifactual "sham contract" of state power.[40] On this basis, one can see a
loose parallel between, on the one hand, use value and social contract,
and on the other, exchange value and sham contract. Jameson also
provides clues for considering Rousseau's contribution to understanding the independent role of human subjectivity. He quotes Rousseau:

> The repeated contacts between men and various entities, and be-
> tween the entities themselves, must necessarily engender in the
> mind of man the perception of relationships.[41]

And Jameson elaborates: The social contract thus involves the
apprehension of others as having the same subjectivities as oneself
(that is, having pity, desire, sympathy).[42]

Although Jameson is a literary theorist, not a social scientist, there
is a meeting of minds here. Eagleton, likewise a literary theorist, states
the metatheoretical point even more strongly: If subjectivity and social
reality are inseparable, there can be no question of asking where ideas
come from or how to pose questions about social reality.[43] Margaret
Archer, a sociologist and cultural theorist, puts the problem this way:
"Compacting structure and culture defies and defeats analysis, and
collapses praxis with meaning, and renders history uninterpretable."[44]

To put it another way, if we view action and order as "nothing other than what exists in people's heads,"[45] this precludes the distinction we need for theory and practice.

Rousseau has become central in cultural politics. Following a line of scholarship, I contend that Rousseau is not mere text but that he offers a useful concept for social theory. But then questions arise: How do we know what other people's subjectivities are? How do we know what engenders the perceptions of relationships? If we take Rousseau's axiom seriously, we must therefore take subjectivity seriously.

Anthropology to the Rescue

For Geertz, the issue lies not so much in the axiom of subjectivity, but rather in the practice of it, namely finding a common ground of understanding and discourse with the "others," namely, those who are the subjects of anthropological fieldwork. In a sense, Geertz's problem, as he describes it, is not to form a social contract with someone who is similar but, rather, with someone who is different. He wants to understand Emawayish, the Ethiopian poet, well enough to allow her to tell her story so that he can convey it to Western readers. "Text positivism" (and do note here, the polemical word returns) requires that Emawayish is a coauthor in the project and fully depicts things as she sees them and in a way that Geertz, too, can understand them.[46] Thus, in contrast to Gouldner, for whom Positivism posed problems for the theorist that require reflexivity, Geertz maintains that Positivism is a problem for the empiricist. "Facts" are obtained through subjective understanding as it lies in the discovery of agreement between the people who are being described and the describers.

Geertz terms this *dispersed authorship* and there is "the simple assumption that although Emawayish and her poems are, of course, inevitably seen through an author-darkened glass, the darkening can be minimized by authorial self inspection for 'bias' or 'subjectivity' and she and they can then be seen face to face."[47] Coming to terms with subjectivism for Geertz is indistinguishable from attempting to "get things right," yet it also enlarges the possibility of discourse among people who are in many ways quite different from one another but who recognize the problem of mutual coexistence, and of, somehow, getting along. Being reflexive, in other words, attends to substance, not to explanations that account for it.[48]

Enlarging on the other end, reflexivity requires that we make demands on theory for its political, social, and ethical significance. To illustrate, Service advocates the dispersion of no-strings-attached capital to assuage the economic inequalities that violate cultural legitimacy.[49] Peter Blau looks to the prospects of the randomized confounding of individual differences—in status, income, ethnicity—so that voluntaristic social relations will be increasingly enhanced.[50] David Harvey suggests the possibilities of fusions of social and political movements that transcend particularisms and differences.[51]

SUMMARY

The recent infusion by cultural studies is a means, in my opinion, of recouping the part of intellectual history that we missed, namely, the subjectivism of the various romantic movements of the nineteenth century. But we should be aware of what we are attempting to recoup as the nineteenth century was a mosaic of conservatism (Nietzsche and Wagner), simplicity (Thoreau), style (Beau Brummel), and melancholia (Baudelaire and Schopenhauer). I have attempted to argue that a critical enterprise requires subjectivism but can be undermined by it as well. If there are no facts, that is, no assumptions about objective conditions, then the sociological project founders on the hermeneutic dilemma that there is no systematic meaning. On the other hand, a denial of subjectivity is to make Comte's assertion that the people whose lives we want to study are incompetent to speak for themselves.

Gouldner warned that high-science sociology, which is the heir of Positivism, serves to defocalize the ideological dimensions of decision-making, diverting attention from differences in ultimate values and from the more remote consequences of the social policies to which its research is harnessed.[52] Since Gouldner wrote, individual utilitarian assumptions have been placed in the arena of contention, with the central problem firmly rooted in a strong axiom of maximization. By assuming that people are self-interested, there can be no chance of the provision of public goods, as the pursuit of rational self-interest leads to free-riding on a grand scale. Rational choice theory is an ambitious attempt to do away with collective utilitarian assumptions, but the main difficulty, it seems to me, is that it fails to comes to terms with fairness, which is what political economy is all about.[53]

Karl Marx and Jean-Jacques Rousseau are extremely helpful in my arguments throughout this book. They each have one foot in the Enlightenment project and another in the romantic backlash. They are also useful for epistemological reasons because they begged questions that have become special problems in contemporary sociology, and I attempt to deal with a few of these. Are people rational? Are they "by nature" social? Is there an analytical distinction between *homo socios* and *homo economicus*? Can we deal analytically with frameworks for ethics and morality? Without providing answers, I try to identify a range of issues that I believe are relevant.

On the basis of the considerations discussed in this chapter, I define what I mean by mapping or elementary cooperation. As Rousseau posits, when people have contacts with one another, a modicum of communality develops. If we then take into account Marx's more sophisticated axiom—in the beginning there was exchange—it boils down to the idea that some differences (inclinations, interests) exist, so that mapping recognizes differences and capitalizes on them. Thus, the axiom in which I lodge the concept of the social contract comes from Marx (use value), but the elementary first step is from Rousseau, namely, we perceive basic human similarities, and this perception makes it possible to empathize and to communicate with one another about our similarities and differences.

NOTES

1. Voltaire was born in 1694 and died in 1778, about a decade before the beginning of the French Revolution.
2. Letter of November 30, 1735, to Abbe d'Olivet. Quoted in John U. Nef, *Western Civilization since the Renaissance*. New York: Harper [1950] 1963, p. 277.
3. François de Voltaire, *Candide*. Chicago: Henry Regnery Co., 1949, p. 100.
4. Ibid., p. 2.
5. Alfred Cobban, *In Search of Humanity: The Role of the Enlightenment in Modern History*. New York: George Braziller, 1960.
6. Ibid., pp. 220–221.
7. Auguste Comte, *The Positive Philosophy*. Trans. Harriet Martineau. London: Routledge & Kegan Paul, 1893, p. 37.
8. Alvin W. Gouldner, *The Coming Crisis of Western Sociology*. New York: Basic Books, 1970.
9. Ibid., p. 92 (emphasis added).
10. Ibid., p. 102.
11. Alvin W. Gouldner, *Patterns of Industrial Bureaucracy*. New York: Free Press, 1954.
12. Alvin W. Gouldner (ed.), *Studies in Leadership*. New York: Harper, 1950.
13. Gouldner, *The Coming Crisis of Western Sociology*, op. cit., p. 484. *Positivism*, it can be added, is a slippery term. When it is often taken to mean that a social

scientist accepts empirical data as "real," Gouldner centers attention on the problems of theory. Clifford Geertz, as will be discussed below, shifts attention back to empirical data.

14. Ibid., pp. 494–495.
15. Alvin W. Gouldner, *Enter Plato: Classical Greece and the Origins of Social Theory*. New York: Basic Books, 1965.
16. Ibid., pp. 112, 387.
17. T. B. Bottomore, *Sociology as Social Criticism*. London: George Allen & Unwin, 1974, pp. 87–88.
18. Gouldner, *The Coming Crisis of Western Sociology*, op. cit., p. 490; also see Alvin W. Gouldner, *The Two Marxisms*. New York: Seabury Press, 1980, p. 24.
19. Bottomore, op. cit., p. 54.
20. Raymond Williams, *The Long Revolution*. New York: Columbia University Press, 1961, pp. 48–49.
21. Georges Lefebvre, *The French Revolution Vol 1. From Its Origins to 1793*. Trans., Elizabeth Moss Evanson. New York: Columbia University Press, 1962, p. 38.
22. Anthony Giddens, *The Constitution of Society*. Berkeley: University of California Press, 1984, p. 334.
23. Jeffrey C. Alexander, "Analytical Debates," pp. 1-30 in Jeffrey C. Alexander and Steven Seidman (eds.), *Culture and Society*. Cambridge: Cambridge University Press, 1990.
24. See Tzvetan Tudobov, *The Deflection of the Enlightenment*. Stanford: Stanford Humanities Center, 1989.
25. Margaret S. Archer, *Culture and Agency*. Cambridge: Cambridge University Press, 1988, pp. 68–69.
26. Jean-Jacques Rousseau, *The Social Contract*. Trans. and Introduction, Charles Frankel. New York: Hafner, 1947 [1762].
27. For a summary about this debate, see Irving M. Zeitlin, *Ideology and the Development of Sociological Theory*. Englewood Cliffs, NJ: Prentice-Hall, 1987, pp. 19–28.
28. Rousseau, op. cit., p. 5.
29. Ibid., p. 79.
30. Ibid. pp. 124–125.
31. Karl Marx, *Capital: A Critique of Political Economy*. Ed., Friedrich Engels. Trans., Samuel Moore and Edward Aveling. New York: The Modern Library, 1906, pp. 46–47, 54.
32. Karl Marx, "On James Mill." Excerpt from Karl Marx and Friedrich Engels, *Historisch-kritische Gesamtausgabe Werke, Schriften, Briefe*, Vol. 1 (3), pp. 425ff. Translation in David McLelland (ed.), *Karl Marx: Selected Writings*. New York: Oxford University Press, 1987, pp. 115–123.
33. David Harvey, *The Limits to Capital*. Chicago: University of Chicago Press, 1982, p. 14.
34. To put it simply, exchange value is the commodification of labor; whatever meaningful differences exist among individuals are imposed by the logic of

production. We could say that a critique of exchange value, in other words, required this initial abstraction.

35. Herbert G. Gutman, *Work, Culture and Society*. New York: Random House, 1976; Eric Foner, *Politics and Ideology in the Age of the Civil War*. Oxford: Oxford University Press, 1980, p. 29.

36. Although Rousseau was from a poor family, he early acquired a wealthy patroness, which might account for his discounting of the importance of work!

37. Paul de Man, *The Rhetoric of Romanticism*. New York: Columbia University Press, 1986 [1984].

38. Jacques Derrida, *Of Grammatology*. Baltimore: Johns Hopkins University Press, [1967] 1974, pp. 158–159.

39. As Jameson notes, the deconstruction of Derrida and that of de Man differs in that "Derrida's argument requires the political and intellectual precondition that we go on 'believing' in the difference. . . . De Man's fictionality no longer seems to stage that agonizing double bind." Fredric Jameson, *Postmodernism, or The Cultural Logic of Late Capitalism*. Durham: Duke University Press, 1991, pp. 226–227.

40. Ibid., p. 220.

41. Rousseau, op. cit., p. 155.

42. Jameson, op. cit., p. 239.

43. Terry Eagleton, *Ideology: An Introduction*. London: Verso, 1991, p. 219.

44. Archer, op. cit., p. xi.

45. Alexander, op. cit., p. 1.

46. Clifford Geertz, *Works and Lives*. Stanford University Press, 1988.

47. Ibid., p. 145.

48. Clifford Geertz, *The Interpretation of Cultures*. New York: Basic Books, 1973, pp. 443–448.

49. Elman R. Service, "The Law of Evolutionary Potential," pp. 93–122 in Marshall D. Sahlins and Elman R. Service (eds.), *Evolution and Culture*. Foreword by Leslie A. White. Ann Arbor: University of Michigan Press, 1988.

50. Peter M. Blau, *Inequality and Heterogeneity*. New York: Free Press, 1977.

51. David Harvey, *The Condition of Postmodernity*. Oxford: Basil Blackwood, 1989.

52. Gouldner, *The Coming Crisis of Western Sociology*, op. cit., p. 104.

53. See James S. Coleman, *Foundations of Social Theory*. Cambridge: Harvard University Press, 1990, especially pp. 21–23.

3

Competition and Cooperation

The pressure of my business is so great that I have not the time to scratch my head, or even to cut my nails, and so I wear them very long. Heaven help me. This, I say, beloved master, so that your worship may not be surprised that I have not given you an account till now of my good or ill fortune in this [work], in which I suffer from worst hunger than when we two were roaming the woods and wilds.

—MIGUEL DE CERVANTES SAAVEDRA
Sancho Panza's letter to Don Quixote de la Mancha

Rhetorically, by analogy, and metaphorically, the notion of what is and should be "business" has taken on an uncommonly prominent place in the discourse of everyday life. In our society, business is the "market-place." And, it is defended in the name of "individualism," which is rough and ready for what Americans consider advances both personal and collective values: individual achievement and social progress. Thus, the marketplace allows us to eat our cake and have it too. Competition, it is argued, promotes both the ends of individuals and the ends of society. Instead, I contend that the valorization of individualism has undermined democracy and equality, and the rhetoric blinds us to the fact that the big players do not live by the rules of competition. It is my point in this chapter that cooperation pervades economic life just as it does social life. There is no reason to be squeamish about it. Drawing from a point that Amitai Etzioni makes, in contemporary, developed countries, competition does not do well in impersonal, calculative systems of independent actors unbounded by social relations but instead requires social bonds that are strong enough to sustain mutual trust.[1]

27

The centerpiece of the marketplace concept is the idea that each rational actor competes and the outcomes are fair. We make much of the sloth and laziness of those who fail. It is said that each individual enters the fray of competition with the same motivations and keen sense of self-interest. Assuming that the game and the rules are fair and square, we conclude that the losers have no one to blame but themselves. We fail to see that the victims did not make the rules and that the playing field was never level in the first place. The rhetoric becomes shriller as opportunities decline and the distance between the winners and the losers widens.

Perhaps fear of societal failure induces a compensatory preoccupation with the moral justification of individual success. Or perhaps we lack a language that is complex enough to account for contemporary dilemmas that individuals and society face.

The successes of the late nineteenth century and the early twentieth century—growth, expansion, increasing productivity—are increasingly attributed to competition, when in large measure our forbearers were successful because they cooperated to exploit available opportunities. Thus, in contemporary times we look not to cooperation, coordination, and planning, but rather to the market. Competition, we trust, will solve problems of health care, schools, urban decline, peace, and the environment.

Andrew L. Shapiro summarizes the results of what in large measure is our increasing reliance on market mechanisms since around the 1960s. Eschewing planning (intervention and cooperation), the United States has moved into first place in a variety of areas, none of which we should be proud. Namely, in the lineup of developed nations, America is Number 1 in the rate of infant mortality, Number 1 in the percentage of the population without health insurance, Number 1 in the rate of handgun deaths and of rapes, Number 1 in military aid to developing nations, and Number 1 in providing the least humanitarian aid per capita to developing nations. We lead the developed world in low compensation to public-school teachers. Of course, in some important matters, we are also first: We have the highest paid CEOs, and the most per capita billionaires.[2]

Of course, the story is far more complex than I imply. But the point I make is that the rhetoric of competition these days is based on the premise that because our past prosperity appears to be due to the successes of free enterprise, we conclude that the solutions to contemporary problems ought to be an infusion of more of the same.

THE RHETORIC OF COMPETITION

When the Soviet Union dismantled its political apparatus, Americans cheered in the name of free markets. And, tending to confuse democracy with capitalism, our foreign aid to countries in the former Soviet bloc is inexorably tied to their adopting market economies. Moreover, difficult questions about the environment are recast in the terms of worldwide market shares and the control of U.S. companies over dwindling resources. Although many available jobs are temporary and minimum wage, they are expected to spur the motivation of high-school and college graduates. Contemporary domestic politics increasingly is a battle among candidates for press coverage, corporate support, and for demographic groups. As a result, the less that national candidates commit to substantive proposals, the better their chances in capturing large blocks of voters.

Already Americans must and do compete for choice residential locations in order to live in the districts of the best public schools. Unfortunately, there is increasing interest in encouraging schools to compete among themselves. The assumption is that all schools can battle among themselves as equals and the invisible hand of the market will drive out the least efficient and the lowest quality. Unfortunately, the already disadvantaged school districts have the most to lose in this competition because they start with the fewest resources. It is as if we have not learned that marketing strategies command high overhead costs that must be borne by every school. It is as if we have not learned that competition drives fashions and fads at the expense of cooperative planning. Likewise health. By stimulating competition for the consumers' health dollar, the market in esoteric medicine has displaced important programs for preventative care and prenatal health, and discourages physicians from going into primary medicine—what has become the "nickels and dimes" of the health industry.

Moreover, the rhetoric of the marketplace—individualism, self-interest, competition, autonomy, and efficiency—masks the reality that much success in economic life is actually the result of cooperation. States attract industries by providing them with tax breaks, roads, dump sites, and zoning exemptions.

Powerful economic actors establish cooperative relations within their environments for the purpose of establishing control. Recognizing the payoff of coordinative strategies over competitive ones, J. P. Morgan stepped into the fuddle to organize the railroad companies. His investment firm gave massive loans to most of the country's railroad companies. In return for the loans, Morgan settled with their representatives to obtain a seat on each of their boards of directors. In all, Morgan or his proxy held 721 directorships in 112 of the country's largest financial, transportation, and public utilities.[3] Our economic history is very much a story about organizing.

In contemporary times, major economic actors exert more control through coordination and cooperation than J. P. Morgan ever could imagine. In part this is because many more very large industries are able to establish an identity between their own interests and those of the nation. For example, in congressional hearings on a wide range of issues including pollution, safety, industrial health, factory safety, and foreign trade, competing firms, such as Ford, Chrysler, and General Motors, will tend to agree.[4]

The claim is that it is in the best interest of the nation if all auto producers reach consensus on the pace of innovation, the amount of overseas production, and a schedule of phasing in pollution and safety equipment. True enough, this enables them to better control the nature of the competition over the world market of automobiles. But is this in the common interest? Control over the market for automobiles is not all that is at stake. Each automaker is linked with the oil, steel, and banking industries. Coordination and cooperation are viewed as imperative to the nation's economic stability. Minor economic actors are not so advantaged, and they cannot cooperate and organize with such returns. In this sense, minor economic actors are encouraged to compete, whereas major ones have the power and resources to cooperate. Small-scale cooperative strategies, for example, collectives and worker-owned firms, are devalued, whereas large-scale cooperation is disguised.

The rhetoric used for market outcomes is often upstream—progress and the like. The downstream consequences are sometimes forgotten. The domination of market considerations in urban planning has had dire consequences on what were once viable communities. Residents of towns in which plants have closed feel betrayed by the rhetoric of competition, as do people whose neighborhoods were targeted by upscale developers. The justification of marketplace competition in terms of obscure and elusive results—progress—ignores the social costs of its present-oriented (profit-maximizing) methodology. The justification, I will argue throughout this book, hardly makes sense in a world in which the opportunities of individual actors are greatly unequal, and in a world in which we share dependencies that are disguised by the rhetoric of markets.

Cooperation is ubiquitous and social contracts pervade economic and social life. The rhetoric of the free market, however, blinds us to how much cooperation there actually is among major economic and political actors. The debacles of the Department of Housing and Urban Development and the savings-and-loan banks, it has been convincingly argued, were the painful results of a free-market strategy—deregulation—when in fact they were the consequences of unbridled collusion.[5] When informal and invisible cooperative arrangements among major economic actors and government agencies are disguised as the promotion of entrepreneurial innovation and deregulation, the public is reassured that the invisible hand of competition nevertheless prevails. However, a recognition of cooperative action puts the burden of proof on the actors, not on an impersonal market mechanism.

Small-scale and large-scale cooperation require different mechanisms for regulation. Large-scale strategies implicate many communities, firms, and nations, and the importance of planning, accountability, and third-party enforcement looms large. Small-scale strategies have more built-in checks and balances, such as visibility and the clarity of the locus of responsibility. But small or large in terms of scale, cooperation is based on some elementary principles of interdependence.

In this chapter I explore ways of distinguishing between cooperation and competition. The idea of the open market creates the illusion that it is open to all comers. However, this notion disregards initial differences among actors—be they individuals, communities, states, or nations—and disregards their differences in resources, attachments, and interdependencies. The marketplace assumes that people are autonomous actors, but participation in markets further atomizes individuals as they heighten antagonistic relations and discourage attachments. Those aspects of our life that are sociable and responsive to what others do, and are even altruistic, cannot be explained satisfactorily for all purposes by the principle of competition in which self-interest, narrowly defined, dominates. Finally, and perhaps increasingly more important, the by-products of competition—overgrazed grasslands, polluted waters, poverty—will not be solved by more competition.

In making the distinction between competition and cooperation, I contrast economic and social behaviors. I should be at once clear that the comparison is analytical. That is, to illustrate, households, which we consider to be social, not economic, actors, do employ strategies that are just as rational as those employed by economic actors. They use budgets for calculating strategies for accomplishing certain outcomes, such as strategies for subsistence, paying the rent, and planning for holidays.

Behavior within and without large companies is routinely cooperative as any sort of task requires negotiation, give-and-take, compromise, and amiability.

RATIONALITY

The distinction between economic and social life—between competition and cooperation—is frequently displaced by a distinction between rationality and irrationality. This distinction is also often one between the rational individual and the irrational group. The rhetoric of the marketplace that stresses the individual is partly the source for this, but so is a conception of democracy that fails to recognize that citizens are members of many institutional structures. Social scientists are not all that innocent as they have embellished certain notions about individuals in mass society: They ferment trouble as they are swayed by irrational loyalties and ideological fervor (Gustav LeBon); become apathetic and lack rational understanding (Robert Michels and Gaetano Mosca); or are ruled by unconscious forces and instincts (Vilfredo Pareto).

In a peculiar sense, the rhetoric of the market provides us moderns with a paradigm of control that parallels outmoded ones—the elites, the state—on which the conservative thinkers of the early twentieth century pinned their hopes. The market is thought to achieve order; it helps to justify why some rise to the top, whereas others do not. The rhetoric of the marketplace chases out a worry about the unreasonable, irrational crowd. A final seduction of marketplace rhetoric is that because it presumably drives incentives, it is believed to achieve efficacious outcomes.

My thesis is that economic behavior of individuals has been reified and is increasingly applied to social behavior and to groups. Individuals in their economic roles have narrow utilities as they pursue ends as they define them. Selling and buying soybeans, picking out sneakers, selecting among a half dozen brands of frozen yogurt, and moving money from stocks and bonds involve a relatively simple calculus. There is usually more than one variable, but economic actors make decisions on the basis of all variables that are known. For example, if the choice is between expensive yogurt with few calories and inexpensive yogurt with lots of them, and the first has the favorite flavor, whereas the second does not, there is a simple matrix of choices. The matrix, moreover, is seen from one perspective, namely, the buyer's.

In contrast, in social life, rationality is not only defined in terms of the actor's perspective and utilities, but also shaped by the perspectives and "utilities" of others. Utilities here are only loosely defined because there are spheres in which we do not have a preference except as others have preferences; sometimes, there are too many dimensions on which to rank; there are spheres in which we choose the lesser of several alternatives because the interests of others are involved; and what appears logical in terms of one outcome may be illogical from another. Highly motivated students often study in groups as they (correctly) know that they learn more that way, even when they know it may change the curve and reduce their chances of getting A's. Workers will cooperate to help slower coworkers even when it reduces their own individual take-home pay. In 1984 the German metalworking union approached the bargaining table to request a 35-hour workweek in order to create jobs for a portion of the 2.2 million unemployed.[6]

The social actor takes into account the ways in which others see the matter, the context of the relation, and what will happen down the road as well. Cooperation has a teleological character because people care about the collective consequences of what they do: If atomistic results were the main consideration, no one would make donations to humanitarian organizations, recycle cans and bottles, stop to assist at an accident, or participate in study groups. Under normal conditions, cooperation is routinized by ordinary institutions, such as staff meetings, traffic rules, town ordinances, the physical layout of buildings, and work assignments, but cooperative strategies surface in dramatic ways under abnormal conditions. Every catastrophic event, such as an accident, a fire, hurricane, or blackout, is accompanied by unexpected acts of personal sacrifice.

In microworlds of social life, cooperation is sustained by bonds of trust and cultural conventions. Knowing the people with whom we wish to cooperate or should cooperate, we put ourselves in their shoes, so to speak. We take their perspectives into account because collective losses and gains are at stake. Friends may engage in turn taking or agree to share. The issue is not so much individual utility but sustaining a friendship or group identity or a common cause. In families, classrooms, neighborhoods, and in organizations, we often engage in cooperative behavior that costs us something with little in return except that the collective enterprise is pushed ahead. Sometimes there are institutional mechanisms, such as written rules, but very often there are none.

On the macroscale, cooperation becomes cumbersome because of the difficulties that any given actor has of fully comprehending the perspectives of other actors. Yet once cooperation is defined as an objective, strangers also mobilize. They do for wars, for emergencies, for political and social movements. People help others whom they do not know, and they will pitch in when another community or neighborhood faces adversity. Very often cooperation has to be prompted by rules or laws, but this does not contradict the point I make. The rules of the marketplace are to ensure that there is no undue cheating when one actor is pitted against another. The rules of social life provide mechanisms of coordinating actors when it's impossible for participants to see the larger picture.

For example, we may have enough sense to know these days that throwing empty bottles into the trashcan is irresponsible, but we need mechanisms and guidelines for recycling. Or, as library patrons, we recognize the obligation of returning books, but life is complicated, so a fine policy is in order. Although it is assumed that atomistic competitors are regulated by "the invisible hand of the marketplace"—namely, adjustments occur naturally owing to the relationship between supply and demand, production, and consumption—the "invisible hand" of social life is a recognition of mutual interdependence. When that recognition is insufficient or difficult, the "visible hand" of institutions advances cooperation.

Therefore, in this profound sense, social life is governed by a more complex rationality than is economic rationality. To wit, because actions in social spheres have implications beyond our personal utilities, we act with others' interests in mind. In yet another sense, the rationality of social life is more complex than that of economic life. Economic actors are specialists. Friends will muddle through, but economic actors know their limits. The electrician will tell the homeowner that to solve plumbing problems one must turn to another part of the Yellow Pages (or, perhaps, in truth, to a cousin who happens to be a plumber). The same electrician will give a neighbor all kinds of advice on everything from what church to attend to the best fertilizer for the lawn.

The fact that an electrician buys groceries on the way home from work does not mean that grocery buying affects work in the electrical shop. In the grocery, at the same time, the fact that the electrician is an employee and not an owner makes not a trifle of a difference to proprietors of the grocery store. Yet the electrician's activities in different social roles—as a union member, with coworkers, with family members, at church—are intertwined in complex ways. This means that the electrician's social calculus is fostered by complex roles in multiple groups. It is hard to say, when push comes to shove, what the

electrician's overriding social self-interest really is, but her or his economic interests are fairly clear, and they are defined in terms of the
possibility of earning a living with electrical outlets and wiring, not
with wrenches and faucets.

Individuals have segmented roles in so many multiple groups that
we cannot say that there is one utility, or one overriding rationality. A
person is, say, a parent, Catholic, son or daughter, neighbor, boss,
employee, poker player, committed Republican. Each role has some
bearing on the way that other roles are played, so that being an
employee has some implications for one's relations with family members, coworkers, and neighbors, and when and where one eats. But in
all these roles a person pays the same price for an apple. We could say
that the self is partialled into many social roles, and into some of these
social roles individuals throw themselves with virtually total abandon,
but into most they do not.

Moreover, these multiple involvements create a sustained ambiguity about priorities of interests and about status so that rules about
bidding and possibilities of underbidding do not necessarily work.
Most of us do not set stock in a single status or accept unified claims to
any particular one. Yet most persons are not tidy bundles of social roles
either. Most individuals preserve some degree of uncommittedness,
which makes it possible to duck into different social roles and form
different affiliations in one sphere when social life in another becomes
unattractive.[7]

In economic life, contracts are made by individuals or aggregates. I
have in mind warranty contracts or sales agreements in the case of
consumers, and wage contracts in the case of employees and employers.
When considering an economic contract, actors calculate what is in their
own best interest and then try to bargain to get the best possible deal.
Formal economic contracts are forged precisely to solve the Hobbesian
problem—to keep competitors more or less honest and to protect
weaker or less-informed parties from the stronger and better-informed
ones. In any event, economic contracts are mostly explicit and formalized with a clear recognition that some participants' rights or interests
are at odds with those of others. The question of contract then is
traditionally based on the idea that actors are autonomous and self-
interested.

Enlightened contract theory tries to identify ways in which initial
advantage is abolished. For example, Rawls's actors are deliberately
blindfolded, and because they cannot thus know or communicate about
their own self-interest, they choose the best collective arrangement,

namely, that the greatest benefits go to the most disadvantaged.[8] This is a major contribution to the theory of economic morality. In this way, Rawls's blindfold is far superior to the invisible hand that brings about inequalities.

A problem, however, is that, when applied to other than economic matters, interests are intricately structured and interdependent. For example, Rawls fails to recognize the importance of differently situated groups who do not rank needs and benefits in the same way. And, in various roles, people will rank their needs and benefits differently. There are men and women, city people, people who like to live in the country, Buddhists, Christians, corporate types, and people who like banjo music, and others who do not. (Then there are corporate types who spend much of their money to improve their country homes, and other corporate types who donate great sums to religious causes.) Neither the invisible hand of the market nor a blindfold will help to minimize differences in needs, interests, and advantage. The point is that economic justice and social justice must take into account the distinctions between markets and social contracts. Distributional issues are more complex in social life than in economic life. Questions of social justice and equity must take into account the knowledge of initial differences (which are often not ranked on one continuum), the fruitfulness of negotiations, a recognition of interdependence among people who have different interests, and the knowledge that people's interests vary as they are embedded in different arenas of action.

The social contracts into which people enter are multiple; many are open-ended as to outcomes; and they evolve over time. They can range from being intimate to being public, or both, like marriage vows. These contracts are enacted within a great many settings, including work organizations (augmenting economic contracts, like labor agreements), political and civic spheres (such as participation in student government), and diverse social institutions (such as the family, neighborhood, or residence hall). Informal, and sometimes formal and even legal, social contracts are crafted to deal with coordinating individual interests and with the general aim of furthering collective goals. Sometimes these lead to political movements, political parties, and trade unions, or just small social clubs. Even when the chief executive officers of DuPont, General Motors, and Chemical Bank, and half a dozen other executives caucus with government representatives to exert influence on a trade bill we could call this a form of social contract, even when it is a form of conspiracy.[9] These arrangements enable people to advance social or antisocial objectives, which, in this case, deal with fostering a congenial business climate. Such examples, however, should not obscure the fact that most social arrangements do not have such prominence but rather simply comprise the muddle of our daily experiences and are, therefore, very much taken for granted. Social contracts are operative when people come together to collaborate, compromise, or cooperate. Social contracts bind as they help to bond.

Historically, working together is far more important than competition. It was through cooperation and collaboration that the first humans were able to adapt to their environments,[10] just as the first economic systems were not based on markets and haggling but on reciprocity and redistribution. In the beginning, the economic system was a mere appendage of social organization.[11]

People strike social contracts precisely because they are different (with varying agendas about what are the means and what are the ends) and vary in terms of age, skills, interests, resources, and so forth. Cooperation is complementary. In contrast, economic contracts are based on the principle that people are identical in that each and every one wishes to advance his or her own self-regarding interests. In this respect, cooperation must give way to mechanisms for peaceful adjudications when there is conflict.

ORGANIZATIONS

People cooperate to do all kinds of things that involve consent and common goals, and this often requires settings in which to do this. These settings can be called organizations. I do not necessarily mean formally constituted organizations, such as a corporation or a hospital, but more generally, dense concentrations of communications and social actions where people hammer out problems of mutual concern. Organizations, in this context, thus include social movements, short-lived community organizations, and elusive social networks. To be sure, formally constituted organizations—such as firms, labor unions, government bureaucracies, banks, universities, and hospitals—are the most enduring forms of social organization and illustrate basic principles of cooperation that are found in less formal ones—neighborhoods and loose social networks. We could say that organizations are created to solve problems of coordination by means of informal and formal agreements, contracts that recognize that people who are very different from one another and initially do not know one another can achieve collective goals. Production and distribution activities, education and science, political control, military power, the distribution of services, religion, and most contemporary leisure activities are lodged in organizations, networks, and associations.

An organization is an assembly of people who cooperate in order to have stable arrangements for ongoing transactions, production, and problem solving. This covers arrangements such as making shoes, publishing a newsletter, balancing the state budget, playing basketball, or running a day care center. It also includes normal routines in families and neighborhoods. When things become complicated or the scale is large, it is necessary and very convenient to have rules, regulations, and written contracts. But, again, this is not only to curb greediness but also to pleat complexities in order to obtain concurrence.

MAPPING

Basic to any social contract is an organizing principle or a way of mapping coordination—that is, establishing connections among people who engage in different tasks, have opposing or contrasting interests, or possess different skills. Mapping capitalizes on some initial differences among individuals, while it overrides or imposes other differences. I draw a distinction here between what we commonly mean by the division of labor in sociology and emergent forms of specialization and coordination. Émile Durkheim's concept, the division of labor, refers instead to the constraints imposed by larger social and economic structures, such as by occupational categories and industries.[12]

I am emphasizing the more open-ended and spontaneous actions that emerge from the differences among people and actions that subsequently alter these differences. For example, we talk about ad hoc or improvisational division of labor: assigning tasks in a committee or among a few students in an off-campus apartment. And we can think of the varied and changing nature of the gendered social roles. Mapping is unlike pure market behavior in that the latter does not create integration, whereas the former does.[13] The incentives to engage in mapping include things such as sharing, exchanging, and collaborating, whereas the paradigm of market behavior is to transact at once, settle the deal, and move on to the next transaction. Mapping often requires incremental amounts of commitment to the group or collectivity and thus helps to achieve cooperation.

Although I do not deny the Durkheimian differences among people that are defined in the terms of large macrostructures, I intend to stress that people participate in creating and shaping specialized roles and that they extemporize when they play given roles. That is, agency, cultural conventions, and social structure are interwoven in micro-worlds, and over the long haul, they are so in macroworlds as well. If it were not the case, the Scottish Highlanders and the Lowlanders would still be feuding; men would always wear ties to the symphony; and average American children would know the difference between what a field of soybeans and a field of alfalfa look like.

Mapping is evident in any social organization, from organizing a peace march to planning a battle. There are always initial differences among individuals that are deemed irrelevant for the social contract, and others that are created. Age may be irrelevant for participating in a peace march, but it is a major consideration in making battle assign-ments. It may not matter who hands out leaflets and who takes the night watch, but such assignments will be made. The range of how sophisticated or how simple coordinative efforts must be is also ex-tremely broad. Mapping is fairly primitive in a peace march, but nevertheless is evident as some people sing songs while other people give talks from the platform. Battles require a fairly complex set of mapping rules based on initial differences in people's skills, training, and experience, as well as many fairly arbitrary assignments.

Given the variety of forms of social contracts and the accompany-ing ways of dividing up the activities, it is important to examine different generic forms of mapping. We should keep in mind that mapping principles are universal in social organizations no matter what the objectives and no matter who is running the show. Moreover, mapping is important insofar as it often breaks down the traditional loyalties of group membership while it fuses new forms of social integration. Organizations erode people's proclivities to form group bonds on the basis of friendship, race, social class, gender, or shared values. It replaces these proclivities with tasks, activities, functions, and hierarchies. Thus, organizations are not for the preservation of a tribe but to carry out activities that transcend particular self-interests, includ-ing many of those that are derived from primal group identities.

Embedded in organizations are cultural understandings as well as control and coordinating mechanisms. Thus, authority is not antitheti-cal to social contracts, although in this context we must simply assume there is consent, leaving problems of power for later. And organizations employ economic contracts—ranging from the simple receipt and ship-ping invoice to the wage contract—to formalize transactions when actors recognize that people do have competing self-interests. A central dilemma for organizations is achieving a balance so that market mechanisms do not wear down the principles of cooperation. The ways in which authority creates problems for social endeavors are discussed in the next chapter. The point to be made here is that, in principle, it is the multiplicity and dynamic quality of social contracts that protect individuals' autonomy and prevent organizations from collapsing into contentious markets.

Organizations are also necessary for markets because markets create problems for the public and the nation-state. Whereas a polity is based on authority and is rooted in diffuse legitimacy, a market is organized around specific bilateral exchanges that lack subsequent obligations and require external regulations, such as contracts and legally binding rules.[14] For example, markets are notorious for their externalities—smokestacks, toxic dumps, deforestation—and organizations created by government are designed to protect the public. And it could be said that organizations created by private citizens help curb abuses by the government and keep issues of public interest on the political agenda.

To trace this argument, we need to examine the structural foundations of organizations—the mapping rules and the nature of social integration in differentiated structures. My starting point is to note that it was not all that long ago that people carried out their entire lives emeshed in encapsulated, polymorphous communities in which people lived single-faceted, generalist roles, were interlocked in redundant and overlapping social networks, and shared a common cultural orientation. Today, we live our lives in packages and participate in great varieties of differentiated social worlds in which we specialize.[15] As moderns, we deal in relations in order to cooperate so we strike social contracts and map out what is to be done and by whom. But it must not be forgotten that we also engage in self-serving endeavors so that happily or not, we must abide by economic contracts.

STRANDS OF INTERDEPENDENCE

Of our classic theorists, it was Durkheim, as I have noted, who clearly recognized the importance of the division of labor for social cohesion; but at the center of the problem for Durkheim was a set of normative constraints that curbed individual self-interest.[16] Enlightenment, for Durkheim, entailed the individual's recognition of bonds of interdependence, but at least as important for Durkheim were the norms of social control that regulated social life. Yet for distinguishing economic behavior, which requires formal constraints and controls, from social behavior, it is arguable that control in social life is not as important as interdependence itself. The social imperative that we have to cooperate because of—and in spite of—differences is sufficient enough reason for people to act fairly reasonably or reasonably fairly. The social contract provides a template for enduring social relations.

This is not to say that social norms of control are not required and important. They are, of course, but departing from Durkheim, we might say that they are needed not so much to curb people's self-interests but as to curb and control organizations as they become unwieldy—too large, too complex, and too powerful. Certainly, formal rules are imperative when social organizations take on market activities, whether this be producing or selling light bulbs or providing services, such as building roads, for taxes. And formal mapping rules are also codified when cooperation is ambitious and involves intricate coordination.

To be sure, there are metaphorical and linguistic confusions that tend to blur the distinction between competition and cooperation. In Little League baseball, youngsters learn the fine techniques of cooperation with the explicit goal of "beating" the other team in the league, and every bond of cooperation within the team disguises a wish among one or more players to be the most outstanding batter. Still this is but a simile of market competition, and the imperative of cooperation, combined with the sublimation of individual interests, prevents anarchy and ensures compliance with the socially agreed-upon rules. There is more at stake than winning, and that is the prospect of being able to play again next week, or next season.

Evident now and again are cases of clear-cut self-sacrifice. Soldiers will shield companions from hand grenades; older children will "cheat" some so younger children have a chance of winning; many law firms take on cases in which clients cannot pay; people will refuse to "name names" even if it means for themselves a serious fine or jail sentence.

Marx recognized far more clearly than Durkheim the distinction between the social contract—the bonds of cooperation among workers—and the economic contract—the formal wage contract. It is this wage contract over which there is fundamental conflict. There is an initial inequality between those who sell labor and those who buy labor and profit from it. It is in recognition of identical self-interests, namely, the objective of all participants to maximize utilities, and in recognition of great initial advantage, that economic contracts must be hammered out.

The social contract, in contrast, is negotiated on the basis of mutual interdependence, a recognition of the importance of social solidarity to achieve cooperation among people who have different interests.[17]

Mapping participation and creating new forms of specialization probably date from the Stone Age, although I would not attempt to prove it. A few examples suffice. Extended families in agrarian Europe engaged in extensive specialization that cut across differences in residence, marriage, age, and generation.[18] The elaborate division of labor among artisans, architects, and glassmakers was so efficient that by the thirteenth century it took workers only about 40 short years to build the large and exquisite cathedral at Salisbury.

P. K. Misra provides rich details about the ways in which the Gadulia Lohars, a nomadic community in northern India, pool household resources for blacksmithing and for raising bullocks.[19]

In many societies in which systematic exchange is institutionalized, the extent of giving ensures cooperative activities and the dispersion of resources. The man who holds wealth gives his cow to a cousin, his boat to a trading partner, and his marriage goods to his son's affines. Giving is the wellspring of continuing social integration.[20] Piotr Kropotkin drew on such examples of cooperation in early societies to argue that mutual aid and mutual support are at the core of social and community survival.[21]

With an increasingly skilled and well-educated population, revolutionary changes in communication, and more varied resources, these early forms of cooperation look anachronistically simple compared with the multiplicity of contemporary forms of mapping. We can consider the ways in which social roles become linked and unlinked by means of mapping and differentiation, and in terms of the spatial and temporal dimensions of activities and their implications for coordination. Some activities must be carried out simultaneously and thereby synchronized. There are others that are organized progressively over time. Still other activities are scattered and thereby loosely coordinated over time and space.

Synchronization

Many social activities involve many people doing different things at the same time in the same place. Sports provide a good illustration of such a form of mapping. When a college team rows, it is clear that there are clearly delineated statuses—specifically, coxswain, feather, "powerhouse," and third, fourth, fifth, sixth, seventh, and eighth positions. Sometimes a school will run a first, second, and third boat, like little production units in a factory. Because each boat is expected to "produce," coaches carefully group people to reinforce certain qualities of rowers and to compensate for others' weaknesses. Although the differences among rowers' responsibilities and skills are fine-tuned, and rowers engage in that fine-tuning, there is no question about who is top dog. The cock screams out commands like a sergeant in a boot camp. The "generals" ride beside in motorized launches, and quite often there is a further delineation of command between head coach and manager, or head and assistant coach. The "submission" to power is inseparable from camaraderie and the spirit of total cooperation.

Members of a firefighters' squadron are similarly highly specialized as each performs a unique task that is carefully orchestrated with what others are doing. This is not to say that each is unable to perform another role, but it is very efficient to know, from the time the station bell rings, who will be in charge of the hose, who will control the hook and ladder, and who climbs into the cherry picker. Operating rooms, fast-food restaurants, orchestra halls, typical mornings in families, and oceanside docks are other sites where the principle of organization involves synchronizing activities that are simultaneous and interdependent.

Synchronic coordination is achieved in any number of ways. People are trained to carry out one task and to coordinate that task with what others are doing. Training is supplemented by devices such as authoritarian leadership—the conductor of an orchestra, the quarterback, the coach. One can see the principle of synchronized mapping in these very simple examples, but in a more abstract way much of work is subdivided this way. A deadline set by management for an annual report sets all departments into action. Their activities may not be so intricately coordinated as the members of a football team, but they all have to be working on specialized-report preparation at more or less the same time to meet the deadline.

As most of us know from play and work experiences, orchestrated activities require a great deal of patience and training, and the consequences of someone "missing a beat" may be nothing short of disastrous. Undoubtedly, one of the reasons why a "performance"—a football game, a parade, dance, or the theater of an operating room—holds such fascination for us is that these are fine-tuned social systems for which synchronization persists as the mechanism of mapping.

Sequencing

Simple or complex interdependent tasks sometimes must have another principle of organization because the sequence in which activities are carried out is important. Restaurants, farms, assembly factories, publishing companies, the film industry, retail stores, and the garment industry all have a complex division of labor, and specialized tasks must be coordinated across time. As one activity ceases, another must kick in.

Just as many of the rules of the market and competition are learned at school, many of the rules of organization and cooperation are learned in play. One such event I remember that turns sequences into a highly ritualized activity is what a Massachusetts summer camp calls "the progressive dinner." Small groups of campers each prepare a variety of never-ending courses, from appetizer (bean pâté and homemade tortillas), soup (mock corn chowder), main dish (dandelion soufflé, fried okra, and sorrel jambalaya), and dessert (watermelon and homemade ice cream). Youngsters enjoy making fun of parents' pretentious dinner parties, but they nevertheless are impressed with their own skills in pulling off such an intricately woven activity. The sharing of the utensils, stove, and space to keep things moving from beginning to end is no small feat of sequential organization. As Zerubavel observes, scheduling of different tasks has become one of the cornerstones of social life in the modern world.[22]

Mapping over time is essential in carrying out activities in many large-scale organizations. It is by sequencing that the modern hospital can get the patient admitted into the hospital, through the tests, into surgery, back into the recovery room, into the hospital room, and discharged. Anticipating the arrival of students on, say, September 1 means that faculty are asked to order books on May 15, the housing office starts making room assignments on June 6, and the classroom assignment office works out its plan by mid-July. Scheduling the first day of school sets backward and forward a wide range of activities that involve the registrar's office, the bookstore, the faculty, the library, and residence halls.

Large commercial establishments work in terms of inventory schedules, production schedules, and marketing and design programs. Once the time of a peak event is known, the division of labor is retroactively and proactively planned. Adding a room on a house means the homeowner, architect, or contractor must plan backward and forward to allow for various workers' different schedules and the logic of construction, leaving allowances for the vagaries of the weather, and recognizing the usual vicissitudes in residents' preferences for colors, cornices, and carpets. The architect or master builder knows that consensus is achieved in incremental steps; it is achieved by projecting the future onto today's planning, and reminding everyone about the consequences of yesterday's decisions.

The same principle applies to government agencies that deal with programs and budgets, and religious organizations that plan for Christmas, Hanukkah, or Ramadan. We all complain about the deadlines and the rules, but without these schedules, systems will collapse. That is, restaurants would serve cold french fries; there would be nothing to feed the cat because the shopping was not done; libraries would not have new books because the orders did not go out; interstate highways that fail to meet at state borders would be built.[23]

Mapping rules become institutionalized, and sometimes lose the purpose for which they were intended. Large bureaucracies, in particular, become encumbered by outdated procedures that are difficult to change. However, mapping rules can also become rituals that we enjoy so much we keep them even when they are quite useless. Complain though some may, traditional weddings, graduation ceremonies, and homecoming have a social persistence, as they are group experiences and metaphors for knitting people together. This is not at all to say that social arrangements are static. They often are dislodged by rapid rates of population change, economic conditions, or technology. To illustrate how technology, for example, changes mapping rules, stores have rapidly adopted computerized cash registers that are capable of instantaneously (and simultaneously) performing the tasks of inventory, credit check, and sales. Not so long ago—and still in stores without these machines—it took many people to perform these tasks. Moreover, they had to be done sequentially. At the same time, factories are introducing production methods that involve principles of mapping so that activities that were once carried out sequentially can now be carried out synchronically, often enhancing worker morale and job skills.[24]

Mapping over Space and Time

Increasingly in modern societies, activities must be coordinated over space and, therefore, over time as well. As the world order shrinks, organizations and people carry out activities in one part of the world that must interlock with activities in other parts of the world. An early example of overspace social integration is illustrated by the couriers of culture who carried technology, learning, and crafts from one part of the world to others. Although the itinerant tradesmen are considered by historians to have been the precursors of modern markets, it can be said that clerics, scientists, musicians, and crusaders were precursors of modern forms of cooperation. Among scientists in England and France, widely dispersed ties helped to form what Bacon called the "invisible college," and this early idea became the template for professional and scientific communications of modern times.[25] Yet these examples of the mechanisms of diffusion involving ideas, culture, and technology are still shy of the on-time coordination required in modern society.

With satellite, telephone, computer, and fax machines, vast new realms of coordination possibilities have been created. This interdependence entails new challenges as it depends on advanced technology, political stability, and a degree of trust among people who rely on translators and who have profoundly different social traditions. The rules about mapping over space have evolved only within the past century, and they have reshaped the ways that social organizations use and are used by markets. Yet this will entail a still greater need for rules for market regulation and control. If economic exploitation of colonies was difficult to curb, the new world order will require far more elaborate regulations and enforcement principles than ever before.

PARTIALLED AND NONPARTIALLED ROLES

These various forms of mapping principles—for example, synchronization, sequencing, and over space and time—entail dynamic interdependence on one or more dimensions, which is a significant departure from what Durkheim described as the division of labor.[26] To illustrate, for Durkheim, hardware stores need suppliers and buyers; physicians need to have mechanics; mechanics need to have physicians. But the social contract extends beyond the obvious fact that to get our own objectives accomplished we need to cooperate. The natural differences in people's interests, talents, skills, and experiences bring about various forms of division of labor that in turn reinforce many kinds of cooperation, indeed, give cooperation a way of expressing itself. Thus, social contracts are based on a multiplicity of differences, not differences in one dimension. To return to the specific example, the PTA may bring together a hardware store owner, physician, and mechanic who together confront the school over a dwindling library budget. The owner of the hardware store may be in competition with the mechanic over the price and supply of auto parts, and the physician may be the ex-wife of the school librarian. Still, they may all attend the same church, while they belong to different political parties. We take for granted such arrangements.

Actors participate in many social worlds, each with its own division(s) of labor, or, in my terms, mapping rules. Each requires a different rationality and affective orientation. Individuals are members of families, households, neighborhoods, work organizations, voluntary associations, leisure organizations, churches, and so on. As people lock into one role, lock out of others, move from one sphere to another, they encounter new constellations of specialized spheres of participation, each bringing with it different participants. To give a concrete example, students segmentalize activities and classes—from morning classes, to their part-time job, afternoon sports or dormitory council, to evening social activities. And there is no single rationality that dominates the day.

Each multidimensional frame of participation involves cognitive specialization, differentiation of authority and social roles, and a distinctive set of priorities and responsibilities.[27] These interlocking roles—each of which is uniquely constituted—give the individual a stake in many different worlds and an autonomy from the overriding claims of one. Perhaps in an agrarian society it was sufficient to have a stake in one or a few worlds, but in contemporary times, occupying one all-encompassing role and rationality is stifling, and, in any case, may be virtually impossible to even attain.

In contemporary society individuals participate in varieties of social and work settings, bringing to those settings the specialized rationalities of other roles. Even in the cherished settings for diffuse emotions and generalized roles, in friendships and the household, external roles intrude and, indeed, are invited, as dinner centers on conversations about what people do outside the family, as a mechanic-uncle volunteers to help fix the car, as Mom dredges up her earlier experience playing softball to help coach Little League, as Dad is called on to help the kids with the computer. Contemporary life would be impoverished without these overlapping and embedded roles.

The social networks that provide the webbing for multiplex roles involve social transactions, just as economic networks involve economic transactions. One difference is that money is not the basis of social transactions.[28] There are other differences, as I have already suggested. A main one is that social transactions are based on the recognition of potentially compatible differences, which in turn fosters trust, whereas economic transactions are based on an acknowledgment that common objectives of maximizing personal utilities engender defensive strategies. As it is said, *caveat emptor*, or the buyer beware.

TRANSACTION COSTS

There is another important difference that relates to the principles of performance in economic and social realms. Efficient markets are those with zero transaction costs—that is, no organizations and costless information.[29] Generalists for local markets (for example, the village store) have low transaction costs because of dense ties with buyers, minimal costs of enforcement, and concentration of control and exchange at one site. Generalists centralize virtually all activities, including production, buying, selling, and accounting work. Economic generalists are not very productive or very profitable, but they are very efficient. With economic specialization and distant markets, a myriad of transaction problems arise. It is necessary to search out to find what prices should be charged for outputs and paid for inputs. In any business, say, that of producing gift cards, there are uncertainties as to who the buyers might be and also about, say, what colors they like and how much they are willing, in the aggregate, to spend on Valentine's Day cards, compared with cards for Graduation Day. Economic specialists are very productive and, all things being constant, profitable as well. They are not very efficient, however, because they must devote many resources to finding out about markets. The village store owner just has to ask the customers, who are known in any event, whereas the producer of cards evaluates the impersonal market long in advance of production, with great uncertainty. That is, the producers for mass markets have high transaction costs.

Social arrangements are very different. Social actors produce (for example, they share ideas and give others support) and they consume (for example, they receive ideas and accept support) in all their social roles. The cost of transacting cannot be distinguished from the payoff of transacting. In our generalist social roles—as citizens—our efficiency does not come at the cost of productivity. In fact, when citizens cooperate as generalists, using the same language and set of public manners, community life and personal life tend to be more efficient and more productive than when citizens are specialists.

However, in our specialist social roles, in occupations, for example, our productivity does not come at the cost of efficiency. Although it is true that specialists must transact a great deal with one another, the transactions are not costly in the same sense that transactions are among economic specialists. There are three reasons for this. First, because people occupy so many social roles, there are cognitive and emotional efficiencies. What we learn and pick up in a classroom, the newspaper, or at a committee meeting only adds to the way we carry out a job—certainly new information never hurt a specialist-person. Second, when people interact as specialists with other specialists, they learn more about how the whole picture fits together. Third, the more specialists interact with one another, the more likely it is that common conventions will emerge to make future interaction possible.

The simple point is that in social relations, the more information the better, and this is achieved through free and easy transactions. In economic affairs, more information ups the costs of keeping secrets; perfect information would lead to monopoly, and imperfect information raises production costs for generalists and raises transaction costs for specialists. Besides this, because relevance is critical in economic life, all economic actors, generalists and specialists, monitor boundaries to keep out what is not relevant. Yet the subjective underpinnings of social life encourage us not to rule out information in premature or arbitrary ways.

The principles of organization—the mapping of activities that are carried out synchronically, sequentially, and over space and time, and that involve multiplexity—imply a great deal for social integration and opportunities for sustaining enduring forms of cooperation. What maintains these social relations are social networks. Like transactions of markets they bind together actors. But social networks do not involve atomistic actors in the aggregate, but interdependent actors in groups of various sizes and interests. Individuals create and participate in social networks, but these networks then take on properties that are quite independent of the people who created them, and this is partly because social conventions emerge when people transact and cooperate.

Discussions about social order and control often veer into discussions about authority, discipline, and power. A recognition of the importance of mapping, however, leads us to look elsewhere for answers about social order and control. Political economy theory increasingly emphasizes contending interests that have to be mediated by the state. This is based on the notion that economic motivations are the basis of the social order. Thus, it is argued that in the Western discourse of power a rationalized system will shape behavior so that behavior is compatible with the system. It is the discourse of a capitalist society that rationality and freedom are not separate from private ownership and individual consumption. But viewing social life as involving mapping shifts the emphasis instead to negotiation and interpersonal communication as the basis of rationality and freedom.

NOTES

1. *The Moral Dimension: Towards a New Economics.* New York: Free Press, 1988.
2. Andrew L. Shapiro, *We're Number One.* New York: Vintage, 1992.
3. Stuart Bruchey, *Enterprise.* Cambridge: Harvard University Press, 1990, p. 343.
4. Mark S. Mizruchi, *The Structure of Corporate Political Action.* Cambridge: Harvard University Press, 1992.
5. For example, see Martin Mayer, *The Greatest-Ever Bank Robbery.* New York: Macmillan, 1990.
6. Edmund E. Byrne, *Work, Inc.* Phildelphia: Temple University Press, 1990, p. 61.
7. One of the pleasures of reading novels is following the psychic and social investments and divestments of a given character, of which only we the reader and the character are aware. The other characters in the novel remain uninformed, which is altogether plausible. The opposite situation—in which we throw ourselves into a role with wild abandon—is commonplace, but not of special literary interest. Nor are friends much interested in the details of our committedness to singleton roles.
8. John Rawls, *A Theory of Justice.* Oxford: Oxford University Press, 1971.
9. Michael Useem discusses the ways in which members of major corporations have issues that transcend the interests of their own companies. See *The Inner Circle: Large Corporations and the Rise of Political Activity in the U.S. and U.K.* New York: Oxford University Press, 1984.
10. Bronislaw Malinowski, *Freedom and Civilization.* Bloomington: Indiana University Press, 1944.
11. Karl Polanyi, *The Great Transformation.* Boston: Beacon Press, [1944] 1957, p. 49.
12. Émile Durkheim, *The Division of Labor in Society.* New York: Free Press, [1893] 1933.
13. Walter W. Powell's discussion of network forms of organization is useful here. See "Neither Market nor Hierarchy," *Research in Organizational Behavior* 12: 295–336.
14. See Charles Lindblom, *Politics and Markets: The World's Political Economic Systems.* New York: Basic Books, 1977.
15. See Ernest Gellner, *Plough, Sword, and Book.* London: Collins Harvill, 1988.
16. Durkheim, op. cit.
17. A form of interdependence in markets is that sellers hope that other sellers will agree to keep the prices up. It is on this point that rational-choice

theorists contend that the extensiveness of members' dependence on one another has no implications for group solidarity (Michael Hechter, *Principles of Group Solidarity*. Berkeley: University of California Press, 1987, p. 49). This is a correct conclusion for market behavior but such cooperation works against buyers' interests and is inefficient.

18. John W. Shaffer, *Family and Farm: Agrarian Change and Household Organization in the Loire Valley, 1500–1900*. Albany: State University of New York Press, 1982.

19. P. K. Misra, "The Gadulia Lohars—Nomadism and Economic Activities," pp. 235–246 in Lawrence Saadia Leshnik and Gunther-Dietz Sontheimer (eds.), *Pastoralists and Nomads in South Asia*. Wiesbaden: Otto Harrassowitz, 1975.

20. Cyril S. Belshaw, *Traditional Exchange and Modern Markets*. Englewood Cliffs, NJ: Prentice-Hall, 1965.

21. Piotr Kropotkin, *Mutual Aid: A Factor of Evolution*. London: Heinemann, 1910. He was arguing against Darwin, but similar charges can be levied against the assumptions of contemporary theory that places individual survival first over that of society. Central in libertarian thinking is the idea of entitlement rights so that the individual's rights and property are in the first instance always protected (see Robert Nozick, *Anarchy, State, and Utopia*. New York: Basic Books, 1974). The denial of social good is also evident in economic theory. In *Studies in the Quantitative Theory of Money* (Chicago: University of Chicago Press, 1956), Milton Friedman argues that individual incentive is to do better than the average, and the implication is that any intervention that undermines individual incentives spells economic disaster.

22. Eviatar Zerubavel, *Hidden Rhythms: Schedules and Calendars in Social Life*. Berkeley: University of California Press, 1981.

23. Which is, in fact, what happened in the 1950s. When the Chicago Skyway was finished, engineers realized that considerable work had to be done to realign the Indiana spur of I90 so that bridge and highway would meet.

24. For example, Arthur Francis, *New Technology at Work*. Oxford: Oxford University Press, 1986.

25. Diana Crane, *Invisible Colleges: Diffusion of Knowledge in Scientific Communities*. Chicago: University of Chicago Press, 1972. Also see Judith R. Blau, "Sociometric Structure of a Scientific Discipline," pp. 191–206 in Robert Alun Jones (ed.), *Research in Sociology of Knowledge, Sciences and Art. Vol. 1*. Greenwich, CT: JAI Press, 1978.

26. Durkheim, op. cit.

27. See Rose Coser, "The Complexity of Roles as a Seedbed of Individual Autonomy," pp. 237–263 in Lewis A. Coser (ed.), *The Idea of Social Structure: Essays in the Honor of Robert K. Merton*. San Diego: Harcourt Brace Jovanovich, 1975.

28. James S. Coleman, *Foundations of Social Theory*. Cambridge: Harvard University Press, 1990, p. 119.

29. Oliver E. Williamson, *Markets and Hierarchies*. New York: Free Press, 1975.

4

The Civility of Ordinary Life

No one can persuade me that it takes a better-paid nurse to behave more considerately to a patient, that only an expensive house can be pleasing, that only a wealthy merchant can be courteous to his customer and display a handsome sign outside, that only a prosperous farmer can treat his livestock well.

— VACLAV HAVEL (May 1992)

The portentous risk to civic life, as Vaclav Havel repeatedly warned, is putting a price tag on it. But what is perceived to be a risk in Czechoslovakia is nothing but ordinary in the West. In the United States the rich have excellent health care, receive and pay for courtesy, and have fine schools for their children. Indeed, race confounds this equation. As Eastern European countries shake free from old regimes of political oppression, corrupt bureaucracies, and lack of economic freedoms, the dangers of "enterprising" social life—when adopting enterprise economies—loom large. Havel warns that emerging economic inequalities may imperil the civic order.

Of course, in the United States civic life has not been completely scuttled by enterprise economy. However, in a period of decline with increasing economic inequalities, the civic order has been jeopardized. What are the social mechanisms that help to maintain civility as common coin? This is a fairly complex question, and social scientists have many answers to it depending on whether they are interested in issues of social justice, communities, neighborhoods, crime, child rearing, and so forth. I choose to deal with the most mundane and commonplace mechanisms that operate at the microlevel of interpersonal relations. These include social conventions, institutionalized means of cooperation, the interdependence of members of weaker groups, and the embeddedness of social arrangements. I also argue that a check on the feasibility of "enterprising" social relations is rooted in the complexity of rationality in social contracts.

SOCIAL CONVENTIONS

In contrast to much of economic life, in social life practices are not established anew on a daily basis, and social cooperation is not renegotiated with every encounter. Social conventions make possible ongoing social relations over long periods of time and over space and that involve different constellations of participants. By social conventions, I cover a wide gamut of taken-for-granted guidelines. Illustrations include the following: rules about starting and ending a conversation, rules about turn taking and face saving, expectations that new members need time to learn and older group members have obligations to share what they know, norms that dominate client and professional relations, and concrete information about how things get done. These conventions, like the structural arrangements already discussed in Chapter 3, integrate elements of social life, and they provide an overarching frame of understanding. Conventions may be made by individuals, but over time, they become independent of the people that made them and even independent of those that use them. For example, compared with Norwegians, people who were born and live in Italy stand closer to one another when they are engaged in a conversation. Norwegians and Italians never think much about it, until they themselves are involved in a conversation with one another. Just the footwork indicates that taken-for-granted social conventions will be modified for this particular social exchange.

Howard Becker provides an exemplary illustration of how social conventions work.[1] When half a dozen or even 100 musicians meet for the first time, they can easily cooperate to make music because a notational system provides them with all the guidelines that they need. Athletes, academics, chess players, and physicians do not need to talk a lot to cooperate (or compete, as the case may be). Specialized social conventions are increasingly international. Baseball, space programs, and entertainment are some domains of activities for which international languages have replaced speaking in many tongues. In some fields in science, the conventions of given disciplines are broken down and rapidly replaced by, or supplanted by, the conventions of new ones. A good illustration would be macrobiology, which attracts scientists whose primary degrees are in many different fields, including physics, chemistry, and biology. In the arts, intergenre cooperation is illustrated by the social underpinnings of cross-over phenomena—classical musicians playing with jazz musicians, opera companies performing gospel music, and Thai choreographers teaching European and American dancers Thai dances.

All social arrangements employ symbols and codes that contribute to efficiency, comprehension, and social cohesion. Organizations that deal with diverse clientele or have a very broad membership evolve semiotic codes that are especially clear so they can be quickly deciphered. The logo of the Red Cross is an example, but so are the architectural codes of urban farmers' markets, McDonald's, mosques, and embassy buildings. One does not need to know Japanese to use the Tokyo subway and rail system, and the same can be said for driving in virtually any country. We attend few big weddings and funerals in our lifetimes, so these events are accompanied with hypercodes that enable people to participate in the rituals without much thinking.[2] In the company of strangers, dialects and accents tend to fall away to provide a more universal idiom. Saussure's distinction between speech and language is useful here.[3] Speech requires only two people, but language is common to all the members of a community and enables them to participate in that community.

There is a marked contrast between the codes of communication in social realms and those in economic ones. In social worlds, we believe the more disclosure there is the better it will be for all participants. In economic realms, nondisclosure is a dominant strategy for securing one's self-interest. This is a source of inefficiency for markets, owing to the high costs of third-party enforcement to maintain more complete if not full disclosure.

THE PROBLEMS OF COORDINATION

At their best, economic contracts are quid pro quo, but when there is asymmetry, as there is in the wage contract, differences in initial economic resources are reinforced by power differences, and the surplus that is generated rebounds to the advantage of the employer. The reason this is often blurred in modern organizations is that there are interdependencies and social resources that are not tied so directly to differences in economic power. Social authority is often a convenience, although it differs from economic power in nontrivial ways. Forms of mapping rely on different means of coordination, ranging from centralized control to full democracy.

On-time synchronized mapping usually requires a high degree of precision. When the hook-and-ladder specialists are getting the equipment ready, the hose specialist must be making sure the pumps, plugs, and hoses are connected. While the design department is planning what sizes and colors the Fall line of refrigerators should be, the marketing department must already be at work considering the advertising strategies. Just as the surgeon dons mask and gloves, the anesthesiologist "puts the patient under," and the surgical nurses attach the patient to the monitoring equipment.

Mapping on-time collective activities is typically a matter of authoritative control. A sergeant shouts out the orders; a memorandum dictates when tasks must be finished; fire chiefs may tip their hats to signal when it is time for firefighters to get to their posts; surgeons merely have to stretch out their hands for the gloves to give the signal that the operation is under way. These kinds of social contracts are not especially democratic as discussion, feedback, and striving for consensus are relatively unimportant when many specialists have to coordinate their activities at precisely the same point in time. (Although democracy may have been what got them here in the first place.)

There may be a great deal of mutual cooperation, bantering about, and joking when we have to meet a common deadline, but the serious transactions are more like one-way orders or strictly under the control of procedures. We each relinquish much autonomy and independence, but only in the colloquial sense of those terms, as we all gain more than we lose. It makes perfect sense to students that if there is one day to register for classes, one way of doing it is to have the A's through D's signing up for humanities classes at 9 A.M., whereas the E's through L's must register for science courses, the M's through Q's line up for physical education classes, and the rest have that hour to sign up in the social science line. Much of social life is turn taking but of the kind that after some finish taking their turn, the others are required to take theirs. We distinguish this authority that is dictated by convenience from power that stems from asymmetry in economic realms, such as unfair employment practices, monopoly, and economic exploitation, in general.

In the case of mapping social arrangements that involve activities carried out over time—sequentially—transactions often follow the contours of decentralized networks as direct communication is important. Relaying a patient from admitting office to surgery to the recovery room is, of course, governed by strict procedure, but participants must be able to efficiently piece together makeshift arrangements if, for example, extra diagnostic procedures are required or if the anesthesiologist cannot be found. In an architecture office, a new project moves efficiently from one stage to the next—from the designer, to those who work on the detailed specifications, then to the engineering specialists, and finally, to the people who coordinate building plans with contractors. This is the theory, at least. But as Dana Cuff insightfully describes, this process involves so many contingencies, feedback loops, and renegotiations that people are ceaselessly involved in redefining their roles as well as the project itself. This involves finessing social arrangements as much as it does finessing the building-in-progress.[4]

Procedures and routines may help supplement the repeated sequences at restaurants, but the informal transactions are all important: "The guy with the blue hat is in a hurry"; "Light on the mustard, hold the garlic"; "Tell her the plate is hot"; "Coffee black for table 6"; "Do we still have the kiwi dessert?" It is difficult to closely control the participants involved in sequential mapping of activities because there are evident reasons for people to adjust to one another's actions. The boss or supervisor who is detached from the ongoing activities can play a greater role as a consultant, mediator, or advisor, and has to rely on the interlocking of lateral roles for the task to be accomplished.

The social coordination of activities carried out over time and space is more complex than that required for activities that are simultaneously or sequentially enacted. Clocks, calendars, technology, and formal contracts enable people to cooperate over long distance. At the same time that formalization becomes important, so does, interestingly enough, trust. International cooperation in economic development, health problems, and scientific research has largely proceeded on the basis of mutual recognition of the complexity of the issues and that any solution must necessarily be the result of collective efforts. It is simple enough to see that these objectives cannot be achieved by markets, owing, first, to the nondisclosure principles on which markets operate, and second, because collective problems are difficult to solve competitively.

I have implied that social power does not exist, or that if it does, it is based on consent. This is clearly not always the case, for it is possible to consolidate social power against the will of the majority of members. Besides piggy-backing on economic power, this is achieved by means of monopolies of social resources (skill, prestige, knowledge), control over uncertainty, and control over the mapping rules.

It is the latter—control over mapping—about which we have the

most to worry. Based on many, many workers' consent over time, it has
the pretentious airs of permanent legitimacy, and, based on general
knowledge of how the pieces fit together, it has the aura of obdurate
omniscience. Because it is the principle of management in large organizations of all kinds, it is useful to explore this form of social power in
some detail.

Herbert A. Simon, in a brilliant and well-known article, discusses
the importance of interdependence and how interdependence enhances
the integrity of the whole and the efficiency of operations.[5] At the crux
of the matter is the notion that the interdependent whole is easier to
control than the collection of parts.

> There once were two watchmakers, named Hora and Tempus, who
> manufactured very fine watches. Both of them were highly re-
> garded, and the phones in their workshops rang frequently—new
> customers were constantly calling them. However, Hora prospered,
> while Tempus became poorer and poorer and finally lost his shop.
> What was the reason? The watches the men made consisted of
> about 1,000 parts each. Tempus had so constructed his that if he
> had one part assembled and had to put it down—to answer the
> phone say—it immediately fell to pieces and had to be reassembled
> from the elements. The better the customers liked his watches, the
> more they phoned him, the more difficult it became for him to find
> enough uninterrupted time to finish a watch.
>
> The watches that Hora made were no less complex than those
> of Tempus. But he had designed them so that he could put together
> subassemblies of about ten elements each. Ten of these subassem-
> blies, again, could be put together in a larger subassembly; and a
> system of ten of the latter subassemblies constitutes the whole
> watch. Hence, when Hora had to put down a partly assembled
> watch to answer the phone, he lost only a small part of his work,
> and he assembled his watches in only a fraction of the man-hours it
> took Tempus.

Assemblies of interdependent elements have the advantage over
aggregations of elements of having integrity, and that integrity is a
property of any well-coordinated system—a mechanical, cognitive, or
social system. When hundreds, if not thousands, of specialized parts
are interdependent, control is easier to achieve.

The morale of the story, as it has been told repeatedly in business-
school courses, is that an organization with interdependence is easier to
manage than one without. Built-in coordination that is achieved by
virtue of interdependence combined with multiple levels of increasingly

encompassing complexity is by far and away the best instrument of control that managers possess. Such organizational interdependence that links parts, units, and levels reduces the amount of time and energy that managers otherwise need to supervise directly.

The other interpretation of this form of social control is that it marginalizes participation and reduces the skills and autonomy of workers. There is engineered social inequality, and the ground rules on which inequality is based are under the control of the manager. Thus, power differences are insidious. We must be careful here and not overstate the case because there are two qualifications that must be made.

First, as with any form of mapping, all participants possess some indifference about the locus of authority and how coordination is achieved. Quite frankly, I happily entrust many decisions to others even when these decisions bear on my own work and well-being. Library acquisitions, computer upgrades, building improvements, and classroom assignments are realms in which I am happy not to be involved (with the proviso that "voice" is an option, as I will later discuss). It might be suggested that in the best of circumstances, complex organizations offer the opportunities of exercising skills and having influence in one domain, while more casually cooperating with others outside that domain of specialization.

Second, authority in any large, complex bureaucracy faces crises of legitimacy now and then, in localized departments or on a grand scale. People are willing to concede autonomy when doing so is practical and consistent with collective perceptions of constraints within the organization and when they have alternatives and opportunities without. Yet people conspire to map new ways of doing things when they can overcome constraints and see that it is in their advantage to do, and if opportunities are not conducive to "exit," many individuals will participate in the conspiracy. Paradoxically, organizations benefit by such machinations as organizations are not watches made up of mechanical parts, but rather are collaborative enterprises in which rational actors each have their own investments in making sure that things go right.

Third, we might ask, who is empowered by interdependence? The person who oversees the organization or members of the organization? This line of questioning makes particular sense when we consider incipient organizations that develop from social movements. The French Revolution and the American Revolution as well as the civil rights and suffrage movements were successful not only because of the linkages among participants but also because participants were drawn from different "places"—for example, organizations, social classes, and communities. Collective strength was not derived from the fact that participants were homogeneous, but because they came from heterogeneous backgrounds and were more complexly interrelated than the elites against whom they mobilized. For example, the civil rights movement drew from black churches, colleges, and traditional civil rights groups.[6] Although initially the suffrage movement was launched by middle-class women, it became successful as ties were forged initially across class and subsequently gender and racial lines.[7] One might conclude that it is not the social solidarity among the powerless but their complementarity that provides organization.

EMBEDDEDNESS OF SOCIAL STRUCTURES

Social structures lend themselves to being viewed in slices. The crew team is a component of the college or university, of an athletics department, and also of regional and national rowing associations. Similarly, the hospital is part of a structure, the institutionalized medical sector, or it can be viewed as a differentiated component of something else, a university or municipal government. The hospital also is involved in "joint ventures" with research institutes, other hospitals, and government agencies. However the structures are defined, the boundaries are unstable because the coordination of activities requires overlapping activities and the creation of statuses that bridge different structures.

Peoples' very perceptions about what the relevant structures are will also vary. For rowing coaches, the New England regional conference may be the meaningful organizational framework for organizing a season; the director of physical education views the rowing teams as composing one small unit in an administrative department; student rowers view team participation as a slot in what is otherwise an academic schedule. Staff physicians may consider the hospital in terms of its departments; physicians with courtesy appointments often cannot see further than their own patients; and, in contrast, residents view the hospital as an extension of the medical school.

Accompanying an understanding of the complexity of social units and the fact that people have different relevant organizational memberships and commitments (even when they are ostensibly part of the same organization) is the observation that each individual is a member of many other organizations. The extraordinary richness of organizational life has profound implications for the freedom people have in making social contracts.

ECONOMIC AND SOCIAL RULES

We are now in a better position to fine-tune some distinctions between economic and social behavior. I focus on two differences—the nature of transactions and of rationality—and the consequences of economic opportunities (or absence of them) for social life.

As I have argued, individuals, families, football teams, organizations, neighborhoods, and nation-states all have environments, and they are embedded in larger social structures. Individuals deal with families; football teams with universities; profit-making organizations with other profit-making enterprises and with buyers; public agencies with larger government units and with constituencies.

As cognizant and perceptive economic and social actors, we are aware that we are making decisions and choices. We are, of course, rational with a vengeance, and market behavior demonstrates that just as social behavior does. In markets, people participate to close the deal, to reduce uncertainty, to get their just deserts. People participate in economic markets as if they were single-stranded institutions. We do not buy shoes in hardware stores; companies do not look for accountants to fill jobs for biologists; we cannot even buy much cultural capital in the neighborhood if we forget to mow the lawn. The ends–means nexus is relatively clear in economic markets.

Interestingly, Freud viewed psychic transactions in much the way that economists view market transactions—as reducing a source of uncertainty, as overcoming it by processing it. In social life, in contrast, we keep making more complex contracts, seeking them out on their own accord, with very little reduction of uncertainty. This suggests that the rationalities of wealth maximizing are different from those in social life.

Social contracts are more complicated than economic deals. They are forged with the idea that self-interest must be tempered by the interests of the other and the recognition that persistence of the group requires subordination of short-term individual goals. Social contracts evolve to take into account the circumstances and contingencies of other actors' rational choices (and to react, in an ad hoc way, to irrationalities). Unlike the revolving charge account for which credit lines and service fees are specified in advance of transactions, in the social organization—for example, neighborhood, voluntary association, the work organization—

there are evolving and ever-changing mappings that require new social contracts.[8] This is the case because of turnover, the changing environment, new roles and role constellations, and the emergence of different cultural conventions and the reshaping of old ones.

In social arrangements, rationality is bounded by interdependence and by the consequences of actions that may be long range. This means that people will often stay in organizations even when they are losing most of the battles. There is not one means–ends nexus. Thus, social rationality is very often difficult to discern from an outside perspective, as role identities and personal commitments are complex and individuals carefully adjust priorities and marshall their resources.

Moreover, economic life and social life are confounded with each other. Economic contracts are made in organizations as well as in decentralized markets, and organizations include families as well as businesses. For that reason, the viability of social organizations depends on the economy and vice versa. This is fairly obvious, but it is important to clarify one aspect of this relationship.

Market opportunities, in the aggregate, depend on growth, and without growth competition has a zero-sum outcome.[9] There may be only so many jobs available in a community in a given year; some local merchants close their doors and go bankrupt; if neither the tax base nor rate increases, more elementary-school teachers will not be hired; and when a buyer spends all of his or her year's savings on a vacation there is none left for a new car. In principle, market opportunities can expand only in ways that are related to growth, for example, owing to technological improvements, or to economic development, or by discovery of a vast frontier. Markets that are unrelated in principle—for example, financial markets, job markets, labor markets, educational markets, land markets—share common fates because they are linked to a broad spectrum of economic opportunities.

When growth is frozen, competition results in zero-sum outcomes, as Thurow, Kuttner, and other economists have shown.[10] Yet the absence of economic growth is more serious than that. When people lose in one market they are also disadvantaged in others. With a deteriorating economy, like the one the United States has experienced since the 1970s, resources become scarcer and opportunities increasingly constricted, disadvantage has multiplier effects.

Social relations are seriously impaired by a precipitous decline in the economy. Decline invariably accompanies increasing inequalities in resources and opportunities, and this means that the implicit and explicit understandings upon which social cooperation was earlier based are seriously undermined. The expectations of the disadvantaged are dashed, and the already advantaged try to consolidate what they have, while they fend off contenders and deal with their insecurities. We might say that when the growth of social opportunities is frozen, social cooperation can turn into social conflict. However, social opportunities are more complicated than economic opportunities on which economic growth depends. This makes the analysis all the more complicated and more interesting. I attempt in the next chapter to explore some elementary considerations about the nature of social opportunities.

NOTES

1. Howard Becker, "Art as Collective Action," *American Sociological Review* 39 (1974): 767–776.
2. Stephen R. Barley, "Semiotics and the Study of Occupational and Organizational Cultures," *Administrative Science Quarterly* 28 (1983): 393–413.
3. Ferdinand de Saussure, *Course in General Linguistics*. Edited by Charles Bally and Albert Sechehaye with Albert Riedlinger. Trans. and Introduction, Wade Baskin. New York: McGraw-Hill, [1915] 1966.
4. Dana Cuff, *Architecture: The Story of Practice*. Cambridge: MIT Press, 1991.
5. Herbert A. Simon, "The Architecture of Complexity," *Proceedings of the American Philosophical Society* 106 (1962): 467–482.
6. Doug McAdam, *Political Process and the Development of Black Insurgency, 1930–1970*. Chicago: University of Chicago Press.
7. Ellen Carol DuBois, *Feminism and Suffrage*. Ithaca: Cornell University Press, 1978.
8. Peter M. Blau, *Exchange and Power in Social Life*. New York: Wiley, 1964.
9. Lester C. Thurow, *The Zero-Sum Society: Distribution and the Possibilities for Economic Change*. New York: Basic Books, 1980; also see Kenneth E. Boulding, *Economic Analysis*. 3rd ed. New York: Harper & Bros., 1955.
10. Thurow, op. cit.; Robert Kuttner, *The Economic Illusion*. Philadelphia: University of Pennsylvania Press, 1984; also see Henry Teune, *Growth*. Newbury Park, CA: Sage, 1988.

5

Whence Come Opportunities?

Although located on the edge of Paris in Vincennes, this is one of the only couscous restaurants that also offers home delivery service. Copious, stylish, and not too expensive, owned and managed by Asdin, a charismatic marathon runner from Djerba, Tunisia.

—Paris Inside Out

The source of economic opportunities is growth that is evident in increasing productivity, in new jobs, and in economic investments. This is, of course, much more complicated than I imply here, and economists have widely different views on how economic growth can be achieved. Yet all economists agree that investments, productivity, and jobs define the parameters of economic growth and, thus, opportunities. And, when economic growth is frozen, competition is intense, and the outcomes are zero-sum. That is, some groups gain at the loss of others. In modern industrial societies decline entails increasing inequalities as it hits those first and hardest who are not advantaged by reserves. Declining opportunities affect those most with the least to lose because they do not have the cushion of reserves.

Social life is not as simple as economic life. There are many kinds of social resources. Conventional ones include knowledge, skills, friendships, status, leisure, and family. In fact, we are always pushing the frontiers of invention when it comes to the matter of social resources. Knowing mubbly-peg and being skilled with the hulahoop does not count for much among youngsters these days, but learning Dungeons and Dragons requires being clever and a great investment of time, and experts are widely admired. Social life is not zero-sum because there are endless resources, and if we do not possess a particular one it is easier to invent a new one than to fight about it. Besides, social resources are not so easy to monopolize (although, of course, people try).

There is, still, the blunt connection between economy and social life, and when economic conditions deteriorate, as when many people are unemployed, hungry, and even homeless, the economy sets such severe constraints on the quality of social life that people often take matters into their own hands. This is not called competition. It is called revolution.

To inquire about how people obtain social resources is to inquire about opportunities, for the step from opportunity to possessing resources is very simple, but obtaining opportunities in the first place is quite tricky. As the expression implies, "If someone only gets an inch, they will take a mile." But how do they get the inch? I believe that is a challenging question.

There are two elementary sources of opportunities in society. One is structural, and the other is cultural. The analytical distinction makes sense in terms of theory and empirical examples, although in social life they are profoundly muddled. Structure encompasses all those things that materialize in practice: resources, organizations, jobs, and even ties and networks among people.[1] Culture includes meaning, social labels, ideas, knowledge, and social conventions. The distinction breaks down at the level of mapping in everyday life but is nevertheless very useful as we try to understand how people acquire opportunities (and how their opportunities are constrained).

Considering structure as social positions—social roles, social statuses—is helpful because positions accompany resources, are bound in social networks, and lock into larger structures, including families, organizations, and social classes. Social positions also have an immediate relation to culture, as social labels help to delineate cultural boundaries and are accompanied by expectations of what people do and what they expect of others. In a sense, opportunities are realized by achieving positions, which play the pivotal role in social structures of all kinds; besides, cultural meanings articulate the way we map activities in the terms of positions. The premises of my argument are not deterministic because people have many positions, which creates considerable slippage, and cultural meaning is not something that stands still. Throughout this chapter an important minor theme is the tension between social structure and culture. Sometimes we look to structure to understand equality or inequality, and sometimes we look to culture.

CULTURE AND GROUP MEMBERSHIP

People are members of groups, which are components of social structures, and that gives them cultural identities and cultural name tags as well. Opportunities are created as membership identities and name tags are redefined, broadened, clarified, or obfuscated. For example, these days we would not say, or write, "the doctor, he . . ." unless we, in fact, refer to a male physician. It is an acknowledgment of changes in American society, but the language we use about group membership is significant in its own right and has social consequences.

Culture creates opportunities through defining and redefining boundaries of group membership. Sometimes vagueness and uncertainty with respect to cultural definitions and boundaries make it possible for a group to eke out a niche in the ecology of opportunities. Following the Revolution, Americans groped for a style that would be appropriate for the new nation. Repudiating European models, artists and builders turned to classical sculpture. George Washington in a Roman toga may now appear downright sappy, but the label and the history that the sculpture brought to mind helped to establish the symbols of a new national identity and served the purpose of showing England and France what America was not.[2]

Kenneth Cmiel provides historical evidence to show that the transformations in American language in the eighteenth century created for planters, shopkeepers, and all sorts of "middling folk" opportunities to participate in civil society. The "breathing space," he explains, for baroque displays of eloquence and for the educated gentry was restrained at the top by fear of reviving aristocratic traditions, and at the bottom by the diffusion of reading skills and the expansion of education.[3]

Being successful in acquiring normal recognition of membership helps a previously unnoticed, stigmatized, or disadvantaged group to secure social and economic resources and then to procure some symbolic basis for a distinctive cultural identity. Some ethnic minorities, such as Italians and Swedes, experienced considerable success in the nineteenth century in this way, and others, such as Asians and Jews, did in the twentieth century.

The agility of cultural minorities—the "Real Granolas," "Hippies," Brooklynites, "Valley girls," urban American blacks, and assimilated Asians—of simultaneously playing off the mainstream and the sidestream culture demonstrates how people create intricate social lives.

Versatility in language or dialect, lifestyles, and demeanor offers a means to cross from one culture to another at the drop of a hat, but it also suggests that groups assimilate as and when they choose to.[4]

But neither is the mainstream culture at rest. Take the matter of dress and fashion. It seems that the increasing tendency for people to dress for the occasion—and not for status—creates the kind of informality that decreases distance among people of different social backgrounds. The repudiation of conspicuous consumption encourages a cultural equality, or at least cultural ambiguity, just as the improved standard of living during the nineteenth century permitted "passing" by the acquisition of fashion and accoutrement that had earlier been monopolized by the upper class. Ever since the abolition of sumptuary rules, fashion has played a role in helping to bring about cultural equality.[5]

Often, the politics of securing equality or group recognition depends on a successful cultural campaign for the assertion of differences. At other times, the politics of securing equality involves a full-scale effort to eradicate old cultural identities and to establish full membership in the broader social-cultural order. Occupational groups create new titles for themselves for this purpose. For example, library schools redefine their students' prospects with specialties in "management information systems." Commercial art programs prefer the title of Design Studies. Home economics has found new lodgings in programs in Nutritional Sciences and Child Development.

Group labels are used to make claims for identity and distinctiveness and to mold group solidarity—African-Americans, Chicanos, Native Americans, Croats, and Serbs. Such cultural techniques for drawing differences emerge out of structural disadvantage or isolation. The embellishment of differences in tradition and historical experiences is a strategy for recognition and redress, and when success ensues, the origins of labels tend to melt away or the labels assume new meaning. The instant that the Beatles were knighted, Queen Elizabeth threw over existing conventions about what constituted meritorious service in aristocratic tradition. North Carolina's country kids were once known as the poor, illiterate, barefoot farmers' sons who worked in the tar factories owned by wealthy northern industrialists. Now Tar Heels—the curse of that work—is used to promote the state's thriving research and industrial capabilities, and, needless to say, its top-ranked university athletic teams.

Sometimes success is based on claims for cultural distinctiveness with the implicit assertion that recognition of differences will enhance group members' identities and contribute to the vitality of social life in general. Throughout American history, ethnic groups attempted to turn disadvantage into advantage by cultural means—for example, newspapers, secret societies, celebrations and festivals, and cuisine. Groups use both strategies, assimilation, and separateness to gain both cultural acceptance and distinctiveness. To wit, women argue different sides of the issue, some making claims for the uniqueness of women owing to biological and physiological differences (leading to the conclusion that women have superior socioemotional skills that make them better managers than men), whereas others argue that the difference between men and women lies only in institutional sexism.[6]

The subtleties of culture are profound, which makes the matter of molding symbolic systems of identity and community an extremely fine-textured affair. It also means that the cultural attributions that we fashion about others are laced with subtle nuances of which we are barely aware. My own best example of this is an undergraduate's research paper from a course in social methodology. The student's hypothesis was that television commercials exhibited forms of racism. I was convinced, along with the student, that this was likely. Sampling evening time slots, he meticulously recorded minority and nonminority representation in commercials. To our surprise, the proportion of blacks in commercials was just about equal to the proportion in the general population. It was also evident that blacks were cast in similar occupational, family, and consumer roles as whites. My ambitious and perceptive student was not convinced. A new hypothesis emerged, was tested, and was confirmed: Namely, African-Americans did not frequently talk for themselves, as off-camera voices were dubbed over their activities. Whites, he found, were more likely to do their own talking. Deeply embedded in our society are the cultural codes of privileged statuses.

THE ECOLOGY OF STRUCTURE

Social structure creates positions of opportunities in many ways. One is through a vacuum, a hole in the edifice, which is not filled or which others have decided not to fill. For example, historically, the difficulties of establishing market ties between cities or between dominant ethnic groups created new chances for stigmatized groups, namely, groups that were marginal by virtue of religion or ethnicity to become successful as itinerant tradespeople. These groups have been called "middle-men minorities" by Edna Bonacich.[7]

Cheap land and untapped resources of the West in the nineteenth century offered clear opportunities for East Coast farmers, whose plots were too rocky and too small to farm, for fortune hunters in search of gold, and for European immigrants. The presence of farmers, fortune hunters, and immigrants, in turn, offered opportunities for others—for traders, railroad companies, and evangelists.

The increasing expansion of industrial firms during the twentieth century created white-collar jobs in management that the native-born, college-educated filled, and as they left blue-collar jobs, these provided opportunities for the sons and daughters of American farmers and for unskilled immigrant groups.[8]

Occupations emerge in the interstices of other occupations' markets in which there are underserved or unsatisfied consumers. For example, dissatisfaction with the bureaucratization of medicine, combined with the lack of medical care in rural settings, gave midwifery a chance to recover in the twentieth century. The increasing incidence of new ailments among the urban middle classes—ranging from tennis elbow, shin splints, fatty deposits, to anxiety about careers and divorces—led to the overflow of patients in the offices of established medical specialties, and this, in turn, created marvelous opportunities for the creation of new specialties, such as amateur-sports medicine, dermatologic surgery, and many psychiatric specialties.

Whereas the expression is "necessity is the mother of invention," it is actually the recognition of opportunities of that necessity that, in fact, parents inventions. Early baseball was a nasty and rowdy affair, and injuries were commonly the result of fans throwing glass pop bottles at players, and players hurling them back. It did not take paper manufacturers long to seize the opportunity. About 1920, such businesses convinced club owners to give up pop bottles for their newly invented paper cups.[9]

The term *window of opportunity* captures the idea of such a structure, although it conveys the namby-pamby idea that one contemplates an opportunity. I want to express, more strongly, the idea that an opportunity is a niche, cranny, nook, or recess in which there is space to occupy. Opportunities are for the seizing, not for the viewing. The ecology of structured opportunities is based on a principle of vacancy, and vacancies are created when there is a frontier, personnel turnover and attrition, demand, hiatuses among existing markets, expansion or growth, and the recognition of new necessities.

POSITIONS AND THE INTERSECTION OF STRUCTURES

To paraphrase Georg Simmel, we could say, it is the position that makes the person. His point is more precisely this:

> [There is a] deeper justification of the proverb: "If God gives somebody an office, he also gives him the mind necessary for it." For precisely, the "mind" required for the occupancy of higher positions exists in many men, but it proves, develops, reveals itself only once they occupy the position.[10]

We will forgive the early twentieth century gendered malaprop to ask, with Simmel, why it is that "the position makes the person"? It implies that if you plunk the average person, more or less suitably prepared, into a position of responsibility, the person will behave responsibly. If you plunk the average person, more or less suitably prepared, into a position filled with opportunities for graft and corruption, it is not unlikely that the person will take advantage of those chances. Finally, if you plunk that same person into a job that is tedious and boring, that person is unlikely to make much of it.

This is the argument that individual attributes are trivial; or, as the sociologist would say, human capital factors—for example, education, skills, experience—are not all-important, given sufficient opportunities.

Melvin Kohn and Carmi Schooler find that for a broad category of jobs within an organization, social class, education, and family background make less of a difference for performance than do the opportunities that people have in their jobs.[11] The implications of White's and Sørensen's investigations are that moving up the ladder in an organization depends on a vacancy opening up, and not only—or always primarily—on education, talent, experience, and so forth.[12] A further refinement of that work is that for a given pool of workers, promotion chances depend purely on luck even though workers vary in terms of their human capital.[13]

Jobs also shape the way in which people are likely to respond to situations. People with jobs that are on the firing line and who continuously face conflicting expectations—such as waitresses,[14] secretaries,[15] or cab drivers—are likely to react to cross-pressures with aggression or emotional outbursts. Jackall reports that when the opportunities for immoral behavior in large corporations are profound enough, most everyone acts immorally.[16] One interesting line of research in criminology leads to the conclusion that the likelihood of crimes is the result of opportunities for committing them.[17] For example, in neighborhoods where many people are at home, say, watching television, there are fewer robberies than in places where people go out in the evening and homes are empty.[18]

For those who are not convinced that the opportunities of positions have imperative command over distributions of aggregate behavior, a simple exercise shows that there is a tautological inevitability to this assumption. As the number of people in the population of any place increases in a linear fashion, the number of possible interactions among the members of the population increases exponentially. To give a specific example, as the number of people increases from 2, to 3, to 4, to 5, and then 6, the number of possible connections increases exponentially from 1, to 3, to 6, to 10, and then 15. This inevitable consequence of population growth has wide-ranging significance. Although the individual does not have more direct connections than there are other individuals, there are many more total connections.

That is, compared with people in small groups, those in large ones have many more friends of friends, many more direct and indirect connections, and much more access to information and resources. Positions are also more partialled up, as I later show, as people specialize in some ways with some of their acquaintances and in other ways with other of their acquaintances. A person in a given position in a group of 6 people can play 15 roles, whereas in a group of 2, there is much role consistency in that single relationship. Interestingly, the implications of structure for positions are cast deterministically, yet the enhanced mapping opportunities among people increase the indeterminacy of group life.

These exponential density effects have far-ranging implications for the group, city, or neighborhood. As size increases, the number of strangers must grow faster than the number of people who are friends because there is an upper bound on the number of friends one can possibly have. Large groups and cities are relatively more impersonal, and increasingly many relations are distant and fleeting.[19]

Places differ in systematic ways in terms of their demographic composition—the relative numbers of people of different ages, occupations, races, and ethnicities. This also figures into opportunity structures. In large cities, in which there are usually excesses of females, the average woman's marriage chances are lower than otherwise. A given group size has consequences in the short and long run. Members of large cohorts—such as the postwar baby boom—experienced extremely large class sizes in elementary and high schools, and the numbers in the cohort may come close to exceeding the numbers of available jobs, or, at least, generate stiff competition for the jobs that are available.[20] When mandatory retirement policies were rescinded, the prospects for job mobility of many vice-presidents and assembly-line workers with low seniority plummeted. As we shall later see, if the middle class declines, the chances of upward mobility will be severely curtailed for those who are working class in origin.

POSITIONS AND CULTURE

Positions, as Simmel observed, are the niches of opportunities, but in the phrase, "positions create the person," positions are not only parts of structures, but they also, as Le Goff argues, express themselves symbolically and are the objects of cultural interpretation.[21] Again, we must be careful and remember that this is a dynamic and holistic relation, even though there are analytical distinctions that can be drawn. In general, cultural expectations that accompany positions play a role in enhancing or diminishing opportunities. Social labels, or cultural definitions, are often the vehicles for obtaining or exploiting opportunities. The position that is embellished with codes of power and dignity, and empowered with high expectations, is very different from the one that is not. Thus, we talk about "dead-end" jobs as ones that are truly specious and ostentatiously void of opportunity. We also refer to the "figurehead," or "the front," for unauthentic positions. The "fast tracker" creates expectations of future success.

Social labels have consequences that alter situations in profound ways. When teachers are told in advance of the school year that some particular kids are "slow" and other particular ones "bright"—when, in fact, they have about the same grades and achievement scores—at the end of the year, the labels become the realities. Even in the psychology laboratory when lab technicians are told that some rats are "experienced in learning experiments" and other rats are "naive and inexperienced"— when actually all the rats arrived just the day before from the rat farm— the lab technicians will unwittingly create real differences among the rats by handling them differently. The "smart, experienced" rats receive more petting and handling, which apparently spurs the motivations of rats.[22]

Social opportunities, including those that ensue from labels, have consequences that are independent of individuals. They create expectations to which people conform, in terms of which people strive to achieve, or to which they simply acquiesce. Thus, opportunities are defined by social labels and expectations, just as they are lodged in social arrangements, such as interpersonal networks and organizations.

The luck or misfortune of any given individual depends on very large structures of opportunities. I stress *large* because their lack of immediacy and remoteness makes it unlikely that people see that their fortunes or misfortunes are tied to such large structures. However, our lives are not only carried out within very large social systems, but they are also implicated in many microsocial systems, an argument that will be fleshed out in the next section. Yet neither luck nor misfortune makes so much sense when we consider the cultural conventions writ large or small. The knife of agency—individual and collective—whittles away at the untoward results of happenstance. In the long run, luck is recognized for what it is, and the lucky ones are called to account to justify themselves, and justice norms are mobilized when it is recognized that persons' fates are the result of what has been unforgettably described as "the slings and arrows of outrageous fortune."

STATUS AND ROLE

The duality of status and role—position and behavior—allows us to see clearly how any one position relates to other positions, how individuals fill more than one position, how positions entail social networks, and how networks delineate organizations and also are embedded in them. At the same time, culture is both context and constituent of status-role as social conventions articulate with status and social expectations accompany role relations. Robert K. Merton's classic essay provides the theory for status and role, and the imagery that makes them such a powerful set of concepts. The individual occupies several statuses, some of which involve, say, organizational participation and others that involve participation in other social systems, such as the family or voluntary association. In each of these statuses, the person has not one but a set of role relations.[23]

For example, Sara, who is an elementary-school teacher (a status), has role relations as a teacher with other status incumbents—parents, other teachers, students, the principal, the school nurse. Sara has other statuses. She is also a parent, works for the local Cub Scout troop, is a daughter, and is actively involved in a community club, and in each of these statuses, Sara has a wide range of role relations.

A point made by Merton is that there is a potential for conflict that may arise owing to discrepant expectations on the part of role partners or by virtue of occupying multiple statuses.[24] A college student is well aware of the incompatibility between his or her statuses, when for example, an employer expects the student to work during exam time, when parents think that the student should come home weekends, and when a close friend needs help in moving precisely the night before a major term paper is due.

Yet Merton also sowed the seeds for understanding how complex status sets and multiple role relations enhance well-being. For example, just as there are high rates of occupational and geographical mobility, there are also high rates of status mobility; exiting a status has distinctive advantages and problems, for example, for nuns who leave and join the secular world, for the new retiree, and the recently wed. The term *leaving the closet* captures the notion of new opportunities of different structures.[25] Some exits occur quite "naturally," as 17- and 18-year-olds leave home, graduate from college, and find their first jobs. Others are voluntary as people withdraw from friendship groups and join others, quit jobs and take others. A major point is that changing opportunities accompanying voluntaristic choices and those entailed in the life course and other transitions means that people lead unexpectedly interesting and complex lives. Although as map makers, we make voluntary choices, these are made on the basis of opportunities that are already available, and choices lead to statuses that are accompanied by their own opportunities.

Rose Laub Coser has developed other far reaching implications of the theory for understanding how occupying multiple statuses entails an enrichment of our microsocial worlds and, paradoxically, for autonomy and individuality. As Coser writes:

> To the extent that an array of relationships with the different demands, expectations, and orientations requires from a person an effort to differentiate and to synthesize, a process of individuation exists.[26]

To wit, membership in complex status sets is a source of individual autonomy, cognitive complexity, and adaptability. This in turn suggests a wellspring for the continual supply of diversity of experience, at least at the level of the individual. Culturally, all people must be different, owing to their distinctive constellations of roles and statuses that are, moreover, ever changing over time.

Another consequence of membership in complex role sets is that it enhances tolerance as individuals acquire cosmopolitan perspectives and become aware of the pluralities of others' situations. When many people have multiple involvements and are anchored in varieties of social settings, there are relatively more contacts among people with different backgrounds and interests, which may not be a cause of cultural diversity but is clearly requisite to the tolerance of such diversity.[27] The paradox of autonomy turns on the point that membership in complex status sets promotes the capacity of choice (as agency) and sustains sufficient ambiguities about what people actually do choose. This, in turn, undermines, or at least considerably reduces, the effectiveness of social control and authority, as individuals are knowledgeable and competent. In complex social arrangements, people make decisions, disagree, and dissent.

NETWORKS

Each status set accompanies role relations involving strands of connection with others. Some relations are instrumental (to get a job), some are charged with emotion (with spouse or lover), some involve love and great responsibility (as for a child), some are reciprocal (in a student study group), some are profoundly asymmetrical (the general and the enlisted recruits come to mind), whereas some are confrontational (the strikers and management at the automobile assembly plant). These social relations and networks involve the many mapping rules of social contracts as outlined earlier and often tie together diverse social settings—work organizations, neighborhoods, families, and voluntary associations.[28] Thus, networks are a source of social glue just as they provide individuals with resources and are a means whereby we get things done.

All such ties, potentially, are the sources of opportunities, but various types of ties provide opportunities of different kinds. Far-flung acquaintances provide superior sources of information about jobs[29]; coworker relations are precisely what provide the rich underlife of impersonal and bureaucratic organizations[30]; and community networks form the dense underbrush that provides cities and citizens with resources for mobilizing soup kitchens, town parades, political campaigns, and interdenominational youth programs. Because networks are so informal, exclusion is a problem, and individuals and groups are easily disadvantaged by lack of access. Compared with men, women are handicapped in job searches, owing to their more impoverished organizational networks,[31] but may be advantaged in old age by the friendships they have cultivated.[32] Urbanites have more far-flung acquaintances than people who live in rural and suburban places,[33] and sharing the unusual and grave problems of poverty, poor families may develop more self-help networks than middle-class families.[34] Cultural diffusion over space is obviously a way that networks decrease the distance between core and periphery, city and hinterland, and, thereby, potentially break up entrenched inequalities and asymmetries of dependence.[35]

CULTURE, ORGANIZATIONS, AND THE DIVISION OF LABOR

According to Weber, people's actions are oriented and justified by prevailing modalities of legitimization, and legitimation is rooted in some form of social organization.[36] Legitimation is essentially cultural consensus about prevailing social patterns. Throughout most of history, dominant patterns of religion, family, locale, and trading were rooted in the belief that action was to be guided by the sanctity of tradition: Thus, economic development moved like a snail as social and political life was more to be conserved than to be adjusted to changing circumstances or new instrumentalities. The divine right of kings helped to shelter practices of feudal hierarchies just as the continuity of social life was linked with sacred and enduring religious and family traditions. One could just as easily mention modern values that are as questionable as the divine right of kings, but these values—consumerism, and status seeking, for example—accelerate change rather than impede it.

The emergence of world trade, science, and improved communication was incompatible with such a world view, and in the early stages of industrialization, a new outlook emerged, centering upon the practical, the efficient, and the pragmatic—how to devise new means to connect with chosen ends. This, according to Weber, meant collective rationality. We can accept Weber's argument about collective rationality of modern life even if we assume that pastoralists, hunters and gatherers, and nomads are also rational. That is, all people at all times have preferences and make choices within the constraints of institutional arrangements.[37] The point is that increasingly, as institutions are held to be secular—not sacred—and mutable—not fixed—and increasing in number—not limited—each individual finds himself or herself involved in making more and more choices and decisions. Tradition matters less.

Weber's other point is that the collective arenas in which people make choices exhibit a rationality; that is, large organizations (1) exhibit internal interdependence and (2) advance collective ends. In practice, this combination poses contradictions. First, enterprise in organizations involves a division of labor and differences in authority. According to Weber, this is the structural and orderly consequence of collective rationality, for unless there is specialization and authority relations it would be hard to achieve common goals. Second, enterprise in large, complex organizations involves community of equality in the sense that we all buy into the grand plan and cooperate, and in the sense that rationality is granted to each and every member. The full implications of the contradiction between the division of labor (differences in authority, among other things) and equality are far-reaching. Yet, here, I shall focus on Weber's own example, the formal organization, or as Weber called it, the bureaucracy.

A bureaucracy (as a theoretical model) is defined as a set of statuses, the occupants of which have rights and responsibilities that are defined by formal provisions, charters, rules, constitutions, or laws. First, people are not themselves the wielders of power, but power resides in offices that are delineated by contracts, legal codes, and written rules, and, most important, by a prevailing legitimacy or agreement that formality and the division of labor rebound to the collective advantage. Second, although individuals may have their own personal agendas, there is consensus about organizational goals and the means to obtain them.

Besides organizing congeries of offices (statuses or positions), a bureaucratic plan delineates a division of labor among departments, subunits, and hierarchical levels. And, to ensure that centrifugal forces entailed by the specialization created by these forms of the division of labor do not undermine the integrity of the organization, mechanisms of coordination are devised to offset such forces. These include rules and regulations, committee structures, administrators and clerks, memoranda, conference calls, and computer networks.

It is fairly clear that the structural underpinnings of the division of labor lead not to equality—the principle of community—but rather to enormous inequalities—of pay, authority, perks, responsibilities. Some might say that company picnics, departmental lunches, weekend retreats, and company baseball games take the sting off the consequences of the division of labor and hierarchy. I do not believe it for a second. The effects of the structural arrangements on generating and sustaining inequalities are unquestionably great.

At the same time that an excessive and arbitrary division of labor can erode the clarity and the logic whereby opportunities are created, there are other structural mechanisms that help to recover opportunities. It is interesting that they lie in indeterminacy, namely, in uncertainties and slippages within structures.

For example, what helps to balance the power between those who wield authority and those who do not is that the latter often control sources of uncertainty.[38] In simpler societies, work roles could be clearly defined in fairly unambiguous ways. Farmers, shopkeepers, and silversmiths had clearly defined jobs that entailed apprenticeships, experience, and training that were fairly precisely linked to what they did to "make a living." With industrialization, the expansion of the service economy, and organizational complexity, work roles often are not congruent with stereotypical training.

Some occupations have relative independence from organizational claims by virtue of their esoteric training. Professionals, such as accountants, pharmacists, lawyers, and doctors, exercise judgment and carry out work that is very complicated. An advanced mastery of codified knowledge gives some professionals, such as engineers, a precision and control that many other workers do not have. Some professionals work in areas that are unpredictable owing to the uniqueness of each case. These include various fields in the human services, such as social work, psychiatry, and the ministry.

Within complex organizations, this distinction involving uncertainty and routine applies to occupations that require less education as well. Most everything is somewhat esoteric and complex to people whose training is in general management, and, therefore, managers depend on clerks, computer specialists, and most everyone else. When lower participants control uncertainties that management does not understand, management becomes dependent upon them. Owing to specialization, generally, each occupation controls uncertainties that create dependence by others. Robert Zussman demonstrates that nurses and technicians acquire enhanced authority, professionalism, and discretion as physicians become increasingly dependent on their skills.[39]

Technology, as we know, is an instrument of control that in the past has reinforced inequality. For many reasons, notably for improved efficiency but also for control over workers, entrepreneurs introduced technology in the watch-making industry, textiles, arms production, and in agriculture, that radically changed the nature of preindustrial crafts. Although romanticism about preindustrial craftwork is to be avoided, a long history of scholarship documents how modern technology, perhaps typified most frequently as "Fordism," degraded the work process and led to worker alienation.

Increasingly new technologies—robotics, just-on-time production, computerized production—have been widely adopted by Western European countries and Japan and more slowly by American firms. This leads to indeterminacy of control. Generally, besides offering advanced sophistication, they appear to offer all workers relatively more autonomy and control, opportunities to improve skills, and also foster decentralization in the workplace.

EQUALITY AND DIVERSITY

Because organizations are based on consent and the recognition that participants are rational (without which consent is impossible), the collectivity recognizes equality, and it also recognizes communities with diverse interests. We take these one by one, first, equality, and next, diversity.

As members of the organization, we agree that we all have the same basic rights and protections—to be evaluated on the basis of our training and experience, not on the basis of personality, family connections, or characteristics that are extraneous to the job. We have the right to appeal unjust decisions, to hold each and every member accountable for his or her actions. The notion of equality defines rights of membership and legitimizes a social contract in which all have obligations. I have already examined how the social contract entails bonds of cooperation among people who do different things.

Implicit in the organization—indeed, implicit in the modern social contract—is the notion of fairness. In the abstract, individuals enter into a given work contract with the idea that it is the best alternative, and once so entered, they have certain rights—of appeal, of a private life outside of work, of the protective clauses stated in the work contract (hours, benefits, pension plan, and so forth). Similarly, managers and owners have obligations and are bound by law and contract not to abuse authority. Weber had a notion about fair contracts that continues to have heuristic value. We can even tie Weber's conceptions about structure and fair contracts into recent research on the impartiality of opportunity structures. As I earlier indicated, research on vacancy chains suggests that mobility in an organization is purely a function of empty positions, not of human capital (education, training, and so forth) that people bring to their jobs.[40] In a highly impersonal way, sustained high levels of attrition pull people up through jobs and levels. At a given level, people have equal chances of advancement.[41] Of course this line of empirical research skirts the issue of culture altogether but suggests instead that there are structural mechanisms underlying equity in the process whereby people acquire positions that provide opportunities.

But it is on this point that the contradiction is resolved. The very idea that luck is involved, overriding the myths we have about the way that bureaucracies and firms work, would be preposterous were it not for strong equality assumptions.[42] Elites must be convinced that there are no means to ensure their reproduction if they could, or that the means they have are not superior to chance alone. And members of the collectivity must be convinced that chance is as fair a principle as any other in making distinctions.

Yet large-scale organizations, bureaucracies or cities or corporations, are also communities based on diversity, not merely on a collectivity with an overriding rationality. This point has been suggested earlier as I described the multiple affiliations of people that result in overlapping communities, each organized in terms of different objectives and each composed of people with different affiliations, interests, and backgrounds. This means that people may have authority and high social standing in one group and little authority and low social standing in another group. Recognition of this pattern is recognition of the impossibility of sustaining consolidated inequalities.[43]

WAGE CONTRACTS AND SOCIAL CONTRACTS

On the one hand, I have argued that equality has a special urgency, is even imperative, in modern society, and opportunities are achieved both through structure and through culture. Recognition of group membership, the replenishment of vacancies, the myriad of group affiliations, the reworking of linguistic labels, social networks, and the legitimacy of rights all play a role in understanding how people acquire opportunities. Implicit here was the notion that mapping activities in the terms of elementary social contracts is the way that people exploit and create opportunities. I have also argued that social life is not zero-sum because there are many arenas of action and many social resources, and in any case, social resources are not used up. But social life requires economic resources, and in the realm of economy—unless there is growth—there are zero-sum outcomes. Moreover, the wage contract is fundamentally unequal. The last part of this chapter deals with the way in which businesses have adopted principles of social organization in order to secure legitimacy and thereby to disguise the reality of the wage contract.

Workers, as members of a class, have no alternative but to sell their labor. As de Jasay notes, capital has an acceptable alternative, namely, not to buy labor, and it does not starve if it abstains:

> All the great contracts governing the "relations of production" under capitalism—those between capital and labor, the industrialized and the underdeveloped, the center and the periphery, whites and coloured, urban ghetto and suburbia—are of this unequal sort with no "real" choice but acceptance on the part of the weaker party.[44]

De Jasay's solution resides in bilateral contract with enforcement, which I examine briefly in the last chapter. However, the point of departure here is based on the observation that there are compelling incentives for promoting bases of cooperation, even in profit-making firms. There are historical conditions under which workers' real situations are ruthlessly exploited by owners, and there are historical conditions under which workers' real situations are ameliorated. If all firms were owned by workers, there would be no conflict between the social contract and the wage contract.

Industrial capitalist economies trigger upward mobility, but such economies also generate inequality. This longer story will be elaborated upon in another chapter, but suffice it to say here, there was a brief period in American history when economic inequalities declined. This was between the end of the Depression and the mid-1970s, which makes this period critical for understanding how wage contracts can be reconciled with social contracts.

The New Deal brought in a host of reforms to return workers to their jobs, to stabilize the labor force, to grant power to unions to engage in collective bargaining, and to reduce the ebb and flow of labor, which in turn reduced uncertainties for both labor and management. Firms also embarked on their own programs that reinforced the effects of this legislation. Notably they extended the career concept to blue-collar workers and introduced internal labor markets. These are based on the principle that workers are hired at the bottom of the hierarchy, but with training and experience they are promoted within job ladders, provided with incentives to stay, including fringe benefits and the likelihood of lifetime employment. Increasingly, after about World War II, work of many or even most kinds involved a career, "an orderly sequence of development extending over a period of years and involving progressively more responsibilities."[45] Careers, therefore, had a stabilizing influence, providing security for the worker and the worker's family and for the place of employment. The consequences of this transformation were profound, including an appreciable increase in the dependence of managers on employees and emerging symmetries of trust.

Because careers blur the distinction between blue- and white-collar work, they helped to reduce traditional conflict within organizations, and because career was linked with change over the life course, mobility and advancement were considered to be normal transitions, with expectations of increasing rewards over time.

But that also means that serious economic depressions and firm instability can have more devastating effects on workers' expectations now than under traditional arrangements that were based on underlying antagonisms. There is recent evidence, as I will discuss, that internal labor markets have weakened since the mid-1970s. With the increasing precariousness of the economy since the recession of 1973, firms have jettisoned their internal labor markets in order to maintain the work force flexibility that they had prior to the New Deal.

There is, after all, an intractable contradiction between the fundamental basis of the wage contract and the principles of organization— we have only to compare Marx's understanding of capitalism with Weber's understanding of social organization to realize how that is true. On the one hand, Marx stressed that relations within the firm would always be dictated by contingencies, such as profitability and growth, whereas Weber's emphasis was on the legitimacy of the collective enterprise.

THE OBSCURITY OF DECLINE

Paradoxically, the same division of labor and hierarchy that creates opportunities through vacancies can obstruct opportunities through excessive unclarity in times of decline. Although there is no unequivocal empirical evidence on this, one suspects that without growth and the expansion of resources, complexity accelerates so that jobs proliferate without accompanying means of advancement and sources of meaning. Burawoy, for example, describes the minute division of labor on the shop floor that leads to ceaseless conflict among workers who consider small differences of such great importance that they forget how this plays into the hands of the owners.[46] Under conditions of declining resources, government workers, such as counselors, probation officers, and social workers, have such high case loads that the incentive structure is altered from one of providing services to rubber stamping as many claims a day, a week, a month, as possible.[47]

Increasingly high case loads accompany widened jurisdictions to create a sense of broad-based power, when in fact, very little can be done—is done—for individual clients. A general point is that the excessive proliferation of specialties and the imposition of cumbersome responsibilities are related structural mechanisms that forestall crisis and diffuse conflict. For one thing, these structural mechanisms set workers against one another, for whatever bonds of cooperation they previously developed are destroyed by the contrived division of responsibilities. For another, as Weber long ago noted, specialization that is not rooted in substance will destroy the meaning of work.[48] Under these conditions, organizational ends are cloaked in a mystery of unconnected parts, and rationality is obscured. When growth stops, the likely outcome is a crushing collapse of opportunities that are commensurate with skills and expectations.

THE OBSCURITY OF SLIPPAGE

At the same time that excessive and arbitrary division of labor can erode the clarity of position and the logic of rationality, there are mechanisms that recover people's opportunities. It is interesting that they lie in the indeterminacy, uncertainties, and slippages of social life. As Andrea Tyree writes on the nature of opportunities in America over time, there is always the "reshuffling of the social deck."[49] By this she means dynamic changes in the stratification system in which each group's privilege and status change over time, but the rules remain pretty much the same. As Tyree refers to the importance of family size, urban opportunities, and education for a group's ranking at any given time, I refer in this more general context to the way in which people from different groups—Italians and Greeks, men and women, blacks and Hispanics—have access to opportunities and acquire access to other opportunities in many arenas of social life at any given time and over time. In American society, there has been a pronounced tendency for groups to avail themselves of opportunities. If we follow family genealogies by occupation, there is a stunning lack of clarity.

With much population diversity and social change, culture is ever renewed, rediscovered, and refashioned. Social groups are the agents of this change, but culture helps to hasten and to sustain it. We would only have to compare the language of the small, well-educated, eighteenth-century American elite that Cmiel describes with the language of contemporary television, of the workplace, or of the newspaper to be struck by how dynamic American culture has been.[50]

The unique positions that people occupy by virtue of their multiple statuses and role relations constitute another source of individual autonomy and, therefore, social indeterminacy. This allows for "underdetermination," the prerequisite, according to Zygmunt Bauman, of individual freedom.[51] These are the sorts of considerations that may have bearing on the possible future irrelevance of the now seemingly intractable difference between the social contract and the wage contract.

We might consider that structure creates opportunities through the steady production of vacancies, whereas cultural opportunities arise by means of the delineation and preservation of some differences, and the transformation and destruction of others. Still, the idea of boundaries and niches is useful in discussing opportunities with respect to culture as well. I think it is reasonable to say that we wish to have cultural diversity that is not confounded with differences in social standing, and in economic and political power. We prefer diversity that reflects cultural tastes, political interests and commitments, and differences with respect to opinions, traditions, and intellectual orientations. Cultural diversity helps to counteract the banal uniformity that large-scale markets tend to produce, but, more importantly, provides a hedge against the possibility of crushing authority. The challenge, it seems to me, is how to foster conditions that sustain cultural diversity and, simultaneously, equality of opportunity.

NOTES

1. This working definition is very close to the one elaborated in Harold Fallding's *The Sociological Task*. Englewood Cliffs, NJ: Prentice-Hall, 1968, p. 102.
2. See Michael Kammen, *A Season of Youth*. Ithaca: Cornell University Press, 1978, pp. 106–107; Barry Schwartz, "The Democratization of George Washington," *American Sociological Review* 56 (1991): 221–236.
3. Kenneth Cmiel, *Democratic Eloquence*. Berkeley: University of California Press, 1990.
4. In sixteenth-century Portuguese Western Africa, indigenous males wore

their traditional garb complete with fetishes and pagan symbols. However, mindful of chance encounters with missionaries, they tucked rosaries inside their garb for the purpose of a fast change in presentation. I thank Rekha Mirchandani for this example.

5. Chandra Mukerji, *From Graven Images*. New York: Columbia University Press, 1984.
6. For a summary of the debate among feminists, see, for example, Mirra Komarovsky, "The New Feminist Scholarship," *Journal of Marriage and the Family* 50 (1988): 585–593.
7. Edna Bonacich, "A Theory of Middleman Minorities," *American Sociological Review* 38 (1973): 583–594.
8. See Peter M. Blau and Otis Dudley Duncan, *The American Occupational Structure*. New York: Wiley, 1967.
9. Harold Seymour, *Baseball. Vol. II: The Golden Age*. Rev. ed. New York: Oxford University Press, 1971.
10. *The Sociology of Georg Simmel*. Trans., Ed., and Introduction by Kurt H. Wolff. Glencoe: The Free Press, [1908] 1950, p. 302.
11. *Work and Personality*. Norwood, NJ: Ablex, 1983.
12. Harrison White, *Chains of Opportunity*. Cambridge: Harvard University Press, 1970; Aage B. Sørensen, "The Structure of Inequality and the Process of Attainment," *American Sociological Review* 42 (1977): 965–978; see also Ivar Berg, *Education and Jobs: The Great Training Robbery*. New York: Praeger, 1970.
13. Rachel Rosenfeld, "Job Mobility and Career Processes," *Annual Review of Sociology* 18 (1992): 39–61.
14. William F. Whyte, *Human Relations in the Restaurant Industry*. New York: McGraw-Hill, 1948.
15. Rosabeth Moss Kanter, *Men and Women of the Corporation*. New York: Basic Books, 1977.
16. Robert Jackall, *Moral Mazes: The World of Corporate Managers*. Oxford: Oxford University Press, 1988.
17. Lawrence E. Cohen, Marcus Felson, and Kenneth C. Land, "Property Crime Rates in the United States," *American Journal of Sociology* 86 (1980): 90–118.
18. Steven F. Messner and Judith R. Blau, "Routine Leisure and Rates of Crime," *Social Forces* 65 (1987): 1035–1052.
19. See Bruce H. Mayhew, "Size and Density of Interaction in Human Aggregation," *American Journal of Sociology* 82 (1976): 86–110.
20. Richard A. Esterlin, *Birth and Fortune*. New York: Basic Books, 1980.
21. Jacques Le Goff, *Time, Work, and Culture in the Middle Ages*. Trans. Arthur Goldhammer. Chicago: University of Chicago Press, 1980.
22. Robert Rosenthal and Lenore Jacobsen, *Pygmalion in the Classroom*. New York: Holt, Rinehart & Winston, 1968.
23. Robert K. Merton (with Alice S. Rossi), "Contributions to the Theory of Reference Group Behavior," pp. 279–329 in Robert K. Merton, *Social Theory and Social Structure*. Rev. ed. New York: The Free Press, 1968.

24. Robert K. Merton, "Continuities in the Theory of Reference Groups and Social Structure," pp. 335–440, ibid.
25. This was pursued by Merton's Columbia graduates. See Helen Rose Fuchs Ebaugh, *Becoming an Ex: The Process of Role Exit*. Chicago: University of Chicago Press, 1988; Zena Smith Blau, *Old Age in a Changing Society*. New York: Franklin Watts, 1973, pp. 210–211.
26. Rose Laub Coser, *In Defense of Modernity*. Stanford: Stanford University Press, 1991, p. 25.
27. Peter M. Blau, *Inequality and Heterogeneity*. New York: The Free Press, 1977.
28. For a recent statement on the general importance of networks, see Walter W. Powell, "Neither Market nor Hierarchy," *Research in Organizational Behavior* 12 (1990): 295–336.
29. Mark Granovetter, "The Strength of Weak Ties," *American Journal of Sociology* 78 (1973): 1360–1380.
30. Analyses of organizational underlife can be found in the following: Graeme Salaman, *Working*. Chichester: Ellis Horwood, 1986; Gale Miller, *It's a Living*. New York: St. Martin's Press, 1981; Gary Alan Fine, "The Culture of Production: Aesthetic Choices and Constraints in Culinary Work," *American Journal of Sociology* 97 (1992): 1268–1294.
31. Karen E. Campbell, "Gender Differences in Job-Related Networks," *Work and Occupations* 15 (1988): 179–200.
32. Jane Scott-Lennox, *Sex and Race Stratification in Informal Support*. Ph.D. dissertation, University of North Carolina, 1991.
33. Claude S. Fischer, *To Dwell among Friends*. Chicago: University of Chicago Press, 1982.
34. Carol B. Stack, *All Our Kin: Strategies for Survival in a Black Community*. New York: Harper & Row, 1974.
35. Norbert Elias, *The History of Manners, Vol. 1, The Civilizing Process*. New York: Pantheon, 1979. Cultural integration achieved through diffusion is not without its costs. Alan Trachtenberg indicates how, historically, it has meant centralization of power and the consolidation of corporate elites. See his *The Incorporation of America*. New York: Hill and Wang, 1982.
36. Max Weber, *The Theory of Social and Economic Organization*. Trans. A. M. Henderson and Talcott Parsons. Ed. Talcott Parsons. Glencoe, IL: The Free Press, 1947, pp. 324–386.
37. See Michael Thompson, Richard Ellis, and Aaron Wildavsky, *Cultural Theory*. Boulder: Westview Press, 1990, pp. 22–23.
38. Michael Crozier, *The Bureaucratic Phenomenon*. Chicago: University of Chicago Press, 1964.
39. Robert Zussman, *Intensive Care*. Chicago: University of Chicago Press, 1992.
40. For a comprehensive discussion, see Ronald S. Burt, *Toward a Structural Theory of Action*. New York: Academic Press, 1982.
41. Sørensen, op. cit.

42. Christopher Jencks (with Marshall Smith, Henry Acland, Mary Jo Bane, David Cohen, Herbert Gintis, Barbara Heyns, and Stephan Michelson), *Inequality: A Reassessment of the Effect of Family and Schooling in America*. New York: Basic Books, 1972.

43. Georg Simmel, *Conflict and the Web of Group Affiliations*. Trans. Kurt H. Wolff and Reinhard Bendix. Foreword by Everett C. Hughes. Glencoe, IL: The Free Press, [1922] 1955, especially pp. 140–154.

44. Anthony de Jasay, *Social Contract, Free Ride: A Study of the Public Goods Problem*. Oxford: Oxford University Press, 1989, pp. 17–18.

45. Harold Wilensky, "Orderly Careers and Social Participation," *American Sociological Review* 16 (1961): 521–539, p. 523.

46. Michael Burawoy, *Manufacturing Consent*. Chicago: University of Chicago Press, 1979.

47. Michael Lipsky, *Street-Level Bureaucracy*. New York: Russell Sage, 1980.

48. See Arthur Mitzman, *The Iron Cage: An Historical Interpretation of Max Weber*. New York: Albert A. Knopf, 1970.

49. Andrea Tyree, "Reshuffling the Social Deck," pp. 195–216 in Judith R. Blau and Norman Goodman (eds.), *Social Roles and Social Institutions: Essays in Honor of Rose Laub Coser*. Boulder: Westview Press, 1991.

50. Cmiel, op. cit.

51. Zygmunt Bauman, *Freedom*. Minneapolis: University of Minnesota Press, 1988, p. 41.

6

Economy, Place, and Culture

"Nothing is allowed. Nothing is forbidden," in the words of one inhabitant. . . . Formal boundaries are gone between town and country, between centre and periphery, between suburbs and city centres, between the domain of automobiles and the domain of people.
— HENRI LEFEBVRE, *The Production of Space*

It was not long ago that economic activities exhibited clear, observable, and intelligible spatial configurations; they were geographically distributed in ways that made social sense. The spheres of production and consumption, and also worlds of work, exhibited spatial clarity, as did accompanying means of exchange and communication. Even though urban growth was ruthlessly driven by commercial interests, the nineteenth-century American city was highly legible with clear linkages between workers and their places of work and between merchants and their customers.

Spatial constraints also meant that economic producers were dependent on local populations. Normative regulation was comparatively easy because responsibility and culpability could be traced to a specific place. Individuals, government agencies, households, and economic units had addresses. Sellers and buyers were spatially situated, as were producers and consumers. There were places to revel and places to take the family. Persons and establishments were local and localizable. True, there were wholesalers and "middlemen" who had shady (i.e., spatially vague) lives. However, for the most part, consumers dealt with retailers whose shops they visited and whose owners they addressed by name,

89

just as merchants knew where shoppers lived and asked about their children.

Although industrial life in late-nineteenth-century America was brutalizing for wage earners, the spatial proximity of workers and owners (and the geographical concentration of workers) also enabled workers to confront owners and to organize strikes. There are many explanations for why union membership and strike activity have declined in the United States, but one obvious reason is that these days owners and top managers are "somewhere else." One way to dissipate grievances is to put nothing but lawyers and lots of space in between those who work and those who own.

However, the spatial nature of the economy has been totally transformed within the past century, and this has far-reaching consequences for social relations and cultural frameworks. I do not want to minimize the fact that an increasingly aspatial economy has had disastrous consequences for groups without many spatial options. However, it will be argued that once in the orbit of a global market economy, political and social mobilization by disadvantaged groups will help to raze ghetto walls.

SOME HISTORICAL COMPARISONS

In the Middletown of 1924 that the Lynds describe, economic roles were clearly delineated as were the spatial locations in which these roles were enacted.[1] The boundedness of the economy clarified the spatial terms of social relations. The mapping of cooperative social activities tempered economic competition, just as economic markets helped to delineate the contours and boundaries of cooperation. The extension of this argument is that when there was religious, class, or ethnic conflict, there was a clear spatial base that facilitated organization, but also spatial interdependencies that encouraged compromise.

Not more than a few decades ago, economic transactions were for the most part local, and when not local, could be easily traced in comprehensible ways. No longer. Whereas Sears had one proximate location for its buyers and a universal catalogue, now it is a nonspatial 800 number with widely scattered operations so that its computers must keep track of where a part was built and from where it must be ordered, and then match part with distributor with repair person, and these, in turn, with customer. To get information on the delays at the airport that is located 10 miles away, the phone call for information goes to a city many hundreds of miles away. It takes one aback to meet a neighbor who is employed by a firm located in another region of the country and conducts all business by fax. At the same time, it was not so long ago that we found ourselves in the situation where we would buy a gift in the United States to send to, say, an English relative, who remarked that as the item was made in Ireland, the purchase was economically imprudent. These days no such remark would be made. More likely, the thank-you card mailed from England had been made in Portugal.

Space, as I shall argue, has increasingly less meaning in economic life and, although we are slow to catch on, the deconstruction of space fundamentally alters the rules of economic markets, the nature of social contracts, and the character of cultural life. The deconstruction of space also makes possible social and political movements that have far broader membership bases than ever before in history.

In the recent past, many, if not most, economic transactions in Americans' lives were fused with sociability and trust. What accounted for a good deal of this focused clarity in economic roles and the stable expectations of participants was the spatial underpinnings of the economic and social order. To make theoretical sense of this observation one only has to refer to geographers' work on central place theory,[2] a brilliant extension of the theory of Adam Smith. Earlier, Smith had stressed that sellers in competition with one another are successful through what are essentially organizational means. These means included specialization, high or superior output, and maximizing internal efficiency. However, he also noted that one means of success was spatial. When sellers dominate a niche they capture a market. In the aggregate this means that sellers sort themselves in space.[3]

In nineteenth-century America, when sellers arranged themselves at approximately equidistant intervals, they each captured a spatial market, a geographical turf. In ubiquitous space, suppliers situated themselves in a central location, and, together, they created and controlled a hinterland, namely, a market of consumers. This served to achieve an equilibrium, but a relatively unique sort of equilibrium as it was not based on intense competition nor did it lead to much exploitation on the part of suppliers. This was because parties to exchanges were mutually interdependent, and suppliers' costs of being sanctioned were not worth the risk.

For the time, the reader should know that I am not describing the largest-growing American cities in the nineteenth century, nor even densely populated Europe in the eighteenth century when Adam

Smith wrote. Instead, I refer to the United States in the mid-1800s to the early 1900s when the vast majority of Americans lived in small towns and villages, and either operated family farms or worked in homes and family businesses.[4] There was a vast territory that initially attracted homesteaders and miners, and, then, merchants, traders, artisans, and preachers. The situation I describe, in fact, survived more or less intact until automobiles became commonplace.

CENTRAL PLACES

With a market radius of about 3½ miles, a small central place, composed of a general store, a grain-storage facility, a post office, a public school, and three churches (for good measure—Catholic, Unitarian, and Baptist), could provide the normal living needs for a population living within the hinterland of about 38 square miles. With larger radiuses, a larger central place would include all the things a smaller central place did (the general store, and so forth) but also a physician's office, carriage maker, a shop for sewing needles and other rare notions, a saddle maker, and perhaps a saloon and library (and probably an Episcopalian church, for extra good measure). For yearly trips, the Iowan farmer could go to Ames to buy imported linen, cast-iron pots, and readymade clothes.[5]

The economy of industrializing America had a nice architectonic shape composed of central places and their hinterlands, medium-sized cities, and large hinterlands. Each small central place had a monopoly over a small geographical market, and big central places controlled larger ones. On a relatively small scale, the economy of the central place and its hinterland worked well, as the stakes were clear (and not so very high, by today's standards, in any case), and intimate knowledge of exchange partners enforced the norms about fair prices and trading practices.

This was the situation in which suppliers knew producers, and consumers knew suppliers, and bonds of trust were accompanied with the recognition that economic exchange must involve profitmaking but also that excessive profitmaking would incur the wrath of the members of the community upon whom each supplier depended. The costs to the supplier of relocating were not trivial, as well everyone knew.

In this sense, social contracts were enjoined to ensure that the stable division of labor was regulated under the rather amazing conditions of monopoly, but I stress that monopoly by sellers in scarcely populated places was accompanied by suppliers' healthy dependence on buyers as well. The mapping of social and economic relations was carefully orchestrated to handle, adjust, and fine-tune nonequilibria, injustices, and inequalities. The stable organization of local markets around the season, the weather, the harvest, and the storage of crops was one in which all parties had an interest in maintaining.

Nineteenth-century American cities were more complicated, of course, owing to the vulnerability of immigrants, fierce competition among sellers for the same consumers and valuable land, and absentee-owned businesses. Although economic exchange in large cities did not particularly involve stable relations between buyers and sellers—as competition was stiff and the forces promoting specialization were thus strong—nevertheless, cartographic differences were important. Though taking different shapes in cities compared with rural districts, the spatial patterns in U.S. cities were prominent and important for social and economic life. These patterns reflected the limits and the strengths of early industry, and they reflected the needs and wishes of population groups who differed greatly in terms of economic resources, language, religion, and experiences with urban life. Local neighborhoods formed the meaningful units of social activities, organized around ethnic traditions, social class, family, and consumption.[6] Although the world of work was boring, brutalizing, and exploitative, the haven of the ethnic community provided a framework of trust and stability.[7]

I should also refer here to the dynamic growth of the city whereby the population spread concentrically over time from core, to residential neighborhoods, to fledgling suburbs. With increased prosperity and bumper crops of new arrivals, the upward mobility of some groups (the native-born and established immigrants) accompanied their spatial mobility outward, as they left their lower-priced residences and shops to new immigrants.[8] The theory of urban ecology helps to explain the persistence of neighborhoods and the importance of space for cultural identity,[9] and also the consequences of an expanding economy for urban configurations of market and social relations.[10]

At the same time, throughout the nineteenth century, groups adapted to the ever-expanding exchange patterns embedded in the capitalist economy of U.S. cities. This entailed a new kind of transspatial organization, namely, integration into a wider culture of urban life, consumerism, and middle-class lifestyles.[11] Or one could say, "passing" was easy, even if opportunities for passing were more afforded the children of immigrants rather than immigrants themselves. This dynamic of concentric growth and transspatial urban culture was, as we shall later see, greatly altered when passing was not permitted blacks, or their children, or even their children's children.

Nevertheless, it is in the elementary economies of the nineteenth century that we find the theoretical clues for understanding why the aspatial economies of the late twentieth century have such profoundly different consequences for contemporary social life and culture. Problems of power and dependence—geopolitical and economic inequalities—in contemporary society are intimately related to both the increase in scale and the decline in distances among places. As such inequalities emerge, however, the recognition of interdependencies also becomes apparent.

CORE AND PERIPHERY

When a stable traditional or agrarian economy, initially demarcated by local exchange, comes under the overpowering influence of external industrial economies, there is a rapid realignment of economic forces and increasing asymmetry, as the industrial nation imposes new production techniques, creates consumer markets, and redefines the conditions of labor. Poor in cash, an agrarian country will inevitably welcome factories, switch from a multicrop agriculture to a single crop export, and throw open its borders to virtually any vendor. Thus, sociologists refer to core and periphery, colonial empires and client states, industrial societies and dependent developing countries.[12]

Within the United States the differences between the core and the rural hinterlands were modulated so that the core's influence over rural America never exhibited the same exploitative character as, say, England's power over Egypt and India, or the United States' control over the Philippines and Guatemala.

Nevertheless, there are parallels between international global patterns in the twentieth century and those in nineteenth-century America. In the predominantly rural United States, the equilibria of localized markets were imperilled, and eventually toppled, by increasing scale. As markets became organized over large territories, local niches were increasingly drawn into the orbits of control of distant administrative, political, and financial centers. With the advent of railroads, the telegraph, telephone, and automobiles, the notion of leaving local markets under the control of local (and not very profitable) entrepreneurs hardly made sense to large-scale producers and suppliers. National businesses vied for the control of the hinterland, its consumers, and its resources, and this inevitably led to the diminution of the autonomy and the integrity of local spatialized economies. This process engendered dependence on the part of the periphery—for capital and expertise—but it also involved integration into the larger national economy.

On their part, the elites blundered ahead to gain the competitive edge, to secure national monopolies, and to join previously unrelated economic activities—extraction, transport, manufacture, and distribution. Although many schemes failed, owing to inexperience and the self-destruction of tooth-and-claw competition, the broader scheme of national economic integration fared quite well.[13]

In general, rural America had much to gain by relinquishing local autonomy because participating in the national economy meant access to education and culture, an unprecedented degree of choice among new products, and the availability of services provided by professionals. For the most part, we consider spatial inequalities to have been relatively mild and short-lived. The major exception, however, was in the South. At the end of the Civil War, opportunistic banks from northern cities exerted leverage on the South to grow cash crops and, given the high tenancy rates of southern farmers, could extract huge profits in the postbellum period.

Still, by around the 1920s, the nation as a whole was brought within the regulative and hierarchical orbit of urban-industrial elites, and metropolitan-based finance capitalism set the terms of local economic life. Social historians document how financiers and urban elites established the rules of the nation as a whole and centralized authority. "Men," Robert Wiebe writes, "were now separated more by skill and occupation than by community; they identified themselves more by their tasks in an urban-industrial society than by their reputation in a town."[14] And, as Peter Dobkin Hall observes, although the opportunities afforded by national economy were ones that could not be refused as they offered abundant advantages over provincial life, by the 1920s, the power of the elites had become so pervasive that they influenced every aspect of American life, from child care through diet and career choice.[15] At the same time, sociologists worried about the eclipse of community, the dangers of mass culture, and the crisis of American identity.[16]

Thus, economic forces within America created initial gaps between rural and urban America, problems of cultural integration, and social inequalities (as expressed by rifts between country and city folk and among regions). However, within the United States, the rapid development of universal education, internal migration, and industrialization helped to eradicate pronounced inequalities between the core and the hinterland.

Ironically, the old core, notably, the metropolitan places in the Northeast has been economically surpassed by much of the former hinterland. In search of cheap labor markets, low taxes, and inexpensive land, producers left behind them a wake of urban decay. Having driven up the cost of living in New York, Boston, and Philadelphia (to a point corporate managers feel they themselves cannot afford), major industries have left these cities. They have also left all these cities' problems—including deteriorating infrastructures, overburdened schools, and expensive urban governments—for the poor to solve.

INTERNATIONAL MARKETS

Compared with the nineteenth-century regional economic inequalities brought about by capitalist expansion in the United States, those in the contemporary world are far more serious. Within the United States, the disruptive forces associated with economic expansion were offset by other dynamics related to cultural integration and the sense of a common national identity. As colonial nations—England, Belgium, the Netherlands, France, Portugal, Spain, and then the United States— identified economic resources throughout the rest of the world, they imposed relations of trade and economic dependence that totally undermined local economies.

Exploitative labor practices, single-crop production, and dependence on the colonial power for capital, technology, goods, and services accompanied raised expectations about an improved standard of living. More often than not, great inequalities and some (although often marginal) improvement in economic well-being have been the results of "modernization." Also raised were expectations about self-determination. The consequences of this for political and social strife, and for brutal expressions of nationalism, are well enough known. But the central point here is that the inequalities engendered initially by imperial colonialism and, subsequently, by both communist and capitalist economic expansion were—and continue to be—spatially based inequalities.

Yet market expansion (again, whether under the financing of capitalists or communists) clarified the irrationality of spatial inequalities. For the purpose of indicating that my ensuing argument is based on a relatively optimistic set of premises, I should explicitly state how different conclusions can be drawn from more pessimistic ones. For example, Ernest Mandel argues that the internationalization of capital accompanies the irreversible centralization of control and worldwide patterns of exploitation.[17]

More along the lines that Henri Lefebvre has argued,[18] I believe that integration in global economic markets will, in the long run, destroy the spatial barriers on which current economic inequalities depend. There are two basic considerations. The first has to do with the nature of producers, and the second has to do with the nature of social organization in an increasingly "frictionless" world.

The first point is that producers (capitalists, socialist cooperatives, and entrepreneurs) abhor disequilibria. Armed with the knowledge and experience of competing in the world economy, economic actors will exploit new opportunities wherever they are located. More simply, producers will continue to organize production, and sellers will continue to sell. In the long run, this is an entropic process. Each subsequent round of competition will take place where production and sales are not so intense already.

American capitalists have been doing this all along, and the rationale is simple. Why open a production plant in New Jersey when it would be more profitable to go to Maine? Eventually, gross, spatial macroeconomic inequalities do decline. Maine, too, can be expected to raise its taxes; its workers will demand higher wages; and the price of land will go up. Consequently, Taiwan, say, may look very attractive. This is what I mean by economic entropy. It is not driven by the interests of the periphery, but it empowers the periphery to bootstrap their local economy. One must assume, however, that the places that are abandoned can respond by downsizing older facilities, retraining local workers, and making sites attractive to different kinds of producers. If cities and industries would forge economic agreements for industry-exiting costs, such transitions would be less disruptive than they are now.

The second point is that although economic markets relentlessly expand, so too do the opportunities for social contracting. Markets do not determine people's social contracts, that is, their organizing to cooperate for political and social objectives, but they do increase the incentives and wherewithal for organizing. Competitive economy, I argue, sews the seeds of its opposition, as participation in markets liberates social, political, and cultural intentions from spatial constraints, and from economic domination.

Maple-syrup producers thus organize to lobby for pollution controls in the Midwest to reduce acid rain. Western European nations press the United States to move faster on controls for automobile emissions, and Latin American countries insist that those nations' companies that deforested much of the Amazon must begin ambitious replanting efforts. If we take into account organizations such as Oxfam, Amnesty International, the World Federation for the Protection of Wildlife, Greenpeace, UNICEF, and many others, I think it is clear that people organize to solve what are essentially worldwide issues.

Lefebvre puts the matter a little differently than I do, by emphasizing the importance of "practical spaces" in otherwise dominated space. We might think of these as "safety zones" instead. He contrasts dominated space that realizes economic, military, and political objectives, with "practical spaces" in which particularities assert themselves. Monopoly and global markets cannot possibly intervene and dominate every practical space:

> The fact remains, however, that the proliferation of links and networks, by directly connecting up very diverse places, and by ending their isolation—though without destroying the peculiarities and differences to which that very isolation has given rise—tends to render [global power] redundant.[19]

My argument is that markets do, in fact, help to create "practical spaces" (or "safety zones") because economic enterprises invest in human capital, render local products valuable in global markets, and trivialize barriers in physical space. This argument assumes that social and cultural forces matter once markets have fundamentally expanded social relations beyond the constraints of space.

To a great extent this is immediately liberating as it ends isolation. Sometimes it is not, as historically peripheral groups veer crazily in search of a legitimate claim to some place in the world order and struggle for a social, political, and cultural identity. Both the capitalist countries and the former communist countries created client nation-states for which decades of dependency deprived them of the means and the experience of self-reliance. It is arguable that a nationalist movement is just as much a way of defining a "practical space" in the world order, as participation in international cooperation is an indication that a nation's or group's "safety zone" is secure.

Racial segregation is a bizarre anachronism in twentieth-century America. Later I will trace what social scientists consider to be the relevant historical economic reasons why segregation and racism have persisted in the United States. However, it is consistent with the arguments in this chapter that locational constraints of segregation mean that African-Americans often fail to achieve what Lefebvre calls a "practical space" without which autonomy and free choice are possible. Segregated workplaces, segregated schools, and segregated neighborhoods reproduce alienation and disaffection and are constant reminders of second-class citizenship. It is not merely the practicalities of the lack of access to economic and social resources, it is also the demeaning consequences of not having choice in a society in which choice is widely taken for granted. White Americans experience constraints on choice, of course, but agency within those constraints is still a given. Particularly for inner-city black Americans, possessing agency of choice is remote in the context of pervasive poverty, segregation, and the virtual absence of employers.

It is interesting that support among whites for general principles of equal opportunities has increased, whereas support for specific proposals for implementing these proposals has not.[20] One way of interpreting this is that groups perceive that status enhancement of others is a cost to one's own group and that this perception is magnified in a sluggish economy.[21] Aside from the social justice issues, the long-run costs to society of segregation and concentrated poverty are staggering. They include present outlays for the provision of social services and transfer payments, the costs of involuntary unemployment, the hefty price of the drug economy, and the long-term costs that inferior schooling will incur. Blacks, after all, make up a growing proportion of the labor force.

Yet there appear to be cultural changes that may redefine the relation between minorities and the white majority. Blacks are asserting a cultural identity that transcends ghetto boundaries, which in turn will shape and empower practical spaces. Recognizing that America is unlikely to be a "color-blind" society, black leaders have emphasized that America is biracial, which refocuses the emphasis to coalition and collaboration rather than acquiescence to marginal participation in a white society.[22] The recognition of cultural diversity is a matter I take up in the last section of this chapter. First, it is useful to see the beginnings of the decline of the importance of locale as spatial boundaries fall away. To the extent that many blacks have lesser attachments to places where they live, it is not unimaginable to consider that they may have psychological advantages in a world in which space is not so very important.

THE DECONSTRUCTION OF SPACE

The postindustrial economy includes features that contradict the earlier character of domination by core nation-states. Vast improvements in transportation and communications have meant that producers, suppliers, and moneylenders are relatively footloose, making every market a veritable niche of contention. In principle, it is difficult to secure a monopoly that can be preserved on the basis of spatial dominance. Complex forms of division of labor are increasingly less amenable to geographical mapping. The low costs of disseminating information, the mobility of capital, and a potentially mobile labor force erode spatial monopolies.[23] Postindustrialization has entailed the decoupling of space and economy in three major respects. We can think of products, producers, and consumers. First, any ordinary household appliance, for example, may bear the stamps of dozens of countries, and the efforts of workers for whom no common language is shared. Second, there is the spatial decoupling of space and producers. Main economic producers—that is, manufacturing firms—have left the central cities, and increasingly are leaving their countries of origin for relocation in hinterlands in search of cheaper labor markets and lower rents. Marx was right that capitalist producers increasingly turn their production activities to the hinterlands—the South of the United States where labor is cheaper—and to the Third World—where labor is the cheapest. The deconstruction of space is ever driven by the pressures of capital accumulation, but with expanding opportunities new equilibria can be achieved as the price of labor begins to respond and land prices adjust themselves.

The experiences in the United States illustrate these spatial readjustments. When manufacturing establishments exited from major cities, they did so with the explicit intention of profiting from cheaper labor markets and lower land values. The short-run microconsequences for labor, land, and local governments have been disastrous. But the long-run consequences were different, as is evident in the declining economic inequality between the older core and newer periphery. It is true that producers left behind cities with deteriorating infrastructures, a loss of major services that thrived on primary economic activities, and the decline of jobs for the semiskilled and unskilled.

They also left behind an angry citizenry with considerable potential for mobilization and organization. If we take a long-range view of that potential—in the context of the demographic projections over the next few decades—it is likely that minorities will have political control over major and middle-sized U.S. cities. Under such conditions, corporate actors can be expected to have a new perspective on economic partners and on social justice. The point here is that economic producers maximize their own well-being by finding new, previously unexplored spatial niches. Over the very long run, this helps to level economic opportunities; for example, there is considerable convergence among the regions of the United States. This also inevitably raises expectations, as opportunities expand, and dashes hopes when they contract. However, raised expectations and dashed hopes are precisely what lead to political and social organization. Sometimes this is not as peaceful as one hopes.

Buyers may be the purest expression of the deconstruction of space. With population growth and high rates of mobility, there is a genuine mass market for the sale and consumption of products. Although there may be local consumer markets and tastes based on tradition and nostalgia—bagels in New York, grits in the South, batik in college towns—the serious demand for everything from baseball cards to BMWs is virtually spaceless. It may not be free of class and status, but demand is, for all intents and purposes, liberated from spatial constraints. Consumers shop from mail-order catalogs and increasingly use commercial telecomputing services, buy from anonymous distributors, who in turn buy their products from companies located throughout the world. In these varieties of ways—the internationalization of products, the mobility of the owners of production, and the freedom of consumers—the economy is increasingly freed from spatial constraints. It is likely that the core industrial nations must relinquish some of their economic power. In fact, it is evident that this is already occurring. But this decline must certainly be accompanied with improved mutual good will. That is not at all a bad trade-off.

ASPATIAL SOCIAL CONTRACTS

The full implications of the deconstruction of space are not at all clear. On the one hand, financial control is situated far from production sites, as management and owners may be located in Paris or New York, whereas the firm is located in Korea or Peru, and consumers are located in, say, Italy and the United States. This raises concerns about accountability, the enforcement of economic contracts, and the identification of relevant third parties for control and regulation. Although decentralized producers located thousands of miles away from owners have great flexibility (enhancing the prospects of democratic participation), local workers, including managers, have little influence over truly major decisions, such as being sold and traded on the block.

Long-distance investment is risky and raises the costs of capital and increases the power of owners and money lenders. International investments are also tainted by the prospects of ideological motivations. The greater the spatial distance over which economic bargains are struck, the more political are money and trade. Every country in which the United States has major investments is one in which we advance our political and military interests. Economic actors care not a trifle whether the stocks are owned by Muslims, Moonies, or atheists, or whether engine parts are made by people who wear traditional headdresses or overalls. In fact, economic actors are extremely tolerant. But for the price of protection (for example, favorable trade arrangements), they support national ideological interests. The relevance of such interests, however, is increasingly called into question in the post–Cold War era. Investors and producers have every reason to applaud. And so do workers.

If we start with the premise that spatial constraints are being overcome at a remarkably high rate, or, to put it colloquially, that the world is shrinking, it is not very helpful to bemoan the loss of locale, but rather to explore the likely implications this will have for social relations. First, I ask about the extent to which differences among places are created or imposed. Second, if microconventions are not generalizable to long-distance social mapping, do we have macroconventions that are in the process of evolution? Third, what is the nature of individual identity in a world that is complex and in which relations are far-flung? I argue that the diminution of the importance of space entails the collapse of structural constraints, making agency that much more important. In that respect, structural theorists can posit the existence of constraints, while cheering as these constraints fall away. In their stead, it can be argued, is the emergence of large voluntary communities based on metaconventions of cooperation.

The mapping of social activities and arrangements over such vast spaces in microseconds both presupposes and sustains an equality of rights that never before was possible. Likewise, accompanying equality is a tendency to discount status differences that are unjustifiable in any but the most universalistic terms (that is, in terms of performance or efficiency).

MACROCONVENTIONS

Modernization entailed the mass diffusion of conventions, primarily from core to periphery but also from periphery to core. Economic activities may have arrived in the hinterlands, initially, but close behind came conventional social understandings. These understandings relate to the mundane and the commonplace—about books and libraries, fixing cars and trucks, using kerosene, the use and reuse of automobile tires, using chopsticks, shaking hands, voting, queuing (which Americans do in England), driving on the left, or driving on the right. This is increasingly evident in intellectual and cultural life, as Czech, Latin American, and Indian novelists, poets, and playwrights have a wide following in Europe and the United States. Most Americans became familiar with Beijing opera and Moscow ballet, and American and English rock singers give concerts around the world that incorporate international music styles and international political messages. "We Shall Overcome" is sung in Polish and Sudanese, just as Japanese children play Brahms on the violin, and American children play mah-jongg. Such cultural conventions are diffused through interpersonal contact and make interpersonal relations increasingly easy. Such conventions become the modalities by which people learn to initially communicate with another, and subsequently to cooperate to further social, economic, or political ends. After all, playing baseball, collecting and trading postage stamps, reading haiku poetry, and going to Shakespearean plays are about as international as driving Nissan cars, drinking French wine, and aping Italian fashions.

Many interests transcend national barriers, and although some efforts in promoting international cooperation have failed or are stifled by the interests of powerful nations, others have been extraordinarily successful as they focus on universal objectives, such as health, the environment, peace, the welfare of refugees, or entertainment. There are no absolute limits to international cooperation, as European countries are discovering. The sunk costs involve things that are technically and socially possible, such as learning languages, changing electrical outlets, and tinkering with national myths. The social investments are made on the basis of the presumption of equal endowments—that Spanish or German engineers can compete in the same arena, just as nations each have a vote in the affairs of the European community. It is in this sense that economic markets that are far-flung can reduce economic inequalities and then enhance international cooperation. The costs? Sherry is already dearer in English shops, and there are threats of boycotting bullfights. But every city in Spain has spiffed up its ancient monuments, medieval walls, and extended museum hours; there is no question that Spaniards are economically better off now than even a decade ago.

Economic exchange by itself leads initially, as I have frequently stated, to profound inequalities—between buyer and seller, between banker and borrower, between landowner and tenant farmer, between owner and wage earner, between developer and renter. Yet the greediness of markets expands the hinterlands, disperses ownership, internationalizes products, creates more buyers. This in turn expands the opportunities of social exchange and amplifies demands for participation. Herein lies the seeds of revolt, but also the seeds of claims to social equality. In the case of Europe, this eventually led to virtual union that has eased economic inequalities and extended social and political rights.

With fewer constraints of space, it might be argued that values and norms will lose their persuasive power. Indeed, one theorist, Jon Elster, so posits:

> As a result of social and geographical mobility, social norms lose their hold on people because people spend a larger proportion of their life with strangers who are not enforcing the norms with the same efficacy.[24]

Elster is correct, I believe, that group-based and group-regarding values and norms loose their hold in larger collectivities. But the other way of looking at this is that the distinction between the "we's" and our norms and the "them's" and their norms becomes subject to collective scrutiny. Women and blacks will not tolerate laws that perpetuate discrimination; the elderly assert economic rights; elites are held accountable. It is likely that privileged groups in postmodern societies will be held more accountable, but, perhaps, to the extent that as mapping cooperative activities becomes more challenging and intricate, and social relations become more complex, that incentives for accountability will bolster normative constraints. When the forms of interdependence thrive, norms of monopoly and dominance are hard to sustain.

The ideology of cultural relativism emphasized that intergroup normative understandings were difficult if not impossible to achieve. Although group values were seen as relative to unique social and economic contexts, which encouraged a sort of "liberal" perspective on group differences, cultural barriers precluded moral connections between the "we's" and the "them's."[25]

We might consider that a framework of cultural pluralism is more realistic than that of cultural relativism, for it suggests that cultural groups are equal participants in the global civic order. This is the recognition that there is a contextual (place) validity of different lifestyles, beliefs and values without insisting that they are constrained and governed by context. Thus, various discourses have unexpected ways of emerging, overlapping, and interconnecting. It is, I believe, useful to think of space-free social contracting.

NOTES

1. Robert S. Lynd and Helen M. Lynd, *Middletown*. New York: Harcourt, Brace, 1929.
2. Walter Christaller, *Central Places in Southern Germany*. Trans. Carlisle W. Baskin. Englewood Cliffs, NJ: Prentice-Hall, [1933] 1966; Edward Ullman, "A Theory of Location of Cities," *American Journal of Sociology* 46 (1941): 853–864; Brian J. L. Berry and William L. Garrison, "A Note on Central Place Theory and the Range of a Good," *Economic Geography* 34 (1958): 304–311.
3. See Edgar M. Hoover, *The Location of Economic Activity*. New York: McGraw-Hill, 1963, pp. 284–286.
4. Specifically, the percentage living in towns of 2500 or more in 1850 was only about 15%. By 1910, 25% of the population was urban, whereas by 1990 over 80% was urban. Janet L. Abu-Lughod (*Changing Cities*. New York: Harper-Collins, 1991) provides a clear summary of historical demographic trends in the United States.
5. Adapted from examples in John E. Brush, "The Hierarchy of Central Places in Southwestern Wisconsin," *Geographical Review* 43 (1953): 380–402, and Arthur E. Smailes, "The Urban Hierarchy in England and Wales," *Geography* 29 (1944): 41–51.
6. Herbert Gans, *The Urban Villagers*. New York: The Free Press, 1962; Michael Young and Peter Willmott, *Family and Kinship in East London*. London: Routledge & Kegan Paul, 1957.
7. Ira Katznelson, *City Trenches*. New York: Pantheon, 1981.
8. In the long run, this process was altered. Federal urban policy subsidized suburban development, and the "trickle-down principle" whereby inner-city housing declined in rental value was altered by the speculative value of deteriorated housing stock. See Sam Marullo, "Racial Differences in Housing Consumption and Filtering," pp. 229–254 in John S. Pipkin, Mark La Gory, and Judith R. Blau (eds.), *Remaking the City*. Albany: State University of New York Press, 1983.
9. Louis Wirth, *The Ghetto*. Chicago: University of Chicago Press, 1969; Harvey Zorbaugh, *The Gold Coast and the Slum*. Chicago: University of Chicago Press, 1937.

10. Robert E. Park and Ernest W. Burgess, *Introduction to the Science of Sociology*. Chicago: University of Chicago Press, 1921.
11. Gunther Barth, *City People*. Oxford: Oxford University Press, 1980.
12. Immanuel Wallerstein, *The Modern World-System III: The Second Era of Great Expansion of the Capitalist World-Economy, 1730–1840s*. Orlando, FL: Academic Press, 1989.
13. Hope T. Eldridge and Dorothy Swaine Thomas, *Population Distribution and Economic Growth, United States, 1870–1950*. Philadelphia: American Philosophical Society, 1964.
14. Robert H. Wiebe, *The Search for Order, 1877–1920*. New York: Hill and Wang, 1967, p. xiv.
15. Peter Dobkin Hall, *The Organization of American Culture, 1700–1900*. New York: New York University Hall, 1984, p. 3.
16. Arthur Vidich, *Small Town in Mass Society*. Garden City, NY: Doubleday, 1958; David Riesman, *The Lonely Crowd*. New Haven: Yale University Press, 1950.
17. Ernest Mandel, *Late Capitalism*. Trans. Joris De Bres. London: New Left Books, 1975, pp. 310–342; see also Harry Braverman, *Labor and Monopoly Capital*. New York: Monthly Review Press, 1974.
18. Henri Lefebvre, *The Production of Space*. Trans. Donald Nicholson-Smith. Oxford: Blackwell, 1991.
19. Ibid., pp. 378–379.
20. Gerald D. Jaynes and Robin M. Williams, Jr. (eds.), *A Common Destiny: Blacks and American Society. A Report of the Committee on the Status of Black Americans*. National Research Council. Washington, DC: National Academy Press, 1989, pp. 113–161.
21. See M. B. Brewer and R. M. Kramer, "The Psychology of Intergroup Attitudes," *Annual Review of Psychology* 36 (1985): 219–243.
22. See William Darity, Jr., "What's Left of the Economic Theory of Discrimination?" pp. 335–373 in Steven Schulman and William Darity, Jr. (eds.), *The Question of Discrimination*. Middletown, CT: Wesleyan University Press, 1989.
23. There are limits to the mobility of labor. However, increasingly technology allows people to work at home; in some industries, middle and top management personnel are rotated through different establishments. In some countries, notably Japan, door-to-door sales replaces retail operations; direct selling accounts for 75% of the new car purchases. (See Nicole Woolsey Biggart, *Charismatic Capitalism*. Chicago: University of Chicago Press, 1989, p. 173.)
24. Jon Elster, *Nuts and Bolts for the Social Sciences*. New York: Cambridge University Press, 1989, p. 162.
25. See Clifford Geertz, *Works and Lives*. Stanford: Stanford University Press, 1988, pp. 129–152; also George Lakoff, *Women, Fire, and Other Dangerous Things*. Chicago: University of Chicago Press, 1987.

7

The Wherewithal of Social Class

Taxes are what we pay for civilized society.
—*Compañia de Tobacos v. Collector,* 275 U.S. 87, 100 [1904]

According to Sir Arthur Salter, an early champion of laissez-faire economics, the narcissism of economic actors is quite sufficient for regulation:

> The normal economic system works itself. . . . Over the whole range of human activity and human need, supply is adjusted to demand and production to consumption, by a process that is automatic, elastic and responsive.[1]

This was written in 1921, prior to the world depression of 1929, and it was clearer to the next generation of economists—including those with such otherwise different views as Joan Robinson and Frank Knight[2]—that economic controls and regulation were imperative. The market must be consciously regulated, or there are pathological problems with monopoly, exploitation, and skewed advantage. A main reason is that buyers are not perfectly knowledgeable, and a second is that economic interdependencies are far too complex for economic actors to know all the consequences of their decisions. We recognize the importance of third-party enforcement, tariffs, trade laws, taxes, and laws to maintain a civic-minded and civil economy.

An early critic of unregulated markets was, interestingly enough, Charles Darwin. As is well known, he maintained that survival of plants and animals depended on opportunities for unmitigated competition.[3] That is, natural selection worked, according to Darwin, so long as there was sufficient variation among species and the opportunity to compete for advantage. This guaranteed survival and increasing adaptability. Yet on the other hand, a problem from Darwin's perspective was the opportunistic breeding of plants and animals for market and trade purposes. He was quick to lecture breeders on the long-term consequences of their free-market approach to natural resources.

One theme of my argument is that because the workings of economic markets depend on self-interest all around, and, therefore, competition with the likelihood of ensuring zero-sum outcomes, it is necessary to have formal contracts, laws, and regulations.[4] This will be elaborated in the final chapter. Part of this argument has been anticipated in Chapter 3 by the discussion of organizations and the tension between the wage contract and the social contract. The firm encompasses and confounds the wage contract and the social contract.

In an important sense, the wage contract is unlike a social contract. For workers, a wage contract is not based on choice; it is rather a preference over alternatives, and thereby is deterministic; thus it is "hardly a promising test of the freedom of entering into a contract."[5] Yet each and every one of us also enters into social contracts in which we are not under constraints to make preferences and for which we do not incur fixed opportunity costs (because other alternatives are just as desirable). Social contracts are possible because of the following reasons: (1) the far-reaching complexity of social life and the ways in which our social roles are partialled (and known only to ourselves); (2) the incessant demands for cultural equality, and, indeed, organizational and societal requirements for the legitimacy of equality; and (3) the way in which growing opportunities expand choices and mutualities of regard.

Civility is what tempers, shapes, and empowers social contracts. Although I have insisted that social life and economic life are profoundly different from one another with respect to accountability, individual rights, and mapping rules, it is also true that when there is precipitous economic decline and overall economic insecurity, social contracts are constricted. During periods of economic growth, we are generous all around in our social dealings. However, with decline, our lives become precarious, and we narrow the limits of civility to those whom we trust and with whom we can share our thoughts. This is the basis of secret societies, cabals, but also the wellspring of social movements—social protest, freedom movements, and peasant rebellions.

In order to ground this argument, I attempt to describe the nature of changing class relations in American society in order to show how the expanding middle class developed in an economic matrix that was conducive to civility owing to expanding opportunities. In turn, expanding opportunities helped to sustain a cultural framework that shaped the expectations of the members of the large middle class and its aspirants. Civility more fully interlaces social relations under conditions of less inequality than of more.

It is within this historical and economic context that claims for rights were freely made, obligations widely recognized, and social differences—notably, ones that are based on lifestyle, religion, ethnicity, and race—increasingly tolerated, and, daresay, even encouraged. To be clear from the start, the pace of historical momentum and people's perceptions of it are especially important. Wide prospects of upward mobility may help to blur the cultural definitions of class lines before they do, in fact, become objectively blurred. In contrast, wide prospects of downward mobility probably promote the active cultural makeshifting of class lines.

THE BASIS OF CLASS

It was Aristotle who probably first recognized the importance of the middle class when he drew attention to its buffering role in a stratified society. His claim was that it protected the poor from the exploitation by the rich and powerful, and at the same time protected the rich and powerful from the plots and intrigues of the aggrieved lower classes. "For where some possess much, and the others nothing, there may arise an extreme—either out of the most rampant democracy, or out of an oligarchy."[6]

The conventional wisdom in social science is that a modern industrial economy is the fail-safe generator of a national middle class, just as this national middle class is the lubricant of the industrial urban economy. The economic arrangements that the middle class helped to create and greatly strengthened, it is widely believed, cannot fall prey to oligarchies or give way to anarchy. There is a grain of truth in this, as the origins of the middle class are rooted in capitalism, postulates of individualism, and entrepreneurship. But its success, in my opinion, depended on very different factors: state intervention, and not economic liberalism; expanding experiences with employment, and not ownership; and inclusive cultural values, not individualism.

Ironically, just as social historians have mustered convincing evidence that the American middle class is relatively new, taking shape only after the Civil War, there are indications that the American middle class might unravel only a century and a half later. I intend to briefly summarize the argument that the American middle class originated in the Gilded Age, flourished through the initial decades of the twentieth century, survived the worst of the Depression, and then rebounded after World War II. I will argue that the historical conditions that supported the economic foundations of the middle class have been fundamentally altered and now no longer prevail.

We might consider first the midtwentieth-century middle class that encompassed a diffuse and large segment of the population, including wage earners, government and salaried workers, proprietors, and, indeed, a large number of the near-rich who embraced middle-class values that related to work and achievement, but who more exuberantly expressed a middle-class lifestyle.

The distinctions that earlier helped to define the internal makeup of the middle class—such as the white-collar/blue-collar line and the difference between salaried and wage earners—became increasingly less significant, owing in large part to the expansion of the service sector. So were the internal distinctions within the old middle class, such as between professionals and nonprofessionals, or between entrepreneurs and employees. In the postindustrial service economy of the United States, the line between the middle class and the truly disadvantaged is far more important than that between white collar and blue collar (that is, middle class and working class) or between occupational groups within the middle class (such as professionals and nonprofessionals). By truly disadvantaged, I refer to Wilson's term for the urban underclass,[7] but, as he indicates, it encompasses the casualties of a declining economy, including the rural poor, the homeless, poor female-headed households, the unemployed, as well as impoverished minorities who are highly segregated in large American cities.

Economy or Culture?

The extent to which class is essentially defined by cultural or economic factors remains a powerful debate in the social sciences long after Marx and Engels's work on class in the middle of the last century and Weber's response early in this century.[8] In the social sciences, a rich tradition is devoted to disentangling economic from cultural components of class. While the Lynds, Thorstein Veblen, and C. Wright Mills[9] demonstrated that economic factors defined and perpetuated class lines, Warner, and later, Bourdieu, although in different ways, contended that the real differences were not so much economic as linked to the cultural significance of differences in lifestyles and occupations.[10]

My argument, more in the lines of the work of E. P. Thompson, is that historical contingencies shape the nature of class.[11] That is, class formation depended on economic factors during the early period of industrialization, but the middle class increasingly defined a cultural basis for itself, and cultural factors played an increasing role in shaping consciousness and institutions. But it was the context of expanding economic opportunities that allowed cultural identity to assume such social significance. To be more explicit, lifestyles and institutions that provided the vital cultural identity of the American middle class in its early origins were contingent on a set of unique historical conditions.

Paradoxically, these conditions initially involved great initial economic inequalities, with the concentration of wealth in the hands of a small minority and a substantial proportion of the population living at or below subsistence wages. But this was followed by rapidly increasing affluence and declining inequalities. In the first place, it can be argued that economic disparities are particularly important for the development of class consciousness, but increasing affluence provided the wherewithal for increasing upward mobility, the diffusion of a concept of the civic sphere,[12] and an increasing recognition of benign differences in social origins and lifestyle within an expanded definition of middle class.[13]

Rules about class identity became increasingly flexible as middle-class lifestyle and the cultural codes of the middle class became widely shared while sufficient numbers of people were close enough to—and distant enough from—immigrant origins to celebrate diversity. (In the 1960s and 1970s, it was called "having roots.") Important conditions, especially after the Great Depression, that made this possible include the following: First, New Deal provisions improved the income of workers and expanded jobs. Second, economic growth helped to reduce the differences between the average salaries paid to white-collar workers and to blue-collar workers. Third, dual-career earnings improved family incomes. Fourth, joint earning in a family often makes family status ambiguous.[14] Fifth, family members, say, over two generations, were often extremely diverse in terms of income, education, and occupation. And finally, lifestyle differences were increasingly eroded owing to the wide diffusion of consumer products and broad participation in cultural and recreational activities, such as travel abroad, membership in health clubs, going to rock concerts, camping, and owning a VCR.

THE ELUSIVE AMERICAN MIDDLE CLASS

Without an aristocracy, wrote Alexis de Tocqueville, America was a place where citizens were remarkably egalitarian in their views.[15] When Tocqueville visited America in the 1830s, there were few families of great wealth, but instead (aside from slaves), general economic prosperity shared by farmers, artisans, owners of small manufactures, wage earners, and tradespeople. Although Tocqueville concluded that the line between the laboring and ownership classes was fuzzy at best, he suggested that economic differences between wage earners and "manufacturing speculators" would further decline.[16] Instead, the growing concerns as the century wore on were increasing disparities in economic welfare between the many poor and the wealthy few and between the industrial workers and owners of capital.[17] It was in the midst of these great economic disparities—and concerns about them—that an urban middle class emerged.

The historical origins of the American middle class are somewhat elusive as scholars have considered the important story about class issues in the nineteenth century to be a story about industrial and manufacturing settings. There is no question that the economic conditions created by industrial wage labor, high rates of immigration, and the collapse of the southern economy after the Civil War, combined with the growing wealth of private capitalists, created glaring contrasts between the lives of the rich and of the poor.

Estimates of wealth distribution for northern American cities around 1870 suggest that the top one-tenth of 1% had 15% of the wealth, and over 50% of the population had no real or personal assets.[18] Great inequality was a fact of postbellum America, but it is also the case that there was unprecedented economic growth that affected the prospects of very large numbers of wage earners. While inequalities persisted, wages (in real dollars) increased about 50% between 1860 and 1890.[19]

Increasing prosperity and industrial development generated a need for services—retailers, wholesalers, proprietors, shopkeepers, teachers, professionals, and clerks—that were distinct both from the class composed of industrialists and bankers and from the large class of wage earners and casual workers. In the midst of prevailing inequalities that were generated by industrialization but directly benefiting from the growing affluence (also a product of industrialization) urban white-collar workers emerged as a distinct social class.

The recent work of Stuart Blumin provides a benchmark for research on the nineteenth-century urban classes.[20] What Blumin terms the "elusive Middle Class" emerged in the late nineteenth century out of the congeries of what were called "the middling folk" in the late eighteenth and early nineteenth centuries. These "folk" had earlier included teachers, preachers, and shopkeepers, but without major urban institutions, such as department stores and large banks, there had been too few of them to establish a strong social identity and common cultural orientations.[21]

The middle class was made possible by exactly the same economic conditions that created the wage-earning manufacturing class, specifically, technological developments, industrial growth, and improved overall economic conditions. What distinguished the middle class from the working classes were differences in occupational niches and family configurations, and these were reinforced by residential segregation and differences in household economy.[22]

According to Blumin, what was critical for the emergent identity of the middle class was the slow disappearance of the artisan class, which formed the fragile boundary between white-collar and manual workers. The shrinking numbers of artisans and skilled craftsmen helped to weaken the boundaries between white collar and blue collar, non-manual and manual.[23] Extending this argument, I contend that these are the very structural conditions under which cultural factors became increasingly salient in the development of class identity. The very fact of glaring inequalities between, on the one hand, workers in sweat shops, slaughter houses, and factories and, on the other hand, wealthy industrialists and bankers enabled the "middling folk" to extract and overprice the cultural codes of a white-collar lifestyle.

THE BASIS OF MIDDLE-CLASS CULTURE

Partly because members of the urban working class were themselves residentially segregated by ethnicity and religion,[24] the members of the growing middle class, who were less divided along these lines, could establish neighborhoods based more on lifestyle. This lifestyle drew from upper-class models, but not entirely. The middle class created its own social institutions, such as the public university, newspapers, voluntary associations, department stores, libraries, and business clubs.

In periods of high mobility, defining class membership lines is serious business, requiring cultural edgework that draws from economic and institutional affiliations, and endowing such affiliations with elaborate symbols. Such edgeworking is rooted in self-righteous attempts to distend the boundaries between the respectable middle class and workers, particularly Catholics and Jews. This accompanied zealous efforts to reform beer halls, vaudeville houses, public theaters, and common coquetry.

Late-nineteenth-century culture was strongly rooted in urban ecology. Housing segregation and, therefore, access to amenities helped to fortify differences in lifestyle. Writing on such differences, Trachtenberg describes how housing reinforced the barriers between social classes.[25] Sanitation—now trivial owing to the universality of indoor plumbing—decisively divided houses and neighborhoods, establishing insidious social distinctions.

Yet if access to such amenities established conspicuous class differences, these, in turn, could be elaborated by subtle nuances in cultural expression and lifestyle. If there was one key manifest symbol of the middle class in the decades beginning around 1900, Gwendolyn Wright stresses, it was residence in a fledgling suburb.[26] Suburban neighborhoods took on a special meaning and form of social organization, and those who could afford a house away from crowded tenements bought into neighborhoods that were less clearly segregated by ethnic, racial, and religious lines. The home, "how it was furnished, and the family life the housewife oversaw, contributed to the definition of the 'middle class,' at least as much as did the husband's income."[27] Historian J. M. Burns describes in detail the household routines that as a composite distinguished the nineteenth-century middle-class family from its upper-and working-class counterparts. Education for the boys and proper training for the girls, a maid servant, small families, well-appointed parlors, and a modest carriage were important symbols that delineated middle class from both upper and working classes.[28]

Trachtenberg also draws attention to the cult of domesticity that emerged in the American city in the nineteenth century:

> With the rise of food and clothing industries, domestic labor came to consist chiefly of budgeting and shopping rather than making. From the place of labor for self-support, the home had become the place of consumption. How to be a "lady who does her own work" came very quickly after the Civil War to mean how to be a lady who shops; indeed who sustains herself as "lady" by wise and efficient shopping.[29]

Edgeworking class lines also expressed itself in the most trivial pursuits. The link between social class formation and the mundane affairs of daily life is described in the recent work of cultural historians, most notably in the book by John F. Kasson.[30] Established codes of behavior, he observes, were most highly evolving in the late nineteenth century as self-conscious assertions of bourgeois respectability. Symptomatic of an age with economic affluence and growth were great symbolic differences in social decorum and behavior. Yet much of middle-class life rested on fine points of manners and household management that could be learned very easily from manuals of etiquette and guidebooks for home furnishings. Emotional control, self-discipline, proper public deportment—the moral codes of the middle class—could more readily be cultivated than could wealth, a prominent lineage, or inherited prestige be acquired. Easy acquisition of these behaviors, as Norbert Elias had written, provides a mechanism for social leveling that strengthens the egalitarian character of a society.[31]

DECLINING ECONOMIC INEQUALITIES

Inequalities did not decline before the Great Depression, in part because of sustained high levels of immigration, until the early 1920s with the enactment of a series of immigration acts. However, continued economic prosperity between 1900 and 1930 fostered sufficient opportunities for the expansion of a middle-class lifestyle more broadly than ever before in history. New technologies of the late nineteenth century and early twentieth century brought bicycles, plumbing, electricity, the phonograph, sewing machines, and radio into virtually all urban households. Once gentrified, urban institutions (of many social origins), such as baseball, the penny press, the department store, national celebrations, traveling exhibits (spectacles), and parades, fostered democratic participation as they cut across class and ethnic lines.[32] Even national private organizations that were administered by wealthy elites were remarkably interconnected with the diverse public through dependence on common personnel and institutions.[33]

The decades between 1900 and 1930 were critical for the consolidation of the American middle class. Abundant consumer goods, improved conditions of work, and declines in unemployment led to genuine change in the lives of the working class. Mass credit meant that houses and, a little later, automobiles were within reach of millions of working families,[34] and the restriction of immigration undoubtedly contributed to the sense of security for a largely white, white-collar class. Except for the very rich—who could draw on reserves—and the very poor, notably the blacks—who were the last hired and the first fired—the Depression had a random effect on all groups in the middle, and furthermore, the common hostility against wealthy business leaders probably helped to strengthen the idea of the middle class.

The end of the Depression also meant the beginning of the gradual decline in economic inequalities. The expansion of the numbers of white-collar and salaried workers was made possible by increasing rates of college attendance and the diffusion of social and cultural institutions and the rising incomes of blue-collar workers who could buy into white-collar communities and consumption patterns.

The federated middle class of the midtwentieth century was built on the bedrock of expanding economic and educational opportunities. High rates of mobility permitted the vast diffusion of manners, lifestyle, home decor, and leisure patterns. Nationalism that grew out of World War II probably helped as much to promote feelings of a common destiny as did the virtual universality of Sears and Roebuck catalogs, Victory Gardens, and the wartime switch from butter to margarine. Moreover, the national media were impervious to differences in geography, language, accent, and race. The same media helped to clarify and diffuse a middle-class morality that dictated standards of child rearing, church attendance, sexuality, and appropriate gender roles. Although the American middle class had an initial monopoly on forms of cultural capital in the early part of the century, by midcentury the rules whereby it could be acquired were widely known and readily accepted.

Whereas in nineteenth-century America the initial economic distinction between manual and nonmanual workers could be expressed in symbolic and cultural terms and fortified in urban institutions, residence, and social affiliations, cultural claims to middle-class respectability and success are easily aped and, in the presence of sufficient opportunities for upward mobility, authentically adopted.

My own analysis suggests the great importance of the middle class—not the rich elites—in the recent adoption of cultural practices and the creation of cultural tastes. The main explanation for the diffusion of varieties of culture, including opera and radio, chamber music and television, theater and rock concerts, is the relative size of the middle class. Participation in cultural activities is far more affected by people's education and cultural opportunities in their towns than it is by income. And, regardless of education and income, individuals who live in predominantly middle-class communities are more likely to be consumers of culture regardless of their own class standing.[35] That is, participation in "high-brow" cultural activities is increasingly more a claim for social acceptance than it is a claim for superior status.

THE DECLINE OF THE MIDDLE CLASS

The 1960s was a decade of rights-setting agendas that addressed the needs of those who were not the beneficiaries of the economic growth of the first half of the century: African-Americans, women, Hispanics. Many of these issues rested squarely on marketplace demands, notably, equal pay and equal opportunities. Such claims are completely consonant with middle-class notions that impersonal economic, bureaucratic, and educational institutions must be precisely that—impartial and impersonal. There were, after all, hazy notions that each member of the middle class had made it on these very grounds. Hard work paid off, and should pay off, but the ground rules must be fair and square. The tragedy is that the ground rules changed.

Economists provide the clues as to what happened. The long postwar boom from 1945 to the recession of 1973 was built on a certain stable set of labor-control practices, consumption patterns, and forms of political economic domination that were especially favorable to the middle class. Although economists describe the economic rigidities of this period, the only manifest problem that affected the daily lives of Americans was sustained inflation. The 1973 recession, followed shortly after by the 1975 oil shortage, and a new phenomenon—high inflation and high unemployment—altered the rules of economic life and wreaked havoc with the U.S. economy, especially in major northeastern metropolitan areas. Real productivity declined from a longtime average of 3% to .9%, and remains there; in the middle of that decade unemployment reached over 8%; the percentage without medical insurance grew to 43%; the index of hourly earnings declined by 12% in the short period between 1978 to 1983; and, in the same period, the lowest quintile of the population lost 17% in transfer payments.[36]

During the 1980s, there was a dramatic increase in the numbers of people below the poverty line, as well as a decline in the numbers escaping over that line.[37] By 1988, for example, over 45% of New York City's non-school-age population were unemployed.[38] At the same time, there was also an unprecedented increase in the numbers of workers who experienced job loss owing to firm cutbacks. Between 1981 and 1986, more than five million workers lost jobs owing to job disappearance resulting from plant closings or scale-downs and abolition of positions.[39] During that time there was a dramatic expansion of part-time workers and temporaries. Their numbers doubled between 1980 to 1987, and they expanded to comprise roughly a quarter of the total work force in 1987.[40]

One should also consider the effects of tax policies. Kuttner describes the "bracket creep" that affected the middle and lower classes.[41] Between 1953 and 1974, direct taxes paid by the average-income family doubled, from 11.8% to 23.4% of income, whereas families with four times the average income increased much less (from 20.2% to 29.5%). During the period of 1969 to 1980, the middle class was caught by dramatic inflation and an increase of 92% in Social Security taxes. On the other hand, the most affluent earners experienced tax declines from 77% in 1964 to 28% in 1988. Corporate taxes during this period fell dramatically. The percentage of federal tax receipts from corporate income dropped from 32% in 1952 to an all-time low of 6.2% in 1983. The wealthy continued to benefit as the taxes on unearned income were capped at 50%, and the top rate on capital gains was down to 20%, from an earlier 49%.[42]

Although the secular trend in inequalities began in the 1970s,[43] during the 1980s this trend accelerated owing largely to a steady shrinking of full-time workers in core labor markets and an accompanying increase in peripheral or secondary labor-market sectors. Under the conservative administrations of Reagan and Bush, the conditions of the poor, the working class, and the underclass have been seriously threatened, but the downwardly mobile members of the middle class have been surprised to learn how skimpily sewn the safety nets really are.

For the first time since the end of the Depression, the gaps between the rich and poor and rich and middle are widening. Moreover, there is increasing concentration of wealth. In 1983, the top one-half of 1% of U.S. households possessed about 27% of the total wealth, very close to the 32% just on the eve of the Depression, and almost doubling from the mid-1970s, when this was about 14%. As the average family incomes of those earning around $50,000 or more experienced increases in earnings between 1977 and 1988, the average family incomes of those earning less than $50,000 declined. Summarizing the changes between 1977 and 1988, the Congressional Budget Office reports concluded that the bottom 80% of the population was slipping downward, as the top 20% enjoyed a surge of income and wealth.[44] In short, the rich grew in affluence, the poor grew in numbers, and the middle contracted.

As early as the mid-1970s, Daniel Bell described the members of the middle class as tenaciously clinging to their traditional lifestyle as their economic well-being was being threatened.[45] The data clearly reveal why the members of the middle class feel threatened and the poor feel increasingly discouraged. There are declining opportunities for upward mobility for the daughters and sons of the poor and increases in downward mobility for the middle class and their offspring. College graduates compete with high school graduates for jobs, and high school graduates with high school dropouts. Young, married, dual-career breadwinners cannot afford the down payment on a mortgage, underemployment is excessive, and the numbers defaulting on credit loans and losing health insurance coverage are reaching new highs each year.

Yet we must take note of the cultural context of economic decline. The middle class successfully spawned democratic values, egalitarian patterns of lifestyle and consumption, and an ethos that linked hard work with success and achievement. Just as important, it spawned important codes of civility that made middle-class membership relatively easy to acquire for those with the opportunity to work. The continued viability of the middle class rests on this set of cultural claims just as much as it rests on economic growth and opportunities. Economic decline poses a crisis of authenticity and of legitimacy for the middle class and problems for civility. The ethos of the American middle class, in other words, is contingent on continued prosperity, not on the growing inequalities of the last decades.

THE TRULY DISADVANTAGED AS HISTORICAL VICTIMS

If the middle class is contracting, the underclass and the homeless are expanding in numbers. William Julius Wilson calls this group the truly disadvantaged,[46] and it is increasingly black.[47] Two historical economic accidents account for the predominantly black composition of the very poor in the United States. First, African-Americans, as slaves, drew initially the lowest class position in American society without educational, political, and other resources. Lynchings were reported as recently as 1954,[48] and as late as 1960 Congress had to pass an amendment to enforce the 1954 *Brown v. Board of Education* decision that required desegregation "with all deliberate speed."[49] As recently as June 1992, the Supreme Court declared that many southern states had still not complied.

Second, blacks migrated in large numbers from the rural South to the industrial North after the period of great economic expansion, namely, after the Depression,[50] and their numbers swelled at the time that likely employers, such as manufacturing firms and textile companies, were moving out.[51]

The widespread belief that the middle class had no lower boundary was based in part on the sustained levels of upward mobility of white ethnics at a time when economic opportunities were expanding. However, the fact that the sons and daughters of white immigrants are difficult to distinguish from native-born whites also facilitated mobility and created a middle class that is far more diverse in terms of ethnic origins than its consumer and lifestyles would suggest.

The conditions of ambiguous class membership and ambiguous ethnic identity, along with the expansion of opportunities, are also the conditions on which civility depend. However, when identifiable minority groups became trapped at the bottom of the ladder just as opportunities for economic mobility declined, racism and prejudice reinforced economic realities. Under conditions of economic inequality in which class position is confounded with minority status, a powerful mechanism of distinction is itself skin color and body build, not simply accoutrement, demeanor, and accent. This is the grave situation in other countries where ethnic differences are confounded with residential segregation and economic status, such as Germany, South Africa, Yugoslavia, and Israel.

As advantage begins to slip the grasp of the predominantly white middle class, it is imperative that economic policies are developed to shape opportunities so that the truly disadvantaged are not the third-time victims of economic history.

NOTES

1. J. A. Salter, *Allied Shipping Control*. Oxford: Clarendon Press, 1921, pp. 16–17. R. H. Coase traces the influence of Salter's analysis on subsequent economists and the defense of the view that the economic system "works itself." See *The Firm, the Market and the Law*. Chicago: University of Chicago Press, 1988, p. 34.
2. Joan Robinson, *The Economics of Imperfect Competition*. London: Macmillan & Co., 1933; Frank H. Knight, *On the History and Method of Economics*. Chicago: University of Chicago Press, 1956.
3. Charles Darwin, *The Origin of the Species*. Introduction by Sir Julian Huxley. New York: New American Library, [1859] 1958.
4. This is what Douglass C. North calls "institutions." See his *Institutions,*

Institutional Change and Economic Performance. Cambridge: Cambridge University Press, 1990.

5. Anthony de Jasay, *Social Contract, Free Ride.* Oxford: Oxford University Press, 1989, p. 16.

6. Aristotle, *Politics.* Trans. Benjamin Jowett. New York: Modern Library, 1943, p. 191.

7. William Julius Wilson, *The Truly Disadvantaged: The Inner City, the Underclass, and Public Policy.* Chicago: University of Chicago Press, 1987.

8. Karl Marx, *The Eighteenth Brumaire of Louis Bonaparte.* New York: International Publishers, [1852] 1963; Max Weber, "The Distribution of Power within the Political Community: Class, Status, Party," pp. 926–940 in Guenther Roth and Claus Wittich (eds.), *Economy and Society, Vol. 2.* Berkeley: University of California Press, 1978.

9. Robert S. Lynd and Helen M. Lynd, *Middletown in Transition.* New York: Harcourt, Brace & World, 1936; Thorstein Veblen, *The Theory of the Leisure Class.* New York: Modern Library, 1899; C. Wright Mills, *The Power Elite.* New York: Oxford University Press, 1956; Herbert J. Gans, *The Urban Villagers.* New York: Free Press, 1982.

10. William Lloyd Warner, *Yankee City.* New Haven, CT: Yale University Press, 1963; Pierre Bourdieu, *Distinction.* Trans. Richard Nice. Cambridge: Harvard University Press, 1984.

11. E. P. Thompson, *The Making of the English Working Class.* New York: Pantheon, 1963.

12. Jürgen Habermas, *The Structural Transformation of the Public Sphere: An Inquiry into a Category of Bourgeois Society.* Trans. Thomas Burger with Frederick Lawrence. Cambridge: Cambridge University Press, 1989.

13. Niklas Luhmann, *The Differentiation of Society.* Trans. Stephen Holmes and Charles Larmore. New York: Columbia University Press, 1982.

14. This is true in two respects: Joint earners enhance family consumption and lifestyle, and "mixed-collar" marriages create ambiguous class membership.

15. Alexis de Tocqueville, *Democracy in America. Vol 1.* Trans. George Lawrence, ed. J. P. Mayer. New York: Doubleday, [1836] 1969, p. 266.

16. Ibid., vol. 2, pp. 199–201.

17. See Stanley Lebergott, *The Americans: An Economic Record.* New York: W. W. Norton, 1984, pp. 69–73; Daniel J. Walkowitz, *Worker City, Company Town.* Urbana: University of Illinois Press, 1978; David Ward, *Poverty, Ethnicity and the American City, 1840–1925.* New York: Cambridge University Press, 1972.

18. Lee Soltow, *The Wealth, Income and Social Class in Large Northern Cities of the United States in 1860,* pp. 233–276 in James D. Smith (ed.), *The Personal Distribution of Income and Wealth: Studies in Income and Wealth.* New York: National Bureau of Economic Research, 1975; Robert E. Gallman, "Trends in the Size Distribution of Wealth in the Nineteenth Century," pp. 1–24 in Lee Soltow (ed.), *Six Papers on the Size Distribution of Wealth and Income.* New York: National Bureau of Economic Research, 1969.

19. Clarence D. Long, *Wages and Earnings in the United States, 1860–1890*. Princeton: Princeton University Press and the National Bureau of Economic Research, 1960.
20. Stuart M. Blumin, *The Emergence of the Middle Class*. Cambridge: Cambridge University Press, 1989; also see Stephan Thermstrom, *The Other Bostonians*. Cambridge: Harvard University Press, 1973.
21. Gunther Barth, *City People: The Rise of Modern City Culture in Nineteenth-Century America*. Oxford: Oxford University Press, 1980.
22. Melanie Archer, "Self-Employment and Occupational Structure in an Industrializing City," *Social Forces* 69 (1991): 785–810.
23. Blumin, op. cit., p. 136.
24. Theodore Hershberg (ed.), *Philadelphia: Work, Space, Family, and Group Experience in the Nineteenth Century*. New York: Oxford University Press, 1981.
25. Alan Trachtenberg, *The Incorporation of America*. New York: Hill and Wang, 1982, p. 128.
26. Gwendolyn Wright, *Building the Dream: A Social History of Housing in America*. Cambridge: MIT Press, 1981.
27. Ibid., p. 99.
28. James MacGregor Burns, *The Workshop of Democracy*. New York: Vintage Press, 1985, pp. 119–126.
29. Trachtenberg, op. cit., p. 129.
30. John F. Kasson, *Rudeness and Civility: Manners in Nineteenth-Century Urban America*. New York: Hill and Wang, 1990.
31. Norbert Elias, *The History of Manners: The Civilizing Process, Vol. 1*. Trans. Edmund Jephcott. New York: Pantheon, 1978.
32. Miles Orvell, *The Real Thing: Imitation and Authenticity in American Culture, 1880–1940*. Chapel Hill: University of North Carolina Press, 1989; Mary Ryan, "The American Parade: Representations of Nineteenth-Century Social Order," pp. 131–153 in Lynn Hunt (ed.), *The New Cultural History*. Berkeley: University of California Press, 1989.
33. Peter Dobkin Hall, *The Organization of American Culture, 1700–1900*. New York: New York University Press, 1982.
34. Stanley Lebergott, op. cit., p. 436. For a discussion about the emerging middle class in work organizations, see also John McDermott, *Corporate Society*. Boulder: Westview Press, pp. 181–191.
35. Judith R. Blau, *The Shape of Culture*. Cambridge: Cambridge University Press, 1989.
36. Bennett Harrison and Barry Bluestone, *The Great U-Turn: Corporate Restructuring and the Polarizing of America*. New York: Basic Books, 1988; Barry Bluestone, "The Great U-Turn Revisited: Economic Restructuring, Jobs, and the Redistribution of Earnings," pp. 7–44 in John D. Kasarda (ed.), *Jobs, Earnings, and Employment Growth Policies in the United States*. Boston: Kluwer Academic Publishers, 1990.
37. Laurence E. Lynn, Jr. and Michael G. M. McGreary, "Conclusions," pp. 253–

270 in Lynn and McGreary (eds.), *Inner-City Poverty in the United States.* Washington, DC: National Academy Press, 1990.

38. Kevin Phillips, *The Politics of Rich and Poor.* New York: Random House, 1990, p. 20.
39. Katherine S. Newman, *Falling from Grace: The Experience of Downward Mobility in the American Middle Class.* New York: Free Press, 1988, pp. 23–26.
40. "A Shifting Job Market Is Squeezing the Working Poor," *Business Week,* March 21, 1988, p. 16.
41. Robert Kuttner, *The Economic Illusion.* Philadelphia: University of Pennsylvania Press, 1984, p. 189.
42. Phillips, op. cit., p. 79.
43. Richard Butler and James B. McDonald, "Income Inequality in the United States," in Ronald G. Ehrenberg (ed.), *Research in Labor Economics. Vol. 8, Part A.* Greenwich, CT: JAI Press, 1986; Richard Sobel, *The White Working Class.* New York: Praeger, 1989; Lester C. Thurow, *The Zero-Sum Society: Distribution and the Possibilities for Economic Change.* New York: Basic Books, 1980.
44. Phillips, op. cit., p. 16.
45. Daniel Bell, *The Cultural Contradictions of Capitalism.* New York: Basic Books, 1976.
46. William Julius Wilson, op. cit. The controversies concerning the term *underclass* are reviewed in Michael B. Katz, *The Undeserving Poor.* New York: Pantheon Books, 1989. Briefly, the basic argument deals with whether there is a "culture of poverty" that has been perpetuated by dependency, or whether urban poverty is the consequence of historical and economic conditions. Wilson takes the latter position, but understates, in my opinion, the role of racism. For an important account of the persistence of racism, see Gerald David Jaynes and Robin M. Williams (eds.), *A Common Destiny: Blacks and American Society.* Washington, DC: Committee on the Status of Black Americans, National Academy Press, 1989, pp. 113–160.
47. Blacks, Hispanics, and Native Americans are disproportionately represented among the homeless; see Peter H. Rossi, *Down and Out in America: The Origins of Homelessness.* Chicago: University of Chicago Press, 1989, pp. 122–125.
48. Warren D. St. James, *NAACP.* Smithtown, NY: Exposition Press, 1980, p. 32.
49. Samuel Eliot Morison, Henry Steele Commager, and William E. Leuchtenburg, *A Concise History of the American Republic.* 2nd ed. New York: Oxford University Press, 1983, p. 696.
50. Stanley Lieberson, *A Piece of the Pie: Black and White Immigration since 1880.* Berkeley: University of California Press, 1980.
51. John D. Kasarda, "Urban Change and Minority Opportunities," in Paul E. Peterson (ed.), *The New Urban Reality.* Washington, DC: The Brookings Institution, 1985.

8

The Firm and
Its Contradictions

You have to be tough to want a lot of money. You have to be tough to make money, as everybody knows. But you have to be tough to want it. Money means as much to those who have it as to those who don't. It says that in Money. And it's true. There is a common pool. By wanting a lot, you are taking steps to spread it thin elsewhere.

—MARTIN AMIS, *Money*, p. 263

In this chapter I attempt to show how money—capital—and its transporter—the market—have strayed into social environments in which they are not well suited, with the result that they create considerable havoc both for the economy and for the social environments in which they lodge. Money in this way adulterates social organizations by perverting the grounds of cooperative social life. By infusing organizations with competitive struggle, finance markets undermine the conditions for making social contracts. The underlying premise is *not* that people are corrupt and greedy, although this may be a consequence of these unprecedentedly novel arrangements. A more certain consequence has been prevailing social unease about jobs and earnings, insurance and savings, and the stability of work organizations.

One of the first things students ask when they enter college is will they be able to find a job. They also ask why the economy is so poor. Their concerns are warranted: profits have declined; productivity is at a low rate; unemployment is high. Prices have not fallen. In this chapter, I attempt to provide one explanation for a source of these difficulties.

The explanation requires a rudimentary understanding of firms, markets, and the workings of capitalism.

The firm is an economic entity and is organized around the following economic elements: capital (money), commodities (products and services), and the means of production (technology, land, buildings). The firm also includes labor (workers or employees), which makes it a social entity as well as an economic one. On the one hand, owners and workers have opposing class and financial interests, but, on the other hand, there is considerable identity of interests and incentives to cooperate, as I have argued throughout this book.

Thus, in purely economic terms, the *entrepreneur*[1] owns the capital, the means of production, and hires workers to produce commodities or services to make a profit. It is the rudimentary concept of profit that links the firm to external markets. The *potential for profit* is created by workers: Specifically, surplus value is, put simply, the difference between what workers are paid for their work and what that work is worth—as products or services—in the market.[2] In contrast, the *realization* of profit thus occurs when products or services are sold, in the market and outside of the firm. Entrepreneurs compete with other entrepreneurs to sell products to buyers and buy (as an investor or as a user) land, materials, machinery—again competitively with other entrepreneurs. The entrepreneur also invests capital in capital stock, commodity stock, bonds, and land markets.

In capitalist societies, economic activities are governed by the assumption that actors, as agents, are wealth maximizers. Precisely because money is *made in* the market, outside the firm, the state must play a role in protecting the public and regulating the economy, which it does by means of legislating constraints and facilitating open competition. The state also has more complex roles. It sets monetary policies (that is, whether to have tight or easy money) and fiscal policies (including printing money, taxing, borrowing, budgeting, and spending). This is an issue to which we return later.

The point to be made here is that economic actors are driven by their own self-interest and by the "invisible hand" of the market—demand and supply that generate prices that in turn regulate demand and supply. Although supply is made up of those items—products and services—that were produced in the transformation of potential to real profit, demand originates from what workers are paid in wages and from the profits that entrepreneurs realize.

In early entrepreneurial capitalism, firms could handle production and pricing in a completely decentralized way by means of short-term contracts in markets. And, indeed, in early capitalist societies, selling and buying were carried out in village fairs or open exchange markets. In a sense, this is similar to the way that bonds, stocks, and commodities are sold and bought today, in a freewheeling open and highly impersonal market where prices fluctuate with demand and supply. The early fair and the contemporary stock, commodity, and bond markets are not organizations; they are prototypical models of the way goods and capital are exchanged. They only require atavistic organizations to keep capital and other commodities moving along. Similarly, the self-employed still operate in such markets—trying to buy up cheaply and to sell dearly—and are bound by competitive forces. In the open market of transactions—the village fair or the stock exchange or an aggregate of self-employed entrepreneurs—pricing mechanisms determine the aggregate preference (demand), which in turn affects production and, hence, supply. Thus, external markets are based on a conflict of interest and impersonal competition among buyers and among sellers.

The market often has principles of voluntary regulation, but these are hard to enforce in very large markets. And here enters the state, at least in one of its roles, as "traffic cop," to prevent fraud and monopoly, among other things. Regulations are required to maintain fair competition, to prevent collusion, to ensure disclosure and open information about products, to maintain an explicit pricing mechanism, and to uphold contracts.

COMPETITION

Competition is an interesting concept and pivotal to understanding the market and distinguishing between what is a firm and what is a market. In classical economics, a perfectly competitive market is one in which buyers and sellers—demand and supply—determine the price and the price in turn alters supply and demand. An elegant role that competition plays in economic theory, and even in many real world instances, is that it drives out inefficiencies, such as overpriced items or low-quality products.

The model of competition rests on some important assumptions. There are so many economic units that no single one can affect the price; there is no constraint on mobility; and economic units possess complete knowledge.[3] What is important is that actors are not "nice"; they are purely self-interested. It is for this reason that competition must be impersonal, nonpolitical, and impartial. There are problems when these conditions are not met.

What I have described is the classical conception of the market, and the story is familiar to anyone who has taken a basic course in the sociology of organizations or economics. But it does not require much time for reflection to conclude that the contemporary economy does not work that way. Contemporary profit-making organizations are based on very different principles. Vertical integration, horizontal integration, diversification, and labor contracts are the organizational mechanisms that have transformed and redefined the nature of markets. Moreover, some markets have become more important than others. This will be explored further in this chapter, but the point to be made here is that organizational mechanisms—notably, diversification—alter and sometimes eliminate the pricing system of the market, thereby reducing competition as well as the costs of transacting in an open market.

The bank that owns an insurance firm does not have to purchase insurance plans for its bank tellers. U.S. Steel does not have to haggle with Marathon over the price of oil for its own operations because both are subsidiaries of USX. Phillip Morris executives cover cigarette litigation costs with sales of Log Cabin Syrup, Kool-Aid, Handi-Snacks, and Classic Herb Salad Dressing.[4] The purchasing department at Folger's Coffee does not need to buy bleach for the maintenance staff, nor does its counterpart at Clorox need to buy coffee for the staff, as Procter and Gamble owns them both. Of course, there is a "price" to every unit of capital, labor, and land, but within the firm it is determined by accountants, not by competition.

FIRMS AND MARKETS

I turn to Coase's original essay of 1937, "The Nature of the Firm,"[5] in order to summarize my argument that firms evolved to deal with the anarchy of external market competition, and they did so by internalizing much of that competition. According to Coase's early essay, firms deal with market anarchy and environmental uncertainty by absorbing transaction costs, namely, those costs of exchange that are above and beyond production costs. That is to say, there are many transactions, or exchanges, that were traditionally carried out in markets but are increasingly lodged in firms. According to a more recent essay, Coase states that "firms will emerge to organize what would otherwise be market transactions whenever the costs of organizing a transaction become less than the costs of carrying it through the market."[6] These include any and all transactions that are involved in exchange, such as capital for labor, capital for products, products for profit, capital for reaching consumers (marketing costs), and land for capital. Even when these transactions remain in markets—owing to excessive costs of absorbing them in firms or the impracticalities of doing so—firms nevertheless play a major role in organizing and coordinating them.

This view is consistent with our observation that large firms sometimes buy their suppliers (instead of buying their suppliers' products or their raw materials), and buy their distributors and retailers (that is, buy the means of transportation and purchase outlets and franchises). Firms also hire permanent workers and buy land. Finally, coordination and administration are largely centralized even when production is carried out elsewhere. These examples are important to keep in mind because we shall see later that there is a countervailing trend for which Coase's theory cannot account, although his theory would allow for it.

Although Coase's essay was largely overlooked, Chandler wrote in 1977 that markets had become "invisible," whereas firm-based activities involving coordination, administration, planning, and allocation had become "visibly" placed in the hands of management.[7] Williamson subsequently extended this as a functional theory of the firm: Economic actors can be more efficient if they absorb many of the costs of exchanges and manage rather than directly engage in external transactions.[8] This means that instead of relying on the price mechanism of the external market, the manager directs the resources and hires labor, and instead of purchasing many "inputs," produces them.

In a market, the small, traditional entrepreneur operates through price mechanisms by making new contracts. In contrast, firm managers instead react to price changes and rearrange the factors of production. The tenet of the theory of transaction costs is that internalization reduces uncertainties. My argument is that at some point it transforms incentives to cooperate into incentives to compete, as production priorities are displaced by financial ones.

AN ABBREVIATED HISTORY

Although a main focus of debate about competition is the extent to which it is very imperfect, or only a trifle imperfect, an equally important consideration is where competition is situated. Competition as a form of economic behavior—pure, imperfect, or oligopolistic—is a contemporary invention. Long-distance and local preindustrial trade did not generate prices through competition. Trade was based on dual principles of complementarity and reciprocity, as in the case when residents of medieval towns exchanged handcrafted goods with food-stuffs from the countryside. Or when English linen was exchanged for Portuguese wine. Production was limited by craft guilds and by town institutions to remunerative levels. It was the deliberate action of the state that foisted the mercantile system on what Polanyi calls the "fiercely protectionist towns" by organizing commerce and trade in terms of mobile capital.[9] Thus, until around the eighteenth century and before the development of capitalism, entrepreneurs were localized and were only able to establish small regional monopolies. There were extraordinary barriers to competition, which were not reduced until there were improvements in trade, communication, and banking techniques that mercantilism helped to establish.[10] At the same time, the state had to protect society from the market that it helped to create, and these protections included the introduction of a gold standard, tariffs, poor laws, trade unions, and factory laws.

The market was efficient only for a brief period of time for the economy to be self-sufficient and self-regulating. Conditions that favored a free market in the United States in the nineteenth century included a growing supply of inexpensive labor, free land on the frontier, and the absence of a stabilized foreign currency. Indeed, it is argued that laissez-faire policies never did protect a free market in Europe and did so only briefly in the United States.[11] What we know as modern capitalism has gone through four distinct stages—family owner-ship, managerial capitalism, conglomerate capitalism, and finance cap-italism.[12] Roughly, these periods are the mid- to late nineteenth century, 1900-1945, 1945-1975, and 1975 to the present. In the late nineteenth century, extraordinary advances in technology, the proliferation of pri-vate banks, and protective tariffs made it possible for families to use their fortunes to invest in railroads, then steel, carriage factories, auto-mobile factories, shipmaking, and petroleum production. Organization in the nineteenth century evolved around problems of controlling workers. Unlike European workers, American workers were highly mobile, and the apprentice system was virtually nonexistent. Family owners that managed huge enterprises achieved control through fore-men, who hired and fired workers, set wages and hours, and contracted some work out. Family ownership helped to amass great fortunes, but the highly personal and arbitrary form of organization that evolved was ill-suited to the expansion of those large and impersonal markets that it spawned.[13]

The need to discipline workers, divorce financial decisions from organizational ones, and rationalize operations led to the modern corporation in which professional administrators—managers—took over organizational control, and ownership was assumed by shareholders.[14] The objective no longer was the preservation of the family fortune but instead preservation of the firm's profits. Accompanying these changes was a rationalization of administration. Instead of relying on a cadre of powerful independent foremen, decisions about workers became lodged in the hands of personnel officers. Pay scales, labor contracts, "internal labor markets," and the subdivision of authority routinized internal transactions, reducing sources of great uncertainty.

After the Depression, firms were compelled to adopt policies to stabilize the labor force, which provided further momentum to trends already under way. Labor legislation entailed reducing the differences in employment conditions between white-collar workers and blue-collar workers, establishing ladders for promotion and levels of wage increases, and generally increasing job security. This is what is meant by the internalization of the labor force, which not only created job security for workers but also eased uncertainties for firms.

But another source of uncertainty are products and their distribution. The conglomerate form of organization resolved problems related to production and distribution, and this was also by means of internalization. Namely, firms absorbed the producers and the distributors on whom they depended through both vertical and horizontal integration. For example, automobile companies purchased tire companies and acquired dealerships; oil producers purchased plastics companies; producers of canned foods bought up farms and became agribusinesses.

Paradoxically, what led to the demise of these practices, known as conglomerate capitalism, and what created finance capitalism was antitrust legislation that put curbs on vertical and horizontal integration, notably the acts of 1950, the Cellar-Kefauver Act, and the amendment to the Clayton Act. Designed to prevent intraindustry mergers and monopolies based on families of related products, these acts stimulated interindustry mergers and acquisitions, thereby breaking up firms that were based on similar products and tended to be intraindustry in nature. Thus, initially, finance capitalism was founded on antimonopolistic principles and provided a means of creating organizations that spanned product lines as well as industry lines. In an important sense, it meant the demise of the logic of internalizing transactions that were product-linked.[15]

A CRACK IN THE EDIFICE

Unexpected developments occurred in the early 1970s that resulted from international interdependencies over which nation-states had little control. I have earlier described these as including the oil embargo, a worldwide recession, and the decision to abandon the gold standard. These developments prompted varying reactions by major national economies. In the United States, the government's response was to defer to corporate leaders, although the governments of other countries— notably Japan, Germany, Norway, and Sweden—took more interventionist strategies. This, in retrospect, appears to have better stabilized their economies.

These international changes were more than ripples; they triggered a set of interrelated structural changes in the United States that two economists, Harrison and Bluestone, have described as *The Great U-Turn*.[16] Here are some of the indications of these changes: long-term investments in production—plants, machines, equipment—declined rapidly as short-term investments in capital increased instead; U.S. corporate profitability tumbled; imported merchandise as a percentage of GNP nearly tripled between 1970 and 1980 and has continued to increase. Moreover, although industrial production was virtually flat after 1970, the volume of futures trading has increased twentyfold, while the value of mergers and takeovers exceeded many trillions of dollars in the 1980s. Also, surprisingly, despite the expansion of worldwide production opportunities, global employment by major U.S. firms bottomed out in the mid-1970s.[17]

After decades devoted to organizing internal labor markets in order to create and sustain a stable work force and internal efficiencies,[18] firms began to disband large segments of their full-time labor force while they relied increasingly on part-time marginal workers with short-term contracts. This has resulted in a decline in real earnings and an accompanying increase in economic inequalities. By the mid-1980s, an unprecedented one-third of the full-time labor force had agreed to a freeze in wages or wage cuts.

In short, after three decades of economic growth, the U.S. economy experienced major structural changes in the early 1970s, resulting in declines from which it has not recovered. The large-scale turnaround is complex. One would have to consider the role of international trade, the restructuring of corporate tax laws (which encouraged speculation), high levels of consumer spending accompanied by sustained high levels of military spending, the increase in defense-related research and development at the expense of research and development for industrial purposes, and, also, soaring rates of national debt.[19] One major aspect of the underlying problem was the absence of an international monetary policy, which created a world inflationary spiral of the 1960s, exacerbated by the great extent that U.S. firms had large investments and entanglements in international markets. This generated extreme instability in domestic operations.[20] Another cause of economic decline can be traced to an interconnected set of domestic policies. This includes deregulation (which, among other things, rebounds to depress domestic wages), the retrenchment of public investments (that has resulted in municipal and state budgetary crises), and privatization of public services (which means lack of coordination and inequities).[21]

However, this complex set of causes is less the issue here than the consequences for firms, and then how firms in their turn exacerbated these conditions. Embarked already on a course known as finance capitalism, which entailed, first, conglomerate organization and huge debts for new acquisitions, and then diversification, firms upped the ante by a thoroughgoing internalization of capital markets. The headquarters of corporate organizations became what might be called command economies that controlled and organized their subsidiaries and established financial and monetary policies that guided the operations of their large dependent companies. As Fligstein shows, the history of large companies for the past 20 years has been an orgy of speculative enterprise that involved buying firms, mergers, hostile takeovers, leveraged buyouts, and deacquisitioning. In the short run, investors and lawyers make profits, whereas the profitability of companies themselves has declined. Annual reports of short-term earnings and assets easily disguise these realities.[22]

FIRMS BECOME MARKETS: WHERE IS THE FIRM?

My thesis is that the boundary between the market and the firm virtually disappeared as markets were tamed and internalized by firms. This included, initially, labor and commodity markets, and then money markets, but when the firm becomes a money market, labor and commodities lose their exchange value, which means that the firm becomes simply a place in which financial transactions are carried out. It is not, of course, the case that everyone is fired and production stops, but rather that decision making and policies are dictated by resolving the uncertainties of capital while products and labor are secondary concerns.

Paradoxically, although antitrust legislation reduced horizontal and vertical integration, which discouraged the practice of in-house market pricing for related commodities, it encouraged diversification, which created new practices for in-house market pricing for unrelated commodities. Under these conditions, commodities have no intrinsic or certain exchange value; they are of no real worth to the parent firm or to the firms it underwrites and that produce these goods and services. Yet commodities, like the firms that produce them, are of great value as capital, and in a time when an uncertain and unstable economy discourages long-term investments, capital takes on special meaning, operating as a form of power and as a dynamic conversion force in all other markets. In this way, firms internalize capital markets, while they themselves operate as actors in larger national and international capital markets.

The firm itself can be viewed as an in-house capital market, and each of its subsidiaries as a bundle of money makers (and money losers) that have nothing else in common.[23] Thus, the largest firms—notably, the Fortune 500 companies—have become what Fligstein calls the "central banks" for their subsidiaries, or what I describe as command economies. As Fligstein points out:

> [T]he finance conception of control not only concentrates on diversification, it conceives of the firm in purely financial terms. Each of the product divisions is evaluated on its short-term performance and ability to generate surplus revenue. Growth in the firm is produced by investing in products that provide a relatively high rate of return. When product lines do not perform, they are sold.[24]

Thus, we can consider each major corporation to be a small command economy that controls its own markets. This creates problems of many sorts, as countries that have recently shed their bigger command economies already know. First, a command economy—country or firm—cannot police itself; second, it is inefficient. In the case of American firms, the inability of self-enforcement is most clearly evident in the failure to make investments that do not yield high immediate returns, and the increasing reliance on workers in Third World countries as plants are closed in the United States and domestic workers are laid off.

Indicators of inefficiencies include extremely high debts, a decline in productivity accompanied by an increase in advertising and marketing costs, sharp declines in investments in machinery and plants, and poor and deteriorating rates of profit.

In a genuine command economy, centralized planning and allocation partially circumvent markets, but in any case a command economy does not rely on competition in the same way that a capitalist or quasicapitalist economy does, and which, it is generally now agreed, reduces initiative. The minicommand economies of American firms operate along different lines, creating a peculiar mix of centralized control and intense competition. As we have seen, the prime firm controls the finances for its subsidiaries. And, the prime firm—itself a set of major owners or stockholders—is also a buyer, lender, and seller, thus creating internal competition.

It is important here to point out that internal labor markets are not a capitalist invention, as they occur in large firms in socialist economies as well. David Stark lays out the generic feature of internal labor markets, a means of reducing uncertainties, when he outlines the differences among them under different economic contexts.[25] In capitalist economies, the main source of uncertainty pertains to labor, and thus internal labor markets are organized around a set of bureaucratic rules governing promotion, layoffs, and wage schemes for each of given categories of workers. In contrast, the uncertainties in a socialist economy deal with the external environment, that is, uncertainties in dealing with state regulations and centralized rules dealing with output. Because workers can use "the threat of exit," managers enter into informal agreements with workers to maintain production goals and to achieve consensus. In contrast, within capitalist firms the constraints of impersonal bureaucracy foster workers' compliance, and when there is threat of downsizing, competition ensues among workers, and not between managers and workers. Moreover, owing to the way in which capitalist firms create labor markets, it is all the easier to dismantle them.

To return to the principle of a market, it is sufficient to mention that the very idea of a market is that buyers and sellers are self-interested. The same is true wherever markets are located, outside firms or inside firms. Part-owners of large firms who are also part-owners of other large firms have less stake in any particular firm than they have in their personal assets. This is naturally the case, and we cannot expect that it would be otherwise. But what it means is that the firm becomes an arena of competition among wealth maximizers.

Of course, the firm is not only an economic entity; it is also a social entity. The principle of a market is that it is competitive, and it is so in a highly impersonal way; when markets are digested by firms, they create personal forms of competition. This is because incentives for gain and profit are individualized by co-owners and by contending subsidiaries. Moreover, as buyers and sellers can no longer be distinguished, pricing is no longer competitively established but is so within the command economy of the corporation. A clear example of how these new economic arrangements play themselves out at the expense of firm integrity is described by Fligstein: Because internal firm divisions are subject to the same financial scrutiny that firms are, the competition for survival extends into each component of the corporation, pitting one manager against another, and entire organizations and large departments against others.[26]

Economists and sociologists attempt to understand how organizations harness the uncertainties and irrationalities of what is outside of them. Sociologists describe organizations as if they were distinct from environments,[27] and economists distinguish hierarchies from markets.[28] My argument is that these are now artificial distinctions, and this collapse of the boundary between firms and capital markets has treacherous implications.

Economists and planners are increasingly concerned that the economy does not respond to the decisions of the Federal Reserve that are designed to affect the supply and flow of capital. In a certain sense, the government is enfeebled because it shares financial decisions with the aggregate of major corporate actors. One could say that these actors preempt government by means of their *monetary* policies, insofar as they allocate and redistribute monies to those firms they own and to those to which they outsource and subcontract, and by means of their *fiscal* policies, insofar as they borrow and spend money. Another source of their fiscal power is that they create money by driving up the prices of the firms they intend to buy.

Many of the anomalies of corporate behavior can be understood when we look at the firm in this way. There are some baffling developments in businesses that appear to violate any definition of sensible economic behavior. These provide the clues that the boundary between markets and organizations is in the process of being redefined along new lines. There are general indications that organizations and markets are so intertwined that they are difficult to separate. The underlying observation is that there is competition when cooperation would be more efficient, and there is cooperation when competition would be desirable for enhancing incentives.

The persistence of high unemployment has not appreciably reduced the wages of older and predominantly white male workers, although union concessions have meant they have not increased either.[29] Nevertheless, real average weekly earnings have declined by about 16% since 1973 despite increases in the education of American workers. The most notable changes have included the decline in the numbers of high-wage jobs (especially in manufacturing) and the replacement of full-time workers by part-time and hourly workers, who are predominantly female and minority, exacerbating worker conflict.[30]

Although we consider businesses to be competitive, they in fact tend to speak with one voice and approach a grand consensus on many issues, including foreign trade, capital gains tax, corporate tax, environmental policy, and workplace safety regulations.[31] Burawoy shows how workers become involved in never-ending conflict as they regard their own future livelihood as dependent on the survival and expansion of their capitalist employer.[32] With the erosion of federal regulations governing investments, there is increasing unsavory collusion between, for example, drug cartels, private banks, big-time investors, and government agencies. The Savings and Loan scandal comes to mind, but there are others—the costly overruns of the defense industries, the private gains and the public losses incurred by the Housing and Urban Development investments, and the increasing role played by private investors in bank frauds.[33]

Although we expect trust and the sharing of information within firms and secrecy without, increasingly economists document the way that firm members withhold information within and disclose it without (which, ironically, is dubbed insider trading).[34] The firm was designed to eliminate internal conflict through career ladders, job security, impersonal rules, and legitimacy. Instead, the prevailing practice has become one of notable cut-throat competition. To managers of firms were designated the tasks of legitimizing the rationality of administration, of specialization, and of production activities, yet the world of managers is rife with politics, cynicism, and back stabbing.[35] These are the consequences of the ingestion of market competition.

Accompanying these anomalous (even pathological) patterns of cooperation and competition are indications that inefficiencies are not merely being tolerated but are, in fact, being encouraged. Meyer and Zucker document the increasing tendency for multiunit corporate structures to maintain low-performance firms.[36] This is partly because profits are not necessarily reflected in short-term assets and investment returns, which have higher priority for corporate managers than do either profits or performance. Debts cannot be paid from future profits, and stockholders are interested in today's stock value. Moreover, part of performance is linked to innovation, which requires long-term investments, which are impractical when the entire economy is geared to short-term returns.[37] What appears to account for peculiar forms of cooperation and misplaced competition is the transformation of firms by means of diversification of capital, and the incompatibility between internalized capital markets and enduring social organization.

The argument here is that the firm was so successful that it absorbed competition and up to a point tamed it. But, conventionally, contracts (transactions) within firms are very different from external ones, namely, those that are market-based and, therefore, competitive. Markets are naturally impersonal and based on self-interest, and the effects of absorbing competition within a social entity quite inevitably undermine cooperation.

In trying to describe some of these developments, various terms have been coined: postmodern firms,[38] postindustrial firms,[39] disorganized capitalism,[40] and flexible-accumulation firms.[41] It is unfortunate, I believe, that most of these terms imply an increasingly decentralized character of modern firms and ignore the extent of internal competition. It is the case that as social entities, firms have become more decentralized. This is the result of reducing the numbers of middle managers, encouraging workers to circumvent union negotiations and instead work informally with management, and also by utilizing team production units rather than assembly-line production. These practices can improve worker morale. They do not, unfortunately, address problems of job security.

Furthermore, we must consider the economic context in which decentralization occurs and whether or not it means democratization of the workplace or the downside of economic centralization. I have argued that the firm verges on becoming an economic entity that transcends social organization and production. The decentralization of what might be considered by managers and owners to be uninteresting and unimportant is arguably not in the spirit of workplace democracy.

Large firms are debt-ridden, whereas each merger and each acquisition results in an extraordinary return to investment banks, law firms, brokerage firms, and stockholders. But every merger and acquisition involves more debt in return for asset growth. They are for that reason unprofitable. Ironic though it may be, the countries of Eastern Europe are discovering capital markets while the U.S. firms are destroying them by ingesting them.

Growth by acquisition—rather than by product development, capital investments in technology, and plant replacements—involves high costs of marketing to consumers (the capital costs of advertising have never been higher) and to policymakers (in the form of lobbying and PAC contributions). Whereas the key players might be viewed as highly competitive—which is requisite for markets—the distinction between buyers and sellers is lost in portfolios, and whereas production requires organizations, these appear to be lost to capital markets. However, a clue about where production may increasingly be lodged comes from the literature on entrepreneurship.

SELF-EMPLOYMENT

More and more, large firms are relying on short-term production cycles and short-term planning, as already discussed. They are also undergoing what is termed *restructuring*, dismantling internal labor markets, freezing wages, closing plants, and laying off workers. Firms increasingly rely on short-term contracts, outsourcing, and subcontracting.[42]

This means an increase in traditional entrepreneurship. In less than a decade after 1972 the number of self-employed grew by 25%.[43] This is contrary to the earlier predictions of economists and contrary to the conclusions of many about the indicators of the health of a growing economy. In 1966, Kuznets, for example, had optimistically concluded on the basis of a long-term secular trend that the shift of the labor market to one that was predominantly nonentrepreneurial was part and parcel of the growth of a healthy economy and meant a great improvement in the lives of workers.[44]

Compared with the rest of the economy, the entrepreneurial sector, comprised of the self-employed, has high risks of failure, low returns on investment, high rates of accidents, low profitability, low average wages and benefits, and greater instability of labor. Work by Averitt and Edwards earlier suggested that this economic periphery is the absorption sector for the casualties of a troubled economy,[45] a conclusion that other studies tended to support.[46]

On the other hand, there is some evidence that certain kinds of innovations are more likely to be made by small entrepreneurial firms, including innovations in medical research and computer technology.[47] It also appears to be the case that financial considerations are weighed against other rewards. That is, although the annual earnings of the unincorporated self-employed are less on the average than those of wage earners (a difference estimated to be roughly $4500), Robert L. Aronson summarizes substantial research that shows that the self-employed have higher levels of job satisfaction and report a higher level of autonomy.[48]

The main point here, however, is that the entrepreneurial sector is increasingly composed of service and assembly activities on which large firms depend and which substantially reduce costs for large firms. Specifically, there are savings in overhead, health insurance, pension plans, and in actual capital investments. Subcontracting and outsourcing also reduce long-term commitments in favor of short-term contracts. In particular, industrial homework, which appears to be a high-growth sector of the self-employed, creates huge savings for large companies accompanied by a high potential for exploitation.[49]

Not all developed countries have experienced an increase in self-employment. Germany, France, and The Netherlands have not, for example, and increases in other European communities are traced to immigrants rather than the native-born.[50] Although European countries have experienced the same global economic dislocations that the United States has, the approaches to solutions have been very different. The strategies pursued by most European countries have been to strengthen, rather than to dismantle, the social contracts of economic organizations. The policies in countries such as Norway, Sweden, Germany, Denmark, and Japan are designed to create more security for workers, buffer firms and employees against inflation, and to provide incentives for production-related investments.

I do not want to minimize the complexity of these issues. It is unlikely that a large number of economists would come to an agreement about how to explain the difference in economic outcomes—say, the GNP—between countries that pursue different policies, for example, Germany and the United States. But were the consequences of economic policies for workers under consideration, there would be far more agreement that the United States has not taken "The Best Turn."

SUMMARY

We started with the observation that after steady improvement in the conditions of employment, deteriorating economic conditions combined with disincentives for long-term investment and, instead, opportunities for short-term speculative gain, through mergers and acquisitions, led to the radical reorganization of large corporate firms. The simple way to state this is that capital ceased to be the means of production but an end in its own right. Top management reprioritized firm objectives so that financial investment, and not production, became the prime focus of firm activities. For the social contract among workers, managers, and owners—the organizational framework on which internal labor markets are based—this spells disaster. One can speculate about solutions. For example, one line of research carried out in the 1970s indicated that worker cooperatives, given normal legal and tax protections, may be as efficient as profit-making firms,[51] and in a similar vein, studies suggest that the nonprofit firm can extend its activities beyond the services that it now provides to engage in commercial activities as well.[52] Experience in other countries suggests that internal labor markets can be formalized and protected by the state.[53] Interestingly, they turn on a statist approach that the owners of American firms in fact wholeheartedly embrace, while they try to convince the public that this approach is contrary to the principles of a free market.

NOTES

1. For my purposes in this initial section, the term *entrepreneur* is used to mean owners. It will be clear later on that we must distinguish between shareholders and managers and between those who are entrepreneurs in the traditional sense—the self-employed—and key economic actors.
2. *Capital, Vol. 1*, p. 193, pp. 537–541. The theory of surplus value has been criticized on various grounds. For example, Rosa Luxemburg (*The Accumulation of Capital*, 1951) faulted Marx for not clearly specifying the source of growing demand that capitalism requires for accumulation under conditions of constant or declining surplus value. On the other hand, David Harvey (*The Limits to Capital*. Chicago: University of Chicago Press, 1982) indicates that growing demand can be traced to the credit system, the state, and mobile capital and labor.
3. George J. Stiglier, *The Theory of Price*. New York: Macmillan Company, 1947.
4. The Council on Economic Priorities publishes an annual listing of companies and products, along with a rating of corporate practices. See *Shopping for a Better World*. 3rd ed. New York: CEP, 1991.
5. R. H. Coase's essay, "The Nature of the Firm" was published in *Economica* 4 (November 1937) and is reprinted in *The Firm, the Market, and the Law*. Chicago: University of Chicago Press, 1988.
6. Op. cit., p. 7; also see Douglass C. North, *Institutions, Institutional Change and Economic Performance*. Cambridge: Cambridge University Press, 1990.
7. Alfred D. Chandler, Jr., *The Visible Hand: The Managerial Revolution in American Business*. Cambridge: Harvard University Press, 1977.

8. Oliver E. Williamson, *Markets and Hierarchies: Analysis and Antitrust Implications*. New York: Free Press, 1975.

9. Karl Polanyi, *The Great Transformation*. Boston: Beacon Press, [1944] 1957.

10. Ibid., David Harvey, op. cit., p. 145.

11. Karl Polanyi, op. cit.

12. Stanford M. Jacoby, *Employing Bureaucracy: Managers, Unions, and the Transformation of Work in American Industry, 1900–1945*. New York: Columbia University Press, 1985; Michael Useem, *The Inner Circle: Large Corporations and the Rise of Business Political Activity in the U.S. and U.K.* New York: Oxford University Press, 1984; John McDermott, *Corporate Society: Class, Property, and Contemporary Capitalism*. Boulder: Westview Press, 1991.

13. Recognizing the fundamental significance of the organizational form for profit making, Carnegie stated, "You can take away my steel mills, ores, railroad lines, coal, but leave me one thing and I'll repeat my success. The one thing is organizations." (Cited in James MacGregor Burns, *The Workshop of Democracy*. New York: Random House, 1985, p. 103.)

14. Adolph Berle and Gardiner Means, *The Modern Corporation and Private Property*. New York: Macmillan, 1932.

15. Neil Fligstein, *The Transformation of Corporate Control*. Cambridge: Harvard University Press, 1990.

16. Bennett Harrison and Barry Bluestone, *The Great U-Turn: Corporate Restructuring and the Polarizing of America*. New York: Basic Books, 1988; also see Barry Bluestone and Bennett Harrison, *The Deindustrialization of America: Plant Closings, Community Abandonment, and the Dismantling of Basic Industries*. New York: Basic Books, 1982.

17. For recent summaries, see Barry Bluestone, "The Great U-Turn Revisited: Economic Restructuring, Jobs, and the Redistribution of Earnings," pp. 7–37 in John D. Kasarda (ed.), *Jobs, Earnings, and Employment Growth Policies in the United States*. Boston: Kluwer Academic Publishers, 1990.

18. Simon Kuznets, *Modern Economic Growth*. New Haven: Yale University Press, 1966.

19. Analyses show that these declines are not due to cyclical trends (Gary Burtless, *Earnings Inequality over the Business Cycle*. Washington, DC: The Brookings Institution, 1989), or demographic change (Chris Tilly, Barry Bluestone, and Bennett Harrison, *The Reasons for Increasing Wage and Salary Inequality*. John W. McCormack Institute of Public Affairs Working Paper. Boston: University of Massachusetts at Boston, 1987).

20. Bretton, op. cit., p. 257.

21. Robert Kuttner, *The Economic Illusion: False Choices Between Prosperity and Social Justice*. New York: Houghton Mifflin, 1984.

22. Neil Fligstein, *The Transformation of Corporate Control*. Cambridge: Harvard University Press, 1990.

23. Alfred P. Sloan, *My Years at General Motors*. New York: Doubleday, 1964.

24. Fligstein, op. cit., p. 193.

25. David Stark, "Rethinking Internal Labor Markets," *American Sociological Review* 51 (1986): 492–504.
26. Fligstein, op. cit.
27. Michael T. Hannan and John Freeman, *Organizational Ecology*. Cambridge: Harvard University Press, 1989.
28. Williamson, op. cit.
29. Robert M. Solow, *The Labor Market as a Social Institution*. Cambridge, MA: Basil Blackwell, 1990.
30. Frank Levy, *Dollars and Dreams: The Changing American Income Distribution*. New York: Russell Sage Foundation, 1987.
31. Useem, op. cit.; Mark S. Mizruchi, *The Structure of Corporate Political Action*. Cambridge: Harvard University Press, 1992.
32. Michael Burawoy, *Manufacturing Consent: Changes in the Labor Process under Monopoly Capitalism*. Chicago: University of Chicago Press, 1979.
33. Recent accounts are described in Bryan Burrough and John Helyar, *Barbarians at the Gate: The Fall of RJR Nabisco*. New York: Harper & Row, 1990; and Martin Mayer, *The Greatest-Ever Bank Robbery: The Collapse of the Savings and Loan Industry*. New York: Charles Scribner's, 1990.
34. Douglass North, op. cit.
35. Robert Jackall, *Moral Mazes: The World of Corporate Managers*. New York: Oxford University Press, 1988.
36. Marshall W. Meyer and Lynne G. Zucker, *Failing Organizations*. Newbury Park: Sage, 1989.
37. Fligstein, op. cit.
38. Stewart R. Clegg, *Modern Organizations: Organization Studies in the Postmodern World*. London: Sage, 1990.
39. W. Halal, *The New Capitalism*. New York, 1986.
40. S. Lash and J. Urry, *The End of Organized Capitalism*. Oxford: Oxford University Press, 1987.
41. C. Curson (ed.), *Flexible Patterns of Work*. London: Institute of Personnel Management, 1986.
42. See L. Hirschhorn, *Beyond Mechanization*. Cambridge: MIT Press, 1984; Michael J. Piore and Charles F. Sabel, *The Second Industrial Divide: Prospects for Prosperity*. New York: Basic Books, 1984; Carolyn C. Perrucci, Robert Perrucci, Dena B. Targ, and Harry R. Targ, *Plant Closings: International Contexts and Social Costs*. New York: Aldine de Gruyter, 1988. The implications for workplace safety are discussed in Tom Dwyer, *Life and Death at Work*. New York: Plenum Press, 1992.
43. Robert B. Reich, *The Next American Frontier*. New York: Times Books, 1983.
44. Simon Kuznets, *Modern Economic Growth*. New Haven: Yale University Press, 1966, p. 188.
45. David M. Gordon, Richard Edwards, and Michael Reich, *Segmented Work, Divided Workers*. New York: Cambridge University Press, 1982; Robert Averitt, *The Dual Economy: The Dynamics of American Industry Structure*. New

York: W. W. Norton, 1968; Richard C. Edwards, *Contested Terrain*. New York: Basic Books, 1979.

46. McDermott, op. cit., p. 141; Teresa A. Sullivan, "Women and Minority Workers in the New Economy," *Work and Occupations* 16 (1989): 393–415; Michael Wallace, "Brave New Workplace," *Work and Occupations* 16 (1989): 363–392.

47. Piore and Sabel, op. cit.

48. Robert L. Aronson, *Self-Employment: A Labor Market Perspective*. Ithaca: Industrial Relations Press, 1991.

49. Ibid., pp. 112–114.

50. Jochen Blaschke, Jeremy Boissevain, Hanneke Grotenbreg, Isaac Joseph, Mirjana Morokvasic, and Robin Ward, "European Trends in Ethnic Businesses," pp. 79–105 in Roger Waldinger, Howard Aldrich, and Robin Ward (eds.), *Ethnic Entrepreneurs*. Newbury Park: Sage, 1990.

51. See especially Jaroslav Vanek (ed.), *Self-Management*. Baltimore: Penguin, 1975.

52. See Edward Skloot, "Enterprise and Commerce in Nonprofit Organizations," pp. 380–396 in Walter W. Powell (ed.), *The Nonprofit Sector*. New Haven: Yale University Press, 1987.

53. For example, see James R. Lincoln and Arne L. Kalleberg, *Culture, Control and Commitment*. Cambridge: Cambridge University Press, 1988.

9

Worlds of Fashion, Lives of Leisure

We Must Forgive Fashion Everything, It Dies So Young.
—JEAN COCTEAU, quoted in a Bloomingdale's advertisement
for T-shirts, *New York Times* (August 4, 1991)

Contemporary leisure sheds light on the world of work, in part because work and leisure are so difficult to distinguish on their own intrinsic merits. What is ephemeral leisure for some is ceaseless work for others, and what some consider arduous labor, others consider play. While joking, laughter, and informal bantering ease routines in work settings, some leisure activities, such as a game of timed chess, are carried out with absolute concentration and complete seriousness. The indistinguishability of work and leisure resides in the fact that social contracts pervade and govern them both. If there is one major difference, it is the extent to which leisure is shaped more by its own internal dynamics, whereas work is governed more by external criteria, notably efficiency. This is a matter of degree, of course, but it has important consequences.

What are the parameters of leisure? Some leisure is passive—watching television—and other forms are most certainly not—running a marathon race. There are also differences between people who are paid to entertain and to provide leisure for others and those who are entertained. Another difference is between leisure in which one indulges oneself—reading, gardening, shopping—and leisure that re-

145

quires groups—individuals as audiences or players. Regardless of these differences, social organizations create the opportunities, if not the arenas, for leisure.

PREMODERN AND MODERN LEISURE

Anthropologists emphasize the absence of a distinction between work and leisure in premodern societies, where work, family life, and community tended to be a seamless living experience. According to Applebaum:

> A good deal of time in non-market cultures is taken up with ceremonies, feasting, drinking, visiting, and celebrations. Feasts are approached with the same seriousness as clearing a field, and in some respects it is just as important since it is part of one's obligations to the community.[1]

Such leisure activities—for example, rituals, ceremonies, and festivals—served to strengthen the bonds of the entire group. Linking individuals and families into the broader social order, they provided a mechanism by which an orderly society could maintain itself and served to establish and strengthen fundamental social values. Unfortunately, there are extremely low upper bounds on the numbers that could maintain such activities. According to Radcliffe-Brown, the societies in which these activities could occur with regularity are communities that range from around 250 to 500 individuals.[2] He suggests that collective ceremonies and festivals fail to provide integrative functions for groups that are much larger than this. Beyond this upper limit, there is a division into performers and spectators, into "buyers" and "sellers." Nevertheless, there is every reason to assume that contemporary institutions, such as parades, street festivals, and live rock concerts, provide symbolically and experientially the same sense of collectivity and social integration that were provided by their medieval and other early counterparts, for example, jousting events, religious festivals, and village fairs.

One way in which work and leisure can be distinguished in all societies is the contrast between activities that involve pressure and formal demands and those that do not. Escape from the trading and political life of Athens for a sojourn in the countryside is what Aristophanes dubs "soft and lovely leisure."[3] For the Duc de Maine during the early years of the eighteenth century, leisure was time at Sceaux, that is, time away from the rigid etiquette codes and formalities of state affairs at Versailles.[4]

Firth suggests that in premodern societies the temporal boundaries between work and leisure may be more important than spatial ones, as he contrasts the rigors of the day in a Polynesian village with the casual informality of the evening:

> As the afternoon wears towards evening the social side of the village life becomes more evident. Gradually more and more people stroll down from their houses towards the place where the crowd is gathered on the beach, conversation becomes more general, games start among the young men, wrestling, *fetaki* (a kind of single stick), practicing in the hurling of the *tika* dart. . . . Dusk falls. . . . Dancing, games and conversation on the beach may go on till any hour; there is no conventionally appointed time for retiring, but people trickle off as the desire for sleep comes upon them. And so the day comes to an end.[5]

In modern societies, we make this same distinction, between the demands of where we live and work and the carefree lifestyle of a vacation, of getting away from it all, of escape. This is not unrelated to the idea of social and temporal distance between responsibility and obligations and personal freedom to plan one's own day and schedule. As Zerubavel so convincingly argues, the time away from work is private and discretionary, and it allows individuals the chance to exercise autonomy.[6] There is no better observer of this contrast between work and leisure than a person who works while most other play. Jazzman Danny Barker observes:

> Musicians . . . see so much of life. Things that some of my non-musician friends would enjoy and be amazed at, musicians take for granted. They see life in a raw, nitty-gritty sense. . . . Musicians—they live a night life. . . . So they see things different. They see intrigue. In night clubs, you sit on the bandstand and see all kinds of happenin's. A real depth of life. You see the underworld. You see all kinds of loose livin' people. 'Cause in the daytime, people are more business-like. They tend to other things. But, at night, you see people enjoyin' themselves. To a musician, everyday is like a holiday. It's the good time, and you're playin' for people enjoyin' themselves.[7]

Although I have argued that the differences in leisure between premodern societies and modern ones are difficult to draw on the basis of the way in which people experience and shape leisure in their everyday lives, there are, of course, pronounced differences in other respects. A money economy alters the nature of leisure and also the distinction between private and public spheres that accompanies a market economy. Work roles make people more fully accessible to some others but help to sustain barriers against others, and schedules of work delineate boundaries between public roles and private roles. The growth of cities has had important effects on the mapping of leisure, especially recreational leisure, but also on the supply of institutional-based culture.

In the initial stages of modern capitalism, the line between work and leisure took on special meaning, owing to the cruel conditions of factory work, and the bizarre contrasts between the lives of the idle rich and the poor working class. The relation between work and leisure was viewed by Karl Marx as antagonistic. Disposal time under capitalism, according to Marx, submits to the requirements of capital accumulation, and elites promulgate capitalist ideology through leisure activities while they provide workers with "circuses" to quell complaints about the poor quality of the bread they earn.

My argument, instead, is that there is not an inherent antagonism between leisure and work in contemporary societies, but that realms of leisure can restore some of the excesses to which work is prone. The argument is based on the following considerations: Leisure challenges the excesses of efficiency, infuses risk taking with intrinsic precarious pleasures, and reduces inequalities in a variety of ways.

LEISURE AS ORGANIZATION

As noted, some leisure is produced by some people and consumed by others, whereas other leisure is produced by the same people who consume it. Television, magazines, high culture, and baseball are produced in organizations and sold in markets. Leisure-product work organizations are not so different from any other kind of organization, and we as consumers buy the products or participate as audience members because we cannot produce or create them ourselves, or only with great difficulty. We depend on organizations that supply swimming pools, or sell Monopoly games, or produce the news, and we rely on other organizations to provide activities that are beyond our skills and abilities, such as the sponsors of marathon races and basketball tournaments.

Much, but not all, of contemporary leisure is in some way implicated in the activities of formal organizations and competitive markets.

Other forms of leisure are situated in small informal groups or seeped in community tradition. Leisure activities that are freed from the constraints of bureaucratic organizations and modern markets are of course highly valued, romanticized, and imbued with special power as they are linked with past traditions, individual autonomy, family activities, and ethnic heritages. Such activities are considered to be authentic and often contrasted with degraded leisure of contemporary life.[8]

Production and markets are necessarily bound up with an obsessive concern with efficiency, which is, in the most general sense, the ratio of useful output to useful input. Rates of return of land, technology, capital, and labor are relentlessly calculated by every economic unit, including the farm owner, the industrialist, and the film producer. This is essential to the economic well-being of a society for the sake of subsistence, production, distribution, and profit making, and, increasingly, as we realize, for the preservation of resources.

There are realms of life that are less subject to efficiency criteria. For example, there are many activities in everyday life that are not very efficient, but we engage in them anyway. Sometimes we use candles for dinner, grow flowers rather than vegetables, drink soda instead of milk or juice. Some things have relatively low output for the input we invest, and this is so for one of two reasons: Either the input is so pleasurable that the output is of trivial importance (say, canoeing), or the output is so pleasurable that the disproportionate input is well worth it (say, a 1-day family reunion to which many people travel long distances). Often costs are not so easy to calculate. This story makes my point: A young artist was overheard saying to a corporation vice-president at a gallery opening, "You mean to say that you only work 6 days a week! You must not enjoy what you do."

As I have already noted, everywhere and at all times, play and informality fuse with work to ease tensions, and while this reduces calculable efficiencies, it restores social equilibria.[9] As I have also noted, in some social settings, notably the home, work and leisure are fused owing to the importance of personal relations on which the social unit depends. Kluckholn and Leighton's account of how Navaho families engage in games and work around the hogan[10] is remarkably similar to the Lynds' description of family gatherings that combine barn repair and basketball games.[11] It is interesting to probe how institutions, owing to their internal and relentless constraints for order, impede spontaneity and nonconformity, and simultaneously create products, lifestyles, and meanings that perpetuate the status quo. This discussion has bearing on why cultural industries both resist and promote change, on the ways in which culture exerts hegemonistic control in social life, and, in different ways, destabilizes legitimacy by exposing economic and political fabrications.

THRILLS

Risk taking is central to the world of work, especially in capitalist societies in which corporate financing, venture capitalism, and entrepreneurship all entail risky undertakings and courage to engage in high-spirited adventure. Without entrepreneurial risk taking, there would be very little growth, as illustrated by the invention of the wheel, steam engine, and computers. As Schumpeter describes this risk-taking function:

> [To] reform or revolutionize the pattern of production by exploiting an invention or more generally, an untried technological possibility for producing a new commodity or producing an old one in a new way, but opening up a new source of supply of materials or a new outlet for products, by reorganizing an industry, and so on.[12]

Profits, according to other early economists, were considered to be the reward for risk taking, and nothing more.[13]

The risks entailed in dangerous sports or the willingness to chance it in literature, theater, games, and play are certainly comparable to risk taking in economic life in some respects, but not in all. In business, risk yields (possibly) profits; in leisure it yields, if successful, honor or prestige. However, overstepping practical considerations in favor of creative, risky ones is highly cherished in the arts, science, and sports, and lies very close to the surface of all entrepreneurial innovations. Risk taking poses the same dilemmas in work that it does in play: There is a drama that will take place, but the script is yet to be written as fate and sheer luck play important roles. Very often, the drama is socially ritualized and is subsequently played over again and again in collective mythologies. An example of unnecessary risk taking that is on the boundary of work and play helps to make the distinction I think is useful.

In Bangladesh, going to look for honey requires skill, daring, and considerable courage as the area is infested with man-eating tigers. The activity is infused with religious ritual, and ebullient ceremony and games await the honey gatherers on their return. There are certain similarities here with the "replay" of sporting events, with repeated television coverage of the first trip to the moon, and the ticker tape parades for the return of astronauts and soldiers.

Economic risk taking may be great sport for the risk taker, but efficiency is, after all, the objective. It is not especially lauded, praised, or publicly acclaimed for itself. To the extent that entrepreneurial risk taking is linked with instrumental ends and personal economic gain, there is no fun in it for others. We may envy Carnegie his great successes, but we do not ourselves particularly vicariously enjoy the risks he undertook to achieve them. In fact, we tend to shield our children from the bare bone truths of the costs to others that are often entailed in successful (and failed) risky business ventures.

In cultural life, there is ceaseless change, always undoing routines and altering the rules. "[I]n Fashion," Barthes writes, "work is only a simple reference, then immediately loses its reality."[14] To elaborate a bit on one of Barthes's insights about the semiotics and economy of fashion, it can be said that there is a slow rate of dilapidation in work arrangements and work products because of investment costs, and for reasons of efficiency and accountability. We have stakes in routines and in predictability. This is not the case in the arts—owing to the inherent destructiveness of the avant-garde and the transgressions of popular culture[15]—nor is it true for fashion and design—owing to perpetual turnover. Much of the excitement in sports comes from breaking records, and for the players it is very often breaking their own, not others', records.

Even ordinary play is special because it brackets the transient and nonrepeatable and the nonretrievable. It is the incalculability of fashion, leisure, sports, and the arts that puts them just outside the realm of the reality on which economic life is based.

The leisure industry "blunts the buyer's consciousness" in order to draw a veil of images and meanings around the fashion object,[16] thus conning the buyer into wanting something that he or she does not need. This is a significant part of the argument involving hegemonistic culture. But who after all creates demand for novelty, change, and process? The rational consumers, it might reasonably be argued, are fully aware that this is a co-conspiracy.

Routines predominate in the world of work, whether this is studying calculus alone, doing the dishes at home with other family members, or even doing something "interesting," such as performing neurosurgery or participating in a board meeting. When it is said, "let's get down to business," it means breaking up the fun and restoring routine. And "let's get down to business" undermines the egalitarian nature of high-spirited fun.

Rank and Disarray

If work organizations require hierarchy, work itself is implicated in hierarchies in a far more profound way, namely, the stratification system in which prestige and earnings sort people into classes.[17] Class plays a major role in lifestyle, including where one can afford to live and the schooling choices one makes for his or her children. To an important extent, status that depends on outcomes in labor markets and work organizations, therefore, has a great influence on leisure choices. Going to the theater or ballet, for example, is related to having an advanced education and adequate income. There is an enormous literature in sociology, much of which was written in the 1950s, that discusses the affinity between ranking in work and occupational hierarchies with ranking in leisure activities. Members of the well-to-do elite enjoy cruises, as well as the opera, theater, and dance; the better educated, but less well-heeled, have somewhat less expensive, though more exotic tastes, liking contemporary art and music more than the traditional and authenticated; and, it is said, the lower strata prefer the excitement and the escape offered by movies and television.[18]

Expressing appreciation of the elite arts, like *haute couture* and *haute cuisine*, according to Bourdieu, is a statement of class standing and an investment in cultural capital, as they will buy prestige that authenticates and justifies class position.[19]

I argue, however, that the multistrandedness of social relations combined with the dynamic transformation of fashion in culture continuously undermines the hierarchy of taste and of cultural choices. First of all, each of very many worlds of culture is exceedingly complex and requires knowledge and mastery of conventions. These worlds range from those of amateur archeology, bluegrass music, and film, to the worlds of baseball aficionados and stamp collectors. Increasingly, at least in the United States, there is less coherence between social class and cultural tastes with an expansion in opportunities to visit art museums, and to attend theater, dance, and musical events. Interestingly, where a person lives—a central city, a suburb, or a rural place—apparently makes more of a difference than how much education the person has or how much television he or she watches.[20]

Although there is a notion that going to the opera or visiting a museum is a loftier activity than, say, going bowling, I am not altogether convinced. This is because the producers of high art these days continue to violate the canons of high art—these days the *de rigueur* of architecture is to be found in Disney World, and contemporary painters and musicians draw from the genre of the vernacular—and also because producers of fashion and consumers of fashion take twists, turns, and reversals at a frantic pace that renders cultural hierarchies extremely unstable. Hierarchies of prestige that are based on cultural consumption, cultural display, and cultural knowledge are always in jeopardy. To wit: The flamingos that decorated the yards of working-class families in the 1950s reappear in 1990s San Francisco boutiques, refashioned as costume jewelry; a white faculty member at a prestigious university wears Levi jeans and Tracy Chapman shirts at the department; a French executive in a U.S. firm is told by her boss that her skirt is too short, but her boss apologizes after he returns from a trip to Milan.

It is true that the most highly educated individuals are more likely to have "sophisticated tastes," that is, enjoy cultural forms that are steeped in long traditions and require longer training and more effort to enjoy—for example, Shakespeare, Mozart, modern dance. Audience studies suggest a positive association between education and cultural tastes, although some of that is due to the fact that the most educated people live in large cities.[21] This is the demand side of leisure. On the supply side, the conclusions are somewhat different. The diffusion of the suppliers of culture, both those that specialize in the elite arts— chamber music, opera, museums—as well as regional culture—jazz, bluegrass, and country music—has meant the steady erosion of class-based leisure preferences and activities.[22]

Opportunities are virtually indistinguishable from the geography of supply. Regardless of people's interests in leisure, recreational and cultural pursuits, proximity to supply is a decisive factor in whether they will engage in these pursuits or not. Regardless of individuals' family background, education, and other personal attributes, growing up in a place where there is an abundance of folk music, rap, electronic music, or whatever, will alter the odds that a person will like that particular kind of music.

A main point is that nowadays culture serves to resist conventions, the well-ordered world of practicalness, and the hierarchies of authority. This was not always the case. It was not until the late nineteenth century, when a growing and increasingly well-educated middle class in Europe and the United States challenged the cultural monopoly of the elites.[23]

Later, increasing varieties of art and culture, such as contemporary popular music, traditionally vernacular genre, and the literature, art, and music of diverse societies, began to be recognized in their own right. (I have visions of designers from MOMA and Bloomingdale's waiting at the gates of the Arrival Terminal at Kennedy Airport to meet each returning anthropologist for tips on esoteric fabric designs.) In culture, far more than in the worlds of work and occupations, there is a sustained level of criticism, which moves styles and fashion right along, and, equally important, challenges the conventional standards on which hierarchies are based. Besides, the traditional canon on which elites stake claims is relentlessly eroded, questioned, and often simply ignored.

Thus, people do not engage in cultural activities or participate in worlds of fashion unless opportunities exist. For a great many reasons, culture and fashion generate far more opportunities than do educational institutions, occupations, and organizations. An obvious set of reasons deals with the competition and screening devices that are incorporated in work-related spheres.

One might suppose that the meritocratic bias and emphasis on efficiency in work and organizational settings, compared with leisure and cultural settings, would lead to less discrimination against women and minorities. This is probably not the case. We do know, for example, that the rewards associated with work are unfairly meted out. Women and minorities have lower returns in salaries and wages. When comparing people with roughly comparable jobs (year-round, full-time) and similar qualifications of job holders (a bachelor's degree), women make only about two-thirds of what males make. Comparing black males to white males in comparable jobs and qualifications, this gap is about three-quarters for black males.[24]

Women's opportunities in leisure and cultural realms appear to be superior to their opportunities in work roles. In part because they were traditionally excluded from worlds of work, it was possible to engage in serious "leisure," including charity activities, writing poetry and novels, and, increasingly, athletics.[25] Moreover, in paid leisure and in roles in art industries, women can secure high incomes, and there are niche opportunities for stardom and acclaim. There are few studies that compare the incomes of blacks and whites in leisure industries, but a study of professional basketball players is suggestive. Wallace demonstrates that salary differences among players can be traced to differences in positions played and proficiency, not race.[26] It would be foolish to claim that leisure and the arts are free of the discrimination, racism, and sexism that pervade economic and housing markets, politics, and social life. Yet the relative differences are striking.

EXIT HIGH CULTURE, ENTER POPULAR CULTURE

The study of high culture (like the study of the economy) lends itself to a diachronic analysis, not invariably and not inevitably, but it is generally the case that social scientists who have been concerned with the relationship between culture (art) and society have considered this relation over time. The way in which the "modern," particularly the avant-garde, was viewed was as if each successive development landed in the present, and everything else was declared its antecedents. Taking their cues from art and social historians, sociologists (Arnold Hauser, Pitirim Sorokin) studied high culture as enfolding according to some kind of law, cumulative, sometimes cyclical, but relentlessly evolving in ways that paralleled the history of science, ideas, and material progress.

But "high culture" itself escaped history and did so while critics and historians protested. As critic Clement Greenberg tried to see historical continuity, Jackson Pollack replied that his artworks were "memories arrested in space," and when Ernst Gombrich attempted to see painting in terms of cause and effect, Francis O'Connor said his black-and-white paintings were "pure decoration."[27] In the heyday of internationalism and progressively pure architecture, Robert Venturi pronounced that "Main Street Is All Right."[28] Perceptively, aestheticist Arthur Danto finally said, art has no "right" history, no "privileged" context.[29]

Literary high culture makers also turned their backs on the historical canon as novelists engaged in willful indulgence, self-analysis, and orgies of guilt. All the while modernist literary critics defended The Tradition, writers were bashing history. Milan Kundera starts his novel *The Unbearable Lightness of Being* on a treacherous note: "A Robespierre who eternally returns, chopping off French heads," and then raises the unspeakable, a refugee's nostalgia for Hitler. "Nothing, not a single word," is the last sentence of Saul Bellow's *Herzog*, a book about having no choice. Being forgiven is as important to Joyce Carol Oates, as being loved.[30] And if Updike novels are a bit of kinky fun poked at the middle class, they are also filled with despair, escape, and self-hatred.[31] Modernism rested on both progressivism—there is linear development—and on avant-gardism—that art is autonomous from the realms of mass culture and everyday life. At first, the unreality of the progress myth was recognized by novelists and artists. This was the genre of "blame the victim," but the storyteller and the victim were the same. The Puritan ethic had linked work to guilt, then the consumer society linked work to display, and, finally, artists squared the circle by linking display to guilt. Thus, culture makers explored the undercurrents of family pathology, "real" motivations, and the uncontrollable unconscious. Avant-gardism—continual revolutions in art—in a sense expanded the license for critics, and, speculatively, greatly expanded professional opportunities, as the avant-garde needed to be translated to the public.

More recently, however, artists have eluded critics with repeated shock, recycling, pluralism, and the denial of history, and much of it is polemical and political.[32] If artists were screaming, the "Tradition Is Dead, No More Canon," some critics insist that it still must be there, merely to be discovered by the "best and the brightest." Allan Bloom contends that the ablest of students can see the high-culture literary tradition through prevailing surface confusion. They (the able students) must participate in the essential being of Plato and Shakespeare, although they may explore, if only a bit (and here he cites Bellow), "the debris of modern times."[33] This debris under which the tradition is temporarily buried is multivocal, indiscriminate, and untalented, whereas "the tradition" is carried out at the "20 or 30 best universities" that attract those with "high intelligence" and who are "spiritually free."[34]

As George Lipsitz points out, the traditionalists have insisted on defending a linearity and homogeneity that are not evident in the rich diversity of the modern world. Allan Bloom, Lipsitz notes, assures his readers that rock and roll's entire meaning rests in its rhythm that Bloom confidently explains is reduced to the style of sexual intercourse. Lipsitz fires back: Rock and roll has never had a single rhythm, just as sex never had one style.[35] Lipsitz, is, of course, correct. There is a plethora of them, no matter how you define it.

But if the traditional canon has lost the veracity of its own diachronic, there is a gold mine in the rich particulars and the textured immediacy of popular culture. To make my own views clear about the matter, there is nothing wrong with the tradition, so long as it is assessed in its historical and its present context, but the tradition no longer exists for its makers—for example, artists, novelists, playwrights, and choreographers. The tradition and its analysis elude too easily what is most problematic in the contemporary world, namely, synchronicity, the multiplicity of culture and social arrangements. Lawrence W. Levine writes:

> The blurring of cultural classifications has been accompanied by the
> efforts of producers and performers . . . to reach out to their
> audiences in ways not known since the nineteenth century.[36]

In this sense, postmodernism is a reunification of culture, and a destruction of the difference between the aloof and pretentious on the one hand, and the vernacular and accessible on the other.

Popular American culture is thoroughly well endowed with critical inquiries. It takes only a furtive glance at the grocery check-out counter of *The Globe* or the *National Enquirer* to know that we are not a people to let the powerful and the famous get by with shenanigans, as Reagan had to be reminded to tie his shoelaces and Quayle how to spell "potato." It may be the case that, for the most part, popular culture fails to provide critical analysis of the foundations and causes of our immensely complex economic problems but does an exceptionally good job of telling stories about symptoms. Sociologists are advised to listen carefully.

Much of popular culture resides in reflexive subversiveness, but much of it resides in a sense of play as well, or what Mark Twain described as "whatever a body is not obliged to do."[37] Both *homo economicus* and *homo socious* are pretty serious folks, but that is not the way most of the world is experienced.

Thus, the study of popular culture and popularizing culture has sensitized sociologists to the importance of social cohesion and the particularities of locale. It is in these local facts that we acquire an appreciation of the different conditions under which people live (Herbert Gans, William Foote Whyte), the importance of play and irony (Erving Goffman), of social solidarity (Mirra Komarovsky, Elliot Liebow), of resistance (Douglas McAdam, Manuel Castells), of the way that people improvise (Bennett Berger).

Also for minorities and women, there is now a recognition of distinctive cultural genre. This can be put more strongly. There is a recognition of cultural genre that subvert and challenge the traditional and dominant genre, including feminist poetry, jazz, Motown, rhythm and blues, gospel, and rap. In fact, we now call these "important contributions" to the American cultural heritage, as if they had all the time been integrated in cultural history. They have not been particularly. But cultural reconstruction is all to the good as it provides new frameworks for criticism, fresh cultural meanings, and new economic and social opportunities for minorities and women.

Besides, much of contemporary African-American and feminist

culture is precisely a history about being dominated. This provides the American public the opportunity of reliving and remembering the past as it was lived and known by those who were victims. There is a clear parallel here between cultural life in the United States and that in Germany. Andreas Huyssen, among others, has written about the efforts of German artists to create through their works, a collective *Vergangenheitsbewältigung*, of coming to terms with German history, or remembering and working through a collective (and repressed) experience of dominating and being dominated.[38]

If anything, the U.S. version of *Vergangenheitsbewältigung* is very much a grass-roots affair and popular cultural experience. Consider Billy Bragg, the American black singer, reflecting in the 1990s on the issues of relations between races (but also between nations and classes): "Just because you're going forward, doesn't mean I'm going backwards." "Just because you do better than me, doesn't mean I'm lazy."[39]

If this is reflexive about what is diachronic, it was Woody Guthrie who about 30 years ago elaborated on the importance of the reflexive synchronic. More precisely, Guthrie insists on the subjective and the empathetic (even when it clearly is not forthcoming):

> I've been a-havin' some hard travellin'. *I thought you knowed.* I've been a-ridin' in fast rattlers, *I thought you knowed.* I've been a-hittin' some hard-rock mining, *I thought you knowed.* I've been a-workin' that Pittsburgh steel, *I thought you knowed.* I've been a-layin' in a hard-rock jail, *I thought you knowed.* I've been a-layin' out ninety days, way down the road.[40]

COSMOPOLITAN CULTURE

In general, there is a growing recognition that international diversity is the basis of the world's cultural order. We have impressionistic evidence that this is the case from such examples as the Olympics, the contributions that Third World participants make to dance and music festivals, and the degree to which countries like Japan, China, Brazil, and India have exported their own musical traditions, while often sending performers to participate in music competitions that are steeped in Western traditions. I have argued that culture is not merely escape. It helps to shape new collective reconstructions (*Vergangenheitsbewältigung*) as the authentic past is allowed to surface and as the "other" is discovered.

The media, celebrated by contemporary culturalists, have played an important role in this respect, just as they played an important role in exploring our selective understanding of history. As Alistair Cook, charmingly embarrassed in violating the BBC convention of authenticity, tells his audience:

> While the interlude between Parnell's friendship with Mrs. O'Shea to the time of their adultery was in fact 15 years, it must, perforce, under the constraints of a mini-series format, be compressed to a half hour.

The audience knows it, as Alistair Cook fully realizes. But the point is well taken and must be made from time to time. As Kracauer wrote, history has never been a unified and meaningful set of temporal sequences but is connected in ways that make sense to the present audience.[41] The media demystifies the traditional reconstruction of history, reconstructs its own myths, and thus encourages its audiences to discover history on their own and draw conclusions from those discoveries.

The media's role in collective movements, popular uprisings, and the diffusion of Enlightenment principles cannot be underestimated. For Chinese around the world, "6/4" is the code for the democratic movement; without television, newspapers, and electronic communications, "6/4" would not today be the powerful symbol that it is. History itself has been altered, and space and time have been compressed by the media, as this was possible owing to a global capitalist market. I contend that there may be portentous power here, but at the same time it offers new autonomy and freedom for collective action. The public is not really so dumb as some contend. Equally important, the media create the forms of international understandings that were impossible during the indeterminably long Cold War, increase pressures on political leaders to at least refrain from the most heinous of actions. The public is the world, after all, and newfound sophistication and cultural interdependencies must be taken into account even in the rhetorical strategies of politicians' P.R. point people.

Television is not only implicated in this, it has contributed considerably to this discovery. Television is considered by many as a conspiracy by commercial interests to manipulate tastes and by political elites to pacify the masses.[42] This is, to a certain extent, true: It is undeniable that during the Iraqi war the news was extremely biased as well as censored; major networks fail to offer alternative views on controversial issues, high-quality programming for children, and, with notable exceptions, truly outstanding and innovative feature films and programs.

Nevertheless, the average white child probably sees more black, Hispanic, and Asian children on television than in his or her local school. Worldwide, adults and children are far more informed about other nations, other religions, and global issues than ever before. Whether television watching promotes tolerance and widens people's perspective on the world is a question that is virtually untestable, owing to the absence of comparable survey questions before and after the worldwide dissemination of television. Although television does not especially enliven debate and dissent, it does raise the aspirations of the poor, enlighten the rich, help to diffuse tastes and fads. As Dayan and Katz note, "However hegemonically sponsored, and however affirmatively read, [television media events] invite reexamination of the status quo and are a reminder that reality falls short of society's norms."[43] In general, not only television but also the media, leisure industries generally, and forms of entertainment and sports make the world smaller than it once was and give people a chance to discover they have more in common than they at first think.

In short, the commercial imperatives of the mass media contrive to preserve the hierarchy of the status quo—for the promotion of products assumes consumers understand the rungs of the ladder of cost and resources. Yet in the marketplace of advertising, there is also an imperative to level off price and thereby create mass markets of taste and demand. In this sense, they unswervingly turn ostentatious material emblems of status into short-lived swank. Fashion ever overturns distinction. And the public is unendingly creative to induce commercial advertisers to compete among themselves for new products. These products can range from ones that are trivial and socially irresponsible to the serious and socially correct. All of us have our opinions on this matter, but I will contrast cigarettes and mink coats with preservative-free cereals and cars that have air bags. Intellectually, politically, and ideologically, the mass media are hardly subversive, that is, in any sense of intention and purpose. Yet television has become potentially subversive, and the news often lies in stories about the consequences of corporate greed and irresponsibility, and about political oppression and people's responses to it. We all (that is to mean, all around the globe) shall remember the image of the young person defying a tank during the uprising in Tiananmen Square, the video of a Los Angeles mob of police brutally beating and kicking a black man, and the many news clips of birds and marine life dying on the shores of Alaska following the grounding of the *Valdez*. These news events can be "read" as stories about individual wrongdoing and corruption, yet they are instead often interpreted by the public as exposing the legal, economic, and social contexts in which wrongdoing and corruption are likely to occur. Thus, they encourage audiences to consider, for example, the nature of authoritarian regimes, the inadequacy of laws that might otherwise regulate corporate actors, and the economic conditions that undermine good intentions about better health care and improved schools. In a profound sense, television has increased our awareness of how the interests of the people of the world are uncannily alike.

NOTES

1. Herbert Applebaum, "Theoretical Introduction," pp. 1–38 in Applebaum (ed.), *Work in Non-market and Traditional Societies*. Albany: State University of New York, 1984, pp. 18–19.
2. A. D. Radcliffe-Brown, *Structure and Function in Primitive Society*. Foreword by E. E. Evans-Pritchard and Fred Eggan. Glencoe, IL: Free Press, 1952, p. 204; Fernand Braudel, *Afterthoughts on Material Civilization and Capitalism*. Trans. Patricia M. Ranum. Baltimore: Johns Hopkins University Press, 1977, p. 51.
3. Aristophanes, *The Birds*. Trans. William Arrowsmith. New York: New American Library, 1961, p. 136.
4. W. H. Lewis, *The Sunset of the Splendid Century: The Life and Times of Louis Auguste de Bourbon, Duc du Maine, 1670–1736*. New York: Anchor [1935] 1963, p. 186.
5. Raymond Firth, *We, the Topika*. Abridged edition. Boston: Beacon Press, [1936] 1957, pp. 54–55.
6. Eviatar Zerubavel, *Hidden Rhythms*. Berkeley: University of California Press, 1981.
7. Jack V. Buerkle and Danny Barker, *Bourbon Street Black*. London: Oxford University Press, 1973, pp. 214–215.
8. For a summary of this view, see Patrick Brantlinger, *Bread and Circuses: Theories of Mass Culture as Social Decay*. Ithaca, NY: Cornell University Press, 1983.
9. Rose Laub Coser, "Laughter among Colleagues: A Study of the Social Functions of Humor among the Staff of a Mental Hospital," *Psychiatry* 23 (1960): 81–95.
10. Clyde Kluckholn and Dorthea Leighton, *The Navaho*. Rev. ed. The American Museum of Natural History and Doubleday & Co. New York: Doubleday & Co., [1946] 1962, p. 54.
11. Robert S. Lynd and Helen Merrell Lynd, *Middletown*. Foreword by Clark Wissler. New York: Harcourt, Brace & World, [1926] 1956, p. 149.
12. Joseph A. Schumpeter, *Capitalism, Socialism, and Democracy*. 3rd ed. Harper & Row, [1942] 1950, p. 132.

13. Frank H. Knight, *Risk, Uncertainty and Profit*. London: London School of Economics and Political Science, 1933.
14. Roland Barthes, *The Fashion System*. Trans. Matthew Ward and Richard Howard. New York: Hill and Wang, [1967] 1983, p. 253.
15. See Peter Bürger, *Theory of the Avant-Garde*. Trans. Michael Shaw with a foreword by Jochen Schulte-Sasse. Minneapolis: University of Minnesota Press, 1984; Hal Foster (ed.), *The Anti-Aesthetic: Essays on Postmodern Culture*. Washington: Bay Press, 1983.
16. Ibid., p. xi.
17. See Peter M. Blau and Otis Dudley Duncan, *The American Occupational Structure*. New York: Wiley, 1967; Christopher Jencks with Marshall Smith, Henry Acland, Mary Jo Bane, David Cohen, Herbert Gintis, Barbara Heyns, and Stephan Michelson, *Inequality*. New York: Basic Books, 1972.
18. For an overview, see Bernard Rosenberg and David Manning White, *Mass Culture in America*. Glencoe, IL: Free Press, 1957.
19. Pierre Bourdieu, *Distinction*. Trans. Richard Nice. Cambridge: Harvard University Press, 1984.
20. Judith R. Blau and Gail Quets with Peter M. Blau, *Cultural Life in City and Region*. Akron: Center for Urban Studies, University of Akron, 1989.
21. Paul DiMaggio and Michael Useem, "Cultural Democracy in a Period of Cultural Expansion," pp. 199–226 in J. B. Kamerman and R. Martorella (eds.), *Performers and Performances*. South Hadley, MA: Bergin & Garvey, 1983.
22. Irving L. Allen, "Community Size, Population Composition, and Cultural Activities in Smaller Communities," *Rural Sociology* 33 (September 1968): 328–338; Judith R. Blau, *The Shape of Culture*. Cambridge: University of Cambridge Press, 1989.
23. The exception may be Holland in the seventeenth century. An interesting account is John Michael Montias, *Artists and Artisans in Delft*. Princeton: Princeton University Press, 1982.
24. Robert E. Kennedy, Jr., *Life Choices*. New York: Holt, Rinehart & Winston, 1986, pp. 40–47; Francine D. Blau and Marianne A. Ferber, *The Economics of Women, Men, and Work*. Englewood Cliffs, NJ: Prentice-Hall, 1986, p. 233. Also see Alice Abel Kemp and E. M. Beck, "Equal Work, Unequal Pay: Gender Discrimination within Work-Similar Occupations," *Work and Occupations* 13 (August 1986): 324–348.
25. Kurt Lang and Gladys Lang, *Etched in Memory*. Chapel Hill: University of North Carolina Press, 1990; Arlene Daniels, *Invisible Careers: Women Civic Leaders from the Volunteer World*. Chicago: University of Chicago Press, 1988; also see National Endowment for the Arts, *Artist Employment and Unemployment, 1971–1980*. Washington, DC: National Endowment for the Arts, 1982.
26. Michael Wallace, "Labor Market Structure and Salary Determination among Professional Basketball Players," *Work and Occupations* 15 (1988): 294–312.

27. Rosalind E. Krauss, *The Originality of the Avant-Garde and Other Modernist Myths*. Cambridge: MIT Press, 1986, pp. 234–237.
28. Robert Venturi, Denise Scott-Brown, and Steve Izenour. *Learning from Las Vegas*. Cambridge: MIT Press, 1972.
29. Arthur Danto, *Transfiguration of the Commonplace*. Cambridge: Harvard University Press, 1981.
30. *Because It Is Bitter and Because It Is My Heart* (1990).
31. *Rabbit Run* (1960), *Rabbit Redux* (1971), *Rabbit at Rest* (1990).
32. Hall Foster, *Recodings*. Port Townsend, WA: Bay Press, 1985.
33. Allan Bloom, *The Closing of the American Mind*. New York: Simon & Schuster, 1987, pp. 237–238.
34. Ibid.
35. George Lipsitz, *Time Passages*. Minneapolis: University of Minnesota Press, 1990.
36. *Highbrow/Lowbrow*. Cambridge: Harvard University Press, 1988, p. 245.
37. Mark Twain. *The Adventures of Tom Sawyer*. New York: Simon & Schuster, [1876] 1982, p. 23.
38. Andreas Huyssen, *After the Great Divide*. Bloomington: Indiana University Press, 1988.
39. Billy Bragg, "To Have and to Have Not." Compiled and produced by Kenny Jones. Elektra/Asylum Records, 1988.
40. Woody Guthrie, "Hard Traveling," *Woody Guthrie Sings Folk Songs* (with Leadbelly, Cisco Houston, Sonny Terry, and Bess Hawes). Folkways Records, Album FA 2483, 1962 (emphasis added).
41. Siegfried Kracauer, *History: The Last Things before the Last*. New York: Oxford, 1969.
42. Brantlinger, op. cit.
43. Daniel Dayan and Elihu Katz, *Media Events: The Live Broadcasting of History*. Cambridge: Harvard University Press, 1992, p. 20.

10

The Micrometrics of Morals
and the Macrometrics of Ethics

*If everyone minded their own business, the world would go round a great
deal faster than it does.*
  —THE DUCHESS IN *Alice's Adventures in Wonderland*

It is an established American tradition to belittle the study of morals
and ethics—"Dry," Jefferson said[1]; "subservient to experience," argued
Oliver Wendell Holmes.[2] As for morals in practice, Robert Louis Stevenson said they should be "concealed like a vice."[3] And Henry Adams, in
the same vein, observed that morals are a "private and costly luxury."[4]
As one now reads the writings of early Puritans, the battle of sin and
indulgence appears more like a lively duel than a matter of right and
wrong. Cotton Mather writes, "The diseases of my soul are not cured
until I arrive to the most unspotted Chastitie and Puritie." However, he
quickly exonerates himself by bracketing his sexual appetite for his
third wife: "I do not apprehend that Heaven requires me uterlie to lay
aside my fondness for my lovelie Consort."[5]

Not only the quipsters but even the genuine American philosophers rather let us down. William James conceived as morals in terms of
what is demandable, and everything that is demanded. He writes,

> Since everything which is demanded is by that fact a good, must
> not the guiding principle for ethical philosophy . . . be simply to
> satisfy at all times *as many demands as we can?* . . . *Invent some manner*
> of realizing your own ideals which will also satisfy the alien
> demand. . . .[6]

If truth is today's cash value for James, it was for John Dewey "next day's funding operations," which is to say that what is right tomorrow is what is practical and expedient in the light of today's experiences.[7] The idea that we newly coin our moral standards with shifts in the wind helped to justify the pursuit of pleasure, while it also freed up the individual from social constraints and traditional values. Pragmatic views of morality and ethics were compatible with a nation on the move, the expansion of opportunities, and a vision of progress and overall optimism. American pragmatists might have told Lewis Carroll's Duchess not "*If,*" but rather "*When* people mind their own business the world goes around quite nicely. Thank you."

What James called "truth's cash-value" has a nice ring to it in the context of economic theory that emphasizes the immediate over the long run, places the individual at the center of things, and posits a general equilibrium between individual wants and individual attainments. Pragmatism also enjoyed great favor among psychologists, and behaviorism rested on the tenet that individuals maximize what is rewarding and minimize what is unrewarding. In the light of James's writings, there appeared to be no inconsistency between ethics and the pursuit of pleasure, or between ethics and the accumulation of wealth.

The idea that economic actors should be allowed to maximize their individual utilities ignores the by-products of economic behavior and divorces economics from the larger political and social matrices. Psychological theory, too, severs action from consequences. Although Dewey protested that "a pragmatic intelligence is a creative intelligence, not a routine mechanic,"[8] he nevertheless failed to get out of the logic box whereby the criterion of what is "good" merely involves what is in the individual's gain.

Pragmatism has survived in strains of contemporary public choice theory. Rational actors, it is argued, will cheat, free-ride, and act opportunistically if they can get by with it.[9] Later I will examine the empirical evidence that suggests to the contrary that what people consider to be right or fair usually overrides the temptation to free-ride.

It might be noted here that Adam Smith wrote not only *The Wealth of Nations* (1776) but also *The Theory of Moral Sentiments* (1790). Whereas in the former, Smith defends the pursuit of profits and the importance of self-interest, in the latter, he states his convictions that unregulated competition has untoward consequences.[10] He reminds his readers:

> Man naturally desires, not only to be loved, but to be lovely; or be that thing which is the natural and proper object of love. . . . He

> desires, not only praise, but praiseworthiness; or to be that thing
> which, though it should be praised by nobody, is, however the
> natural and proper object of praise.[11]

Smith Number 1, the champion of economic freedom, juxtaposed with Smith Number 2, the champion of cooperation and conviviality, raises an interesting dilemma for the understanding of morals and ethics. I have cursorily tracked Smith Number 1's influence on psychology and economics (public choice theory), but the problems of conformity and unreflective cooperation are also not insignificant.

DOMESTICATED SHEEP

Sociology and anthropology together "rescued" the individual from individualism, but unfortunately chained the individual to the group. Morals are situated in the local ecologies of norms as groups eke out the standards of living and the conventions for behavior to which individuals are expected to comply. This works quite well in communities in which family, work, and neighborhood are coexistent. Issues about moral conduct are straightforward. Norms about how we treat one another are reinforced throughout this polymorphous community. Family, socializing agents, neighbors, and clansfolk help to define and clarify moral distinctions that guide individual behavior and make group life possible. Micrometrics help to define, clarify, and instill moral codes.

Durkheim's analysis of deviance only makes sense in the context of such a polymorphous, all-encompassing community. In such a community, Durkheim argues, the rule violator can be identified, labeled, and "evicted."[12] The act of eviction strengthens community norms and helps to provide the exemplar case of what is right, namely, conformity, and the exemplar case of what is wrong—deviance. There is no argument with Durkheim about this process whereby moral codes are learned and enforced. Families, schools, and neighborhoods provide the "socializing context" in which moral values and norms of conduct are learned.[13] The "bully," the "cheat," and the "provocateur" are punished, whereas playing by the rules and being cooperative are rewarded. In rearing children, all parents use explicit examples of the "bully," as well as the "ill-mannered," "cheat," "provocateur," and so forth, when defining what is acceptable or not. As Durkheim would say, this serves two functions—to reinforce group standards and to castigate the bully.

This approach has the following implications. A notion of group survival and integrity is a priori, and to the extent that role conformity maintains that group integrity it is itself functional. But if we base a social ethics on conformity to norms we run into problems.

THE KILLING FIELD OF CONFORMITY

Morality is rooted in group membership, loyalty, duty, and obligation. This has not gone merely unnoticed by social scientists, and, indeed, is closely tied to our understanding of socialization, conformity, and compliance with what is expected of individuals. Morality is the stuff of which social roles are made.

Early in Anouilh's play *Antigone*,[14] the prophetic Antigone says to Creon, the King, "You are a *loathsome* man!" In fact, by the time one finishes reading or watching the play (that is, after learning Creon has done away with most of his family and members of the court), one will conclude that this may be one of the biggest understatements in all of literature. King Creon's response to Antigone is a sociological parody: "I agree. My trade forces me to be. We could argue whether I ought or ought not to follow my trade; but once I take on the job, I must do it properly." The modern audience will recognize at once that this is a tragic exaggeration of the oversocialized conception of individuals in which people play their social roles as if they were constrained to do so.[15] In the final chorus of the play, Anouilh describes the situation of Antigone, who plays the enigmatic role of ill-fated conscience: "Well, Antigone is calm tonight. She has played her part." Indeed, only the Guards are left and ". . . they go on playing their cards."

Anouilh's play, of course, has an historical context, namely Nazi Germany and the accounts of French collaborators. Stanley Milgram carried out a series of experiments in which students were told to shock participants in an experiment when they made errors on tests. The participants, paid actors, took the shocks with screams and pleas for the "teacher" to stop. Astonishingly, many continued to shock the actors beyond what we, as detached social scientists, could believe.[16] Yet the results of the experiments seemed to confirm what anthropologists and sociologists claimed all along, that individuals act in conformity with expectations and comply with authority. When individuals participate singly in a science experiment, they will follow the rules that the scientist—a legitimate authority—sets down.

Obedience and morality are closely connected in a social-science theory that explains human behavior by norms and compliance with legitimate authority. Still, the experiment raises important problems about one's response when confronted with a set of expectations that violate conscience. Certainly one aspect of morality deals with obedience and conformity. Without shared conceptions of legitimacy, allegiance to group norms, and compliance with rules, our world would be sheer anarchy. But can we explain people's behavior purely in these terms?

It is helpful to clarify at once why there are limits to generalizing Milgram's findings, to allay readers' concerns about obsessive compulsion to conformity and to anticipate the distinctions I plan to draw. Without the means for interpreting authority and for assessing the short- and long-term consequences of acquiescing, Milgram's subjects may have assumed that the contractual obligations of participating in the experiment obligated them. Conformity was a consequence of a promise and the belief that science does not harm people. This implies a certain suspension of belief.

The tyrant, as Isaiah Berlin observed, can exploit this suspension of belief by manipulating and sustaining the frameworks of interpretation and of judgment. The "demands for cooperation, solidarity, and fraternity" may "obstruct or fail to create conditions which other freedoms, or a larger degree of freedom, or freedom for more persons, [make] possible."[17]

Carrying out experiments similar to Milgram's, but using groups, rather than single individuals, Gamson and his colleagues found that challenge or outright disobedience is a common response to unjust demands of authorities. In groups, individuals adopt an "injustice frame" that grows out of the conviction that "the unimpeded operation of the authority system, on this occasion, would result in an injustice."[18] The curb on illegitimate demands and hegemonic control is established by means of an injustice framework that is collectively defined.

Relevant here is the fact that individuals may play singleton roles, but they are no means themselves singletons, so that individual frames of reference in social life are not atomistically derived. Groups, communities, and society are not simple aggregations of their members. There are, however, distinctions to be drawn. In some groups and relations, partialled roles, such as mother, father, friend, and colleague, accompany unpartialled commitment, such as love, loyalty, and unconditional regard. In other groups, partialled roles, such as supervisor, committee chair, and employee, accompany partialled and conditional commitment.

When we examine the micrometrics of morality, namely, in those worlds where "whole people count," such as in families and friendships, we protect and defend group members against external threats, real or not, while we also are preoccupied about conformity of group members. Thus, microworlds foster trust, obligations, and altruistic behavior rather than, as Dewey and James emphasized, personal pleasure and narrow self-interest. It goes without saying that rationality in microworlds is accompanied by an absorption in the group and group members. Although families provide the prototypical example, large collectivities, such as ethnic and religious groups and ideological movements, can also foster such commitment and intense loyalty. However, on such a large scale, moral claims are nothing short of terrifying.

In contrast, when we examine the macrometrics of ethics—in those worlds in which "part people count"—notably in all those settings in which partialled roles are played with partialled commitment, cooperation problems are important enough that there are reasons to deal carefully with mediation problems relating to conflicting interests, to injustice issues, and to questions about the distribution of collective goods. There must be, after all, a recognition of the fact that people have different bundles of interests and commitments and that the imposition of simple solutions or an overarching set of values is simply unsatisfactory.

There are three essential points here. First, the market metaphor of morality and ethics, on which pragmatism drew with such gusto, simplifies the role of self-interest in social life. In small groups, we are encouraged to make sacrifices for the group, whereas in larger groups, our interests are partialled and segmentalized. This serves both to constrain competition and to encourage cooperation. Second, the small group fosters sufficient collective identity so that injustices from without tend to be resisted. Large groups rely on negotiation, bargaining, adjudication, and conflict as their members hammer out injustice problems. Third, the easy assumption that people comply willy-nilly to group norms must be further clarified. The greediness of microsettings[19] is a problem just as is the plurality of expectations in macrosettings. Most serious, however, is the situation in which the micrometrics of morality are played out in large collectivities. We can think of examples in the United States, just as we can of those in other countries for which nationalist movements and religious groups take uncompromising positions. I pose this problem now but return to it later on.

MAKING SOME DISTINCTIONS

Morality is derived from the Latin word *mos*, meaning custom or mores, although I will emphasize its imperative nature as it pertains to self and its rootedness in local ecologies and homogeneous groups. I am going to define morals as appropriate to small groups, consistent with social-science emphasis on norms and local values. We are moral because we have in-group memberships, and in-groups are the loci in which norms about honesty, personal integrity, loyalty, trust, and reciprocity are learned. In-group frames of reference stay with us, regardless of how sturdy or not those groups are in the present. This is not to say that large groups do not appropriate moral frameworks, for they do, even though this sometimes poses serious difficulties.

Morality is based on two interesting premises. First, it derives its strength from the fact that moral principles have an imperative quality for individuals owing to their connections with particular groups. Second, once group codes are defined as constituting moral guidelines, they beg conformity. The politics of morality are rooted in deep personal feelings about group interests and group insistence on compliance. Some groups condone whereas others condemn such behaviors as prostitution, premarital sex, gambling, smoking, drinking, obscene art, eating animals, eating fish, homosexuality, abortion, and cockfighting. These examples illustrate behaviors that stem from personal convictions and that in the abstract only apply to oneself. What do I care that an acquaintance of mine kills and collects butterflies; another searches art galleries for penises that were severed by Victorians from Greek sculptures; and still another watches "adult" videos? I don't even mind that sheep and chickens are sacrificed as part of voodoo rituals in New York City parks. But let us say that I have a friend who believes that killing animals is wrong and believes a law against such sacrifices should be passed, and another friend who strongly feels that "adult" videos are degrading to women and should be illegal.

Herein lies the problem. In the abstract, morals pertain to one's own behavior and one's own in-group, and they are structurally induced within those little groups in which members participate with unpartialled commitment. Yet in practice, we participate in other realms as well and thereby tread on others' local territories of moral beliefs. Because morals are energized by such strong passions, resolving turf problems requires tact, tolerance, and considerable trust.

Most territories in the modern world, however, are bristling with detachment, or as Simmel would say, people are blasé,[20] and there is no "turf" and, therefore, few turf problems owing to the partialling of commitments. Intergroup and interindividual dependencies give rise to ethical (and legal) problem-solving strategies, which themselves are antithetical to strong moral claims about absolute truths, the preservation of in-group cohesion, and unpartialled commitments. In short, ethics rest on different grounds than do morals insofar as they track coordination and must deal with injustice issues by means of systematic accounting procedures. It is in terms of ethical guidelines that groups and individuals can appeal injustices, and in terms of those guidelines that groups ask its members for more, that is, more work, more tolerance, and more justice.

The mapping of activities assumes existing interdependencies and creates new ones as well, heaping complexity on complexity. In the interstices of complex structures are persons playing unpartialled roles with undivided commitments but also partialled roles with detachment. Moreover, in such complex structures, the rational interests of individual actors matter more in their consequences because there are more individuals whose rational interests are also at stake. Consequentialism is important for the analysis of ethics, generally, whether we are discussing social contracts, as I have been here, or economic markets, which I will also briefly discuss in this chapter.

The etymology of the word *ethics* is helpful. The word is derived from a Greek root *ethike* and has to do with security and housing of those for whom one is responsible. The prosaic origin comes from stalls or barns for the animals. Collective security would be the closest we could come to it, or as Paul Lehmann, a systematic theologian, who traces through its historical roots and linguistic applications, defines ethics, the "cement of human society."[21] In its implications, this conception of ethics both recognizes and transcends the notion of distinctive ethical/cultural systems—Christian, Buddhist, socialist, democratic, Hindi—by drawing attention to the interdependence of individuals, interests, and groups as they still represent their distinctive ethical/cultural memberships.[22] Working backwards to the individual, ethical guidelines must first and foremost recognize this interdependence; actions must take into account their consequences for others who are different from oneself and rest on principles of cooperation.

The litmus test of ethical behavior is that it maximizes beneficial externalities. This puts the onus on responsibility and not on self-interest. Ethical accounting deals with the consequences of the distribution of rights and obligations in a society as much as it deals with the distribution of benefits and "just deserts."

As Rawls explains, there is an efficiency conception of justice that deals with the distribution of benefits in the following way:

> The higher expectations of those better situated are just if and only
> if they work as part of a scheme which improves the expectations of

the least advantaged members of society. The intuitive idea is that the social order is not to establish and secure the more attractive prospects of those better off unless doing so is to the advantage of those less fortunate.[23]

But he adds, the application of this conception requires "that we view persons independently from the influences of their social position."[24] It is on this point that philosophy and social science fail to come to terms, as empirical realities of differences in social positions cannot be willed away, will as we might. There are two issues here. The first has to do with the monopoly of advantage that elites have, and thus their disinclination to ignore the social and economic origins of others. This is the issue of redress. The second has to do with Rawls's conception of a segmented society. This is the issue of simple justice.

Redress

The consequentialist position I am taking raises questions about whether such an equilibrium can be achieved under an efficiency criteria in a society in which there are complex interdependencies that have generated and consolidated differences with respect to multiple resources. We could take as an example Rawls's stipulation that it is possible and permissible on the difference principle to allocate resources in education to improve the expectations of the least favored, but it is not required to even out handicaps so that the competition is fair.[25] However, let us examine what happens historically without the additional stipulation of redress.

We know that education levels have increased and inequality of education has declined, while at the same time income and wealth inequalities have increased. Thus, expectations for returns have been raised, whereas the likelihood of obtaining them diminishes. In the long run, this reduces incentives for people to acquire an education and even to work hard, raising serious problems about justice according to anyone's definition of it. This is a comparison of two distributions—educational equalities and income inequalities—over time, but aggregate distributions conceal interdependencies within a population and likely consequences over the long run. Justice mechanisms decay as inequality of rewards increases, and demands for redress increase as the gaps between effort (education) and reward broaden. We might also recognize that increasing income inequalities over time quite often increases the cost of living for everyone, including those without high incomes. This results in an expansion of numbers within the bounds of eligibility for transfer payments, as individuals in the lowest rungs of the middle-income brackets drop to low-income brackets.

Thus, much and increasing inequality creates conditions under which it is difficult, if not impossible, to apply Rawls's principles for achieving just outcomes. There is some evidence that there is a social calculus of justice in the real world and one that insists on more than Rawls himself requires. During the past 20 years of increasing inequality, the levels of charitable donations and of many kinds of volunteering—activities that reflect collective sentiments of redress—have steadily risen.[26] The work of Jasso is also relevant here.[27] She finds when people evaluate a "just" distribution of goods, such as income, public opinion is strongly in the direction of creating more equality. That is, individuals favor paying the underpaid more and are harshly indignant when people are overpaid for their work. Wolf's analysis of charity and Jasso's research suggests that if Americans would vote for an ideal income distribution there would be much more equality than there is now. Unfortunately, individuals do not create aggregate distributions, just as they cannot create conditions under which the prospects of the already least advantaged are maximized. Prevailing aggregate distributions are the consequences of economic arrangements, political policy, institutional rules, and changing supply and demand, with increasing attenuation between expectations and "deserts" and an increase in the numbers of those least advantaged.

Simple Justice

To return then to Rawls's conception of justice, he draws extensively on formal social-science theory that conceives of society as comprised of multiple, yet independent, groups or strata. In such a conception, justice requires that not everyone must have equal opportunities; instead, "those with similar abilities and skills should have the same life chances." He adds:

> Those who are at the same level of talent and ability, and have the same willingness to use them, should have the same prospects of success . . . irrespective of the income class into which they were born.[28]

Douglas Rae raises, in my mind, the right question: How can we even define a uniform group whose members have initially equal endowments?[29] I have argued throughout this book that the social order is complex and intricate, as groups, and even strata, overlap. Public policy can enhance its objectives by taking this into account. For example, by way of redress, when we improve the wages of women, we also improve the conditions of children. Increasing opportunities for urban entrepreneurs is likely to improve the chances for many blacks and ethnic minorities who live in central cities. Equalizing opportunities and applying justice norms have unexpected beneficial consequences owing to the complexities of social groups and of individuals' memberships in groups.

The Admixture of Morals and Ethics

The paradox is that in a complex society in which there are coexisting in-groups, each in-group can appeal to the structural interdependence that does in fact exist, and to a democratic principle that niche-rights are legitimate. This is where distinguishing morality and ethics becomes problematic. For those who believe that premarital sex is wrong, it is morally reprehensible that college dormitories have condom machines; for feminists, pornographic films and sexist art perpetuate sexism in society; when patriotism takes hold, people become intolerant of dissent and political satire; and the belief that fetuses are babies leads to demands that no one is entitled to an abortion. The game rules can tilt toward downright unfairness as some groups claim exclusive right to the truth and deny the rights of others. Demonstrators of whatever persuasion who shout down speakers in public forums might be an example here. However, interestingly, the game is played in far more clever ways than this. For example, some hunters who claim they do not truck with those who rob banks may, on that basis, work to veto gun controls. And groups who normally discriminate discover that hue is less the issue than having a political ally, a coalition partner on a community project, or buyers for a service.

While we have entered an historical stage of nearly unprecedented moralizing in America, we have also embarked on a collective recognition of the interdependencies in society. The urgency with which people perceive our environmental and ecological problems is an illustration of this. Moral claims about others' behaviors rest on the fragile assumption that peoples' situations are the same, or that there is a single overriding imperative that justifies ignoring differences in a situation. In any process in which moral claims are made in a complex society, the burden of proof resides in the hands of those that contend that there is identity of situations or that the differences among situations are too trivial to be relevant.

It is important to maintain an historical perspective. Until fairly recently, groups were sufficiently segregated that different moralities did not compete so much with one another. Cultural relativism was consistent with group segregation. Middle-class mothers thought that working was wrong for themselves, but quite proper for lower-class mothers; sexual promiscuity was affably attributed to the upper and lower classes; Catholics were readily accorded the right to indulge in having large families; and intellectuals were entitled to be sissies. Interestingly, what probably did more to unite classes and ethnic groups was the specter of communism, and with this common enemy Americans were easily tolerant of group differences and individual variation. The Cold War was what bonded most Americans and sustained a common identity in the post–World War II period. Yet nowadays advancing moral claims is predicated on the assumption that group lines can be unambiguously defined. It is hard to imagine that they can be.

As Wolfe points out, moral decision making involves a lot of talk.[30] It does so because talk defines group membership, boundaries, and identity of members. Paradoxically, as the social order becomes increasingly more complex, moral commitments become more apparently different from one another, and, therefore, increase in the salience they have for group members. But what makes moral stakes more pronounced— the increased salience of the differences among groups—is simultaneously what increases ethical problems and ethical problem-solving efforts as well. The intensity of ethical problem solving likewise raises questions about the relevance—the validity—of moral claims.

THE SUSPENSION OF ETHICS—THE ROLE OF THE STATE

A comprehensive discussion of the role of the state is far beyond my interests, expertise, and the objectives of this book. However, issues involving the state touch down on various topics in a too-important way for me to neglect how they are relevant. An initial problem deals with dependency issues, which would have general bearing on considerations of social and educational inequalities. A second problem bears on the role of the state in economic matters. In a sense, this, too, is a dependency issue because of the asymmetry of power and resources that characterizes the relation of corporate economic actors and the public.

No Exit

Dependency poses moral problems in all social systems, and ethical ones in modern societies as well. Each group and the collectivity condemns members' neglect of children, and supports group interests to look after the aged and the ill. Moral problems of dependence are rooted in the belief that if we share one thing, that is the problem of dependency—each one of us at one time was young, all of us are occasionally ill, and most of us will be aged. We may not as a society handle health and dependency problems very well, but they do have high priority in the public agenda, given a collective empathy about these problems. But there are dependency issues that are interstitial to groups or involve situations in which some members are dominant and unlikely to experience dependencies or to have empathy with those who are dependent. Here is the arena in which the state plays an especially important role. These kinds of dependencies arise from inequalities of knowledge, power, or resources.

Unlike those individuals for which we traditionally care through group efforts or through collective means (the aged, children, the sick), other individuals (the poor, the unemployed, the homeless) are not well-defined aggregates in a large and complex society. The provision of care for nontraditional dependent groups is far from simple. Even knowing who they are is a vast undertaking. The tasks of coordination, enumeration, and providing resources are, it seems to me, the sort of thing only governments can do well. This requires a base of grass-roots mobilization on the part of citizens, churches, and voluntary organizations. However, for reasons of equity, accountability, and continuity of care, the state must play the most important role.

Why Would Markets Be Decent?

The simple market operates pretty much along the lines of the pursuit of economic gain. And why not? Why would a buyer donate a charitable contribution to the seller, or a seller voluntarily reveal defects in the product, or why would a landowner rent property at a rate for which there is no profit? Still, there are market mechanisms that dampen the negative consequences of the pursuits of multiple self-interests. Although ethics in social matters is part and parcel of cooperation, doing well—not simply good—is a fringe benefit of efficient markets.

In an important book, Albert O. Hirschman shows how those with little ostensible power in markets nevertheless have options of exit. This, in turn, sets the automatic trigger response of competition for loyalty. There can be unanticipated consequences that rebound to the advantage of the initially disadvantaged.[31] These options of exit—freedom—arise in economic situations owing to the fact that there are alternatives in a competitive market. In markets, sellers compete with other sellers, and what keeps them from charging too much or selling shoddy products is the fact that people can choose to go elsewhere. This assumes a lot of leisure and knowledge that most of us do not have. But as Hirschman notes, it is nevertheless possible to overcome these difficulties. Not only are companies evaluated by their stock value, their profitability, and the way they package and market their products, but they also are evaluated by their personnel policies (whether they hire and promote minorities and women), environmental impact, use of animals in testing, and a whole lot of other things on which people base their consumer choices. The market analogy extends to organizational membership and the possibility of jobholders leaving jobs and taking others. This assumes that there are jobs available, that we are cognizant of these jobs, and that the jobs are within moving distance. In other words, people have options of exit, but there are problems of available alternatives and knowledge of them.

In other situations, Hirschman suggests that the option of voice is superior. This is the only option in basic social organizations, such as the family, church, society, or a purely monopolistic market.[32]

Yet inequalities in the voice option pose serious problems not fully addressed by Hirschman. We can think of groups that are locked into multiple and reinforcing structures of constraints in ways that voice is hardly a possibility. These constraints are experienced by residents of inner cities who have been victimized by housing policies, racism, and lack of job opportunities. Others are the rural poor who have lost their jobs or farms, have little education, and are otherwise dependent on failing local economies. I have also considered the situation in which the voice of the middle class grows weaker with declining economic opportunities.

In some instances, mechanisms have evolved that guarantee protections in relations of asymmetry. The most enduring examples come from institutions in which there are asymmetries of knowledge and power, and individual welfare is at stake. For example, the Hippocratic oath and the clinical training that physicians undergo is actually a code of ethics governing relationships in which there is asymmetry and in which the whole point is client welfare. Elaborate rules involving confidentiality and the obligations of being trusted are lodged in a variety of relationships that involve similar asymmetries—between lawyer and client, teacher and student. Another example is the elaborate set of human subject protection conditions that govern scientific research in which people are involved. These conditions create obstacles for researchers, such as problems of representative samples and the biases that are created when subjects know the hypotheses of the study, or when it is impossible to have a control group. Nevertheless, these procedures were adopted over some objections with the general recognition in the scientific community that anyone who participates as a subject in scientific research should be fully informed about the purposes of the study and any personal consequences that might ensue.

This example is fairly simple compared with problems of asymmetry in society, yet it conceptually parallels the issue of, for example, the protection of dependent persons whom we try to shield from market competition because they are easily victimized. Children, the elderly, and the ill are special categories in economic life, though they are by no means immune from the destructive effects of competition. These arrangements—codes of professional behavior, guidelines protecting human subjects, and general rules about dependents' exemptions from economic competition—are unusual in that they are self-imposed by the relatively powerful. It is obvious that under most conditions the relatively powerful fail to impose self-restraint unless there are competitive advantages to do so, or the possibility of mass exit is perceived to be intolerable.

We shall later see that the state must play a role in supplementing self-imposed restraint, constraints of competition, and threats of mass exit. It can be briefly noted here, however, that the state has traditionally applied some formal constraints to producers, suppliers, landowners, and service providers in order to rectify asymmetries of information. The state, however, has primarily been concerned with stimulating competition and not especially with creating arenas in which the voice option can be exercised, or even protecting the most disadvantaged and dependent. It becomes increasingly clear that our institutionalized mechanisms for ensuring economic constraints are far less well developed than they are constitutionally allowable. This is due to the fact that economic complexities have far outpaced the rules that evolved to regulate an earlier economy.

The Unanticipated Consequences of Choice

Cooperation

There is some evidence that the recognition of interdependence helps to maintain a cooperative community. The prisoner's-dilemma game has been imported from a technical literature to illustrate that under the conditions of sustained community, people choose cooperative solutions.[33] The problem is simple. Two people are arrested who are alleged to have participated in a crime together. We and the prisoners know they are guilty—say, in committing an act of civil disobedience—but the evidence is flimsy.[34] They are held in different cells and are each told that if they confess, thereby implicating the other, the confessor will be given a free pardon while the accomplice will receive a 20-year sentence. If neither confesses, the evidence is sufficiently mild so that each would get a 2-year sentence. If they both confess, they will each receive 10 years. The "rational choice" for each is to confess, but that then means each would get the 10-year sentence. However, if they act with the assumption of cooperation, neither will confess, and each will receive the mild sentence of 2 years.

When experts, such as economists, play the game once, they play on the basis of rational criteria and confess, but when economists play the game over and over, a cooperative strategy of not confessing develops.[35] Noneconomists, on the other hand, are advantaged by not having a theory of self-interest, and they get to the point more quickly than experts. That is, when "amateurs" play, they often cooperate on the first round contrary to the predictions of game theorists.[36] The matter of cooperation under these conditions is baffling. Sen, an economist, in summarizing the befuddlement of the experts about cooperation, concludes that economic theory misleads us by saying that what a person pursues is personal gain.[37] Instead,

> What a person can be seen as maximizing depends on a certain reading of what he or she takes to be the appropriate control variables and what variations are seen as the right means of control exercised by each player.[38]

In other words, there are departures from the standard behavioral assumption of self-centered behavior, and these involve bonhomie and sympathy for others, or commitments to various causes, or when economic efficiency has nonmarket consequences. People do not always take actions on the basis of short-run self-interest as if all that mattered were market relations. There are long-run advantages to cooperation, and social arrangements depend on cooperation.

A most important reason why we cooperate is that we do not know what the other person will do if we do not cooperate. This uncertainty with respect to *the other person's* behavior generates an incentive to try a cooperative strategy. In many casual situations, cooperative strategies become institutionalized. Opening and holding doors has become more cooperative and less sexist; people dim their bright lights on the highway; queuing at the box office or bus stop is common enough; confused tourists holding maps in their hands are often assisted by locals. These are trivial examples, but they illustrate that complete strangers cooperate even when it costs them something or is inconvenient. They also mirror the far more prevalent instances of reciprocity and cooperation within organized social settings, such as neighborhoods, and work organizations in which virtual strangers, as well as coworkers, develop solutions to achieve common ends.

People cooperate when they recognize the beneficial consequences of doing so, but they also cooperate owing to the consequences of noncooperation. Although not every disaster results in collective cooperation, many, even most, do. It is recognized that the probability of survival is linked to the probability of orderly crowd behavior. There is an increasing disapproval of the use of pitons in mountain climbing, which is probably one of the most interesting examples of cooperation, for it is a form of disciplined behavior that attempts to maximize the pleasure of mountain climbing for future generations of climbers only because it minimizes the harm caused to the mountain. A denial of cooperative strategies is to gainsay that we act with a recognition of consequences. It is, in short, a denial that we are rational *only* in the terms of self-interest.

When Rules Evolve

"The Tragedy of the Commons" has come to serve as a paradigm for situations in which rules are required to ensure cooperation.[39] Common pasture in an English or Colonial New England village was not only common property of the villagers but was also unrestrainedly available to their animals. The more cattle (or sheep or whatever) that were put to graze on the common, the less forage there was for each animal, and more of it got trampled, but as long as there was any profit in grazing their animals on the common, villagers were motivated to do so. Unlike the game of prisoner's dilemma, cooperation does not come naturally as people have no reason to curb their own interests. Collectively they might be better off if they could be restrained, but no one gains individually by self-restraint.

The Tragedy of the Commons provides a textbook illustration of problems that cannot be resolved without a resort to rules and constraints for cooperation. We assume that in the New England town meeting the commons problem was resolved amiably. And, in fact, in some New England towns, including Boston, the commons is now held as a public park, a collective good, in spite of the obvious fact that putting the park on the auction block would go far to solving Boston's immediate financial problems. Rules are designed to take into account the untoward consequences of collective actions.

The Tragedy of the Commons may, in retrospect, appear fairly simple because the consequences of overgrazing ought to have appeared quite obvious to the Boston landholders. In the case of modern societies, the cumulative actions of autonomous individual actors have led to toxic dumps, overused water sources, deforestation, a deterioration of the ozone layer, and the kinds of problems, generally, that are not all that immediately obvious. Identifying them is hard enough, and solving them even harder. Schelling concludes by saying that institutional arrangements must be designed to overcome these divergences between individual interests and the larger society. These include market-oriented institutions—contracts, damage suits, copyrights, rental agreements—but most solutions must originate with government—taxes, legal protection of persons, laws, and regulations.[40]

Few of us would have the courage to get into a roller coaster or an airplane unless we knew that there were periodic safety checks. We trust that the governments to whom we pay taxes are engaged in activities such as monitoring the local water supply and enforcing laws about school-building safety. Deregulation of the marketplace might have some fiscal advantages, but many experts are alarmed about the social consequences.

It is not even clear that regulation and monitoring introduce inefficiencies *given the complexity of our economic order* and, indeed, it is argued by Douglass North that formal economic control may enhance efficiencies because rules and third-party enforcement reveal otherwise unknowns.[41] Let us say that in the absence of regulations and monitoring, Firm A dumps its steel shavings into the city dump, whereas Firm B has devised an efficient and profitable solution by selling its steel shavings to a microchip firm. Third-party monitoring helps Firm A's efficiency by proposing this solution, to say nothing about the public welfare.

But North goes further than this. There are many realms, such as the residential housing market, where without rules—laws involving banks, zoning, realtors, insurance companies—the market would be highly inefficient, and prices would be higher than they are. And, generally without a matrix of rules, markets are insufficiently stable, even though problems of social justice are ignored.

These considerations raise interesting problems for the privatization of public services. The growth of the nonprofit sector has been analyzed as a case of market failure, namely that nonprofits take over as service providers when there is much asymmetry in information or when proprietary interests lead profit-making firms to take advantage of clients.[42] This helps to explain the predominance of nonprofit organizations in many service sectors, such as day-care centers, hospitals, social welfare, and charitable activities. In other areas, we also rely on the nonprofit sector. For example, when we shop around for a nursery school or a university, we rely on accrediting agencies to do much of the information gathering for us.

But increasingly, public-sector services are being transferred not only to the nonprofit, voluntary sector but also to the for-profit sector. This may have some beneficial consequences. It revitalizes local responsibilities as it encourages citizens and firms to take an active role in the problems in their own communities. Corporations are encouraged to have day-care centers and fund local parks, and existing nonprofit service organizations are assuming increasing responsibilities for a wide range of programs. But there are serious problems of accountability, efficiency, and coordination. In the long run, some affluent places will secure far better services for their communities, whereas poor places will lose services. An equally serious problem is that services will be run to promote private interests. It is inevitable when a public-school system is taken over by a university, a fairly benign institution, that university interests—for teaching and research—will preempt the interests of the local community, as education is a public good that is incompatible with university free-riding.

In the example of the commons, it is supposed that every citizen of Boston has one cow. The result of our unregulated economy is that a few have very many cows, and some have none at all. Government regulations, especially our tax laws, housing policies, and unemployment provisions, have augmented inequalities. By doing so, they have drastically altered the consequences of an efficiency calculus that those who work hard have access to opportunities. Although the right to education is deemed just, education does not produce just deserts. Dire predictions will be made about an economy in which there is increasing stagnation of unequal advantage over time. The theoretical and empirical work on justice shows that there is a social consensus that being underpaid is far more outrageous than being overpaid. The calculus of social justice actually does work on the bottom of the social and economic scale, and one supposes it does so because we perceive the consequences of inequality, and the legitimacy of claimants who are owed justice, yet fail to be counted. But an aggregate of citizens does not directly create economic inequalities. Economic actors and political actors, in the aggregate, do.

Social Contracts and Externalities

Industrializing societies simultaneously broadcast rights and interdependencies. Many economic activities create by-products that have notably serious consequences because of social, political, and economic interdependencies. Such interdependencies are not governed by the rules of the market. Some social scientists place a great deal of emphasis on choice.[43] But *choice* is not the word that comes to mind for people who have a foul-smelling smokestack in their neighborhood, are employees of a company in which the managers decide to substitute part-time for full-time workers, are those who placed their savings in a bank that closes, or are homeowners near a new development that creates traffic problems and increases property taxes. There are growing interdependencies between economic producers and the public, who has to bear the costs of producers' externalities. These problems originate because externalities lie beyond market control, but they are insidious owing to the fact that the public is handicapped by lack of information and constraints on choice.

It was in the context of expanding opportunities that the Keynesian welfare state evolved to broaden political and social rights. But the welfare state differed significantly between the United States and Western European nations. The United States was generous with its public education programs and tight-fisted about other social allowances and its economic programs. With few exceptions, social and economic programs were based on the assumption of prosperity and increasing opportunities. It was assumed that short-term unemployment benefits would be satisfactory, that rent controls would ensure housing for the poorest urban households, and that private employers along with public subsidies would cover health-care costs. The 1970s reversed the conditions on which this social contract was based. Moreover, after the

1970s, the rules that curbed the excesses of the market began to deteriorate. Deregulation and corporate refinancing through tax breaks, combined with the withdrawal of federal funds from public housing, public transportation, and early schooling, exacerbated the effects of the deteriorating economy.

The greatest danger to the civic order would be the confounding of growing economic inequalities with basic human rights, such as liberty, self-determination, and welfare. When people prioritize marketlike choices, putting personal economic well-being first, which is tempting in a highly competitive and downwardly spiraling economy, interventionist strategies are all the more important. I contend that it is possible—desirable—to limit the individual's and community's maximization of goods (wealth, property, resources) with the conception that preserving rights—welfare, education, health, liberty—may be jeopardized under the conditions of competition over finite goods. This is consistent with the idea that basic rights are bestowed on individuals qua individuals, but are meaningfully defined and shaped by virtue of initial advantage and disadvantage individuals have as a result of group memberships. And, to paraphrase Isaiah Berlin, the extent to which a group is allowed to have great wealth and power must be weighed against the claims of many other values, such as equality, or justice, or security, or public order.[44]

NOTES

1. Thomas Jefferson, Letter to Robert Skipwith (August 3, 1771), p. 77 in Julian P. Boyd et al., *The Papers of Thomas Jefferson. Vol. 1*. Princeton: Princeton University Press, 1950–74.
2. Oliver Wendell Holmes, *The Common Law*. Boston: Little, Brown, 1881, p. 110.
3. Robert Louis Stevenson, *A Christmas Sermon*. London: Chatto & Windus, 1908, p. 19.
4. *The Education of Henry Adams: An Autobiography*. Boston: Houghton Mifflin, 1918, p. 335.
5. Quoted in Sanford Lyman, *The Seven Deadly Sins*. New York: St. Martin's Press, 1978, p. 75.
6. *The Writings of William James*. Ed. John J. McDermott. Chicago: University of Chicago Press, 1977, p. 623.
7. See Morton White, *Social Thought in America*. Rev. ed. Boston: Beacon Press, 1952, pp. 145–146.
8. John Dewey, "The Need for a Recovery of Philosophy," pp. 3–70 in J. Dewey, A. W. Moore, H. C. Brown, G. H. Mead, B. H. Bode, H. W. Stuart, J. H.

Tufts, and H. M. Kallen, *Creative Intelligence: Essays in the Pragmatic Attitude*. New York: Holt, 1917, pp. 63–64.

9. Gary S. Becker, *The Economic Approach to Human Behavior*. Chicago: University of Chicago Press, 1976.

10. Adam Smith, *The Theory of Moral Sentiments*. Eds. D. D. Raphael and A. L. Macfie. Oxford: Clarendon Press, 1976.

11. Ibid., pp. 113–114.

12. Émile Durkheim, *The Rules of Sociological Method*. Trans. Sarah A. Soloway and John H. Mueller. Ed. George E. G. Catlin. New York: Macmillan, 1938, pp. 65–73.

13. P. W. Musgrave, *Socializing Contexts*. Sydney: Allen & Unwin, 1987.

14. John Anouilh, *Antigone*. Adapted by Lewis Galantiere. New York: Samuel French, 1947.

15. The term comes from a classic essay by Dennis Wrong. See his "The Oversocialized View of Man," *American Sociological Review* 26 (1961): 183–193.

16. Stanley Milgram, *Obedience to Authority*. New York: Harper & Row, 1974.

17. Isaiah Berlin, *Four Essays on Liberty*. Oxford: Oxford University Press, 1969, p. lvi.

18. William A. Gamson, Bruce Fireman, and Steven Rytina, *Encounters with Unjust Authority*. Chicago: Dorsey Press, 1982, p. 14.

19. Lewis A. Coser, *Greedy Institutions*. New York: Free Press, 1956.

20. Georg Simmel, "The Metropolis and Mental Life." In Kurt Wolff (ed. and trans.), *The Sociology of Georg Simmel*. Glencoe, IL: Free Press, 1950, pp. 402–408.

21. Paul Lehmann, *Ethics in a Christian Society*. New York: Harper & Row, 1963.

22. This distinction between morals and ethics that I am making is not one that Plato or Aristotle would have recognized. In classical Greek, *ethike* meant the art and study of moral character, and *moralis* is the Latin translation of the Greek, ethical. For my purposes, Paul Lehmann's modern distinction is a helpful and even necessary one. I am grateful to Professor George A. Kennedy for helping me to clarify this etymological difficulty.

23. John Rawls, *A Theory of Justice*. Cambridge: Harvard University Press, 1971, p. 75.

24. Ibid., p. 511.

25. Ibid., p. 101.

26. Alan Wolfe, *Whose Keeper? Social Science and Moral Obligation*. Berkeley: University of California Press, 1989.

27. Guillermina Jasso, "A New Theory of Distributive Justice," *American Sociological Review* 45 (February 1980): 3–30.

28. Rawls, op. cit., p. 73.

29. Douglas Rae, *Equalities*. Cambridge: Harvard University Press, 1981, p. 73.

30. Wolfe, op. cit., pp. 239–241.

31. Albert O. Hirschman, *Exit, Voice, and Loyalty: Responses to Decline in Firms, Organizations, and States*. Cambridge: Harvard University Press, 1970.

32. Ibid., p. 33.
33. The question of whether people cooperate or tend to maximize their own outcomes has led to a sizable industry. Amaitai Etzioni estimates that there are over 1,000 studies involving the experiment. See *The Moral Dimension*. New York: Free Press, 1988, p. 60.
34. This is Gellner's twist on the game; see Ernest Gellner, *Plough, Sword and Book*. London: Collins Harvill, 1988, pp. 251–252.
35. Ibid.
36. Thomas C. Schelling, *Micromotives and Macrobehavior*. New York: W. W. Norton, 1978.
37. Amartya Sen, *On Ethics and Economics*. Oxford: Basil Blackwood, 1987.
38. Ibid., p. 85.
39. Schelling, op. cit.
40. Ibid.
41. Douglass C. North, *Institutions, Institutional Change and Economic Performance*. Cambridge: Cambridge University Press, 1990, pp. 52–53.
42. Kenneth Arrow, "Uncertainty and the Welfare Economics of Medical Care," *American Economic Review* 53 (1963): 941–973.
43. Milton Friedman and Rose Friedman, *Capitalism and Freedom*. Chicago: University of Chicago Press, 1973; James S. Coleman, *Foundations of Social Theory*. Cambridge: Harvard University Press, 1990.
44. Berlin, op. cit., p. 170.

11

Rights, Goods, and Welfare

The poor can stop being poor if the rich are willing to become richer at a slower rate.
                                                                —MARTIN LUTHER KING, JR.

Where I live [Brooklyn] some Jews are black, and some blacks are Muslims; some whites are Italian and some whites are Muslims. So nobody cares. What's the big deal?
                                        —Personal comment, New York City taxi cab driver

In the last chapters I have suggested that there is a serious problem of confusing a utilitarian calculus of individual human welfare with a theory of rights. Although this argument can extend into very difficult philosophical arguments, I simply want to suggest that a comprehensive view of human rights and community welfare is inconsistent with the right of individuals to amass great wealth, thereby greatly increasing economic inequalities.

When people prioritize market choices over rights, putting personal economic well-being first—which is tempting in a highly competitive and downwardly spiraling economy—I have argued that it places great strain on civicness and civility. Under conditions of nonrestraint, moreover, the Hobbesian utilitarian axiom—people exercise rights to pursue their self-interest to the hilt—seems to be a matter of daily fare.

In contrast with the ease with which utility can be defined—what people wish to maximize—the concept of rights is excruciatingly difficult to define. We can locate utility in the individual actor, but any definition of rights must take into account a social, economic, and legal context. It could be said that Robinson Crusoe had his own utilities, but he had no rights.

Because rights are argued in the pages of virtually every discipline's major journals, including those in jurisprudence, theology, the social sciences, and philosophy, and provide lively topics of discussion in elementary school classrooms and community meetings, we are not sure whether or not we agree on what they are. It can be minimally argued that the Bill of Rights offers a good starting point for an initial definition of legal rights. Thus, we have freedom of speech, of assembly, of due process; guarantees against cruel and unusual punishment; protection from unlawful search and seizure; and laws against discrimination.

Such rights protect the individual against authority and the state but do not address welfare rights. I will argue that in addition to these there are other basic rights, such as those related to education, decent housing, and health, which must be minimally guaranteed in a society that is interested in human welfare. In the technical literature, the line between individual rights (liberties or civil rights), public or collective rights (indivisible benefits, such as clean air), and positive rights (a divisible benefit, such as an educational subsidy) is elusive at best. A case can be made that these categories are somewhat outdated as each category is defined in terms of the individual or an undifferentiated aggregate of individuals, and fail to take into account attributes of individuals.

Michael Freedan's work on rights is helpful as he considers the way that individuals can be given special rights according to given attributes and group membership. These rights are flexible and can be accorded permanently or temporarily according to policy.[1] His wonderfully obvious examples—children, the aged, the handicapped, women, minorities— make it ever so clear that we do, in fact, practice many "rights-conferral" practices without evoking the technical definitions of individual rights, private rights, and collective rights. We think of them in terms of legislated provisions, rather than in the terms of a broader philosophy of rights. However, by stressing the group-based nature of rights, Freedan helps to overcome some of the difficulties inherent in the literature on individual rights (such as trust, accountability, and free-riding).

This is a useful start. Group rights, like individual rights and collective rights, are rather like problems on the demand side of the equation. To put it awkwardly, what about the supply of rights? How can we consider criteria for programs to enhance group rights? Who pays? What is subsidized? When we flip the rights problem on its head, we can rather talk about "goods" and their supply.

PROTECTION OF SOCIAL GOODS

In a recent article, economist William J. Baumol confronts the issue of subsidization to affect supply of goods.[2] The purpose of his argument is not especially to define individual or group rights but rather to distinguish between sectors of the economy. However, I find his argument especially useful for the purpose of an analytical exercise about the supply side of rights, or goods. Baumol contrasts the productive sector of the economy (the sector that makes profit and pays for its own future) with the nonproductive sector that cannot possibly foot its own bills. He discusses stagnant social services, growing needs and costs for medical care and legal services, and the declines in education and in postal, police, and sanitation services. He also includes "repair services, the performing arts, restaurants," and by implication, other service industries, such as baseball, museums, airplane travel, and psychotherapy. His point is that services (unlike production activities) are hard to standardize and are not productive and profitable. This contrasts with, say, making automobiles and shoes. Therefore, Baumol argues that this is the reason that components of the service sector all share symptoms of decline and require economic subsidies. If, say, education were to continue growing at its current rate, 2.9% per year, for the next 50 years, expenditure on education would rise from less than 7% of current GDP to 29% of the GDP. Baumol advocates raising taxes to pay for services that are inherently labor-intensive, hard to standardize, and, unlike activities in the nonservice sector, do not reap productivity gains.

We do not have to be economists to appreciate the fact that providing children with immunization shots, teaching geometry, and cleaning the city streets do not reap a return on investment in the same way that producing automobiles or making detergent does. There are several possible extensions to Baumol's arguments. I contend that he confounds three types of goods: collective goods, private goods, and group goods. (Note, again, that I have explicitly changed the language here from "rights" to "goods," as the topic is supply, not demand.)

Postal services, street repair, and clean air and water are indivisible public goods, and most people would agree that they should be supported by taxes and public subsidies. Health, education, and housing are not public goods in the classic sense of the term but are arguably basic human rights and lie within an expanded definition of public goods.[3] In a broad sense, they can be defined as inalienable rights to the extent that only by ensuring them do we maintain the general welfare and preservation of the society. In a very pragmatic sense, when individuals are denied health and access to education and housing, they are unable to contribute to the future productivity of the society.

Here the notion of rights and goods is confounded in a provocative and important way. Let us take the example of education. Already Americans and their legislators treat elementary and high-school education as a right and a good. If we were to consider that particular categories of youngsters, such as minorities and rural children, are especially needy in terms of educational subsidies, we could further distinguish between group rights and individual rights (and from the suppliers' viewpoint, group goods and individual goods). This suggests that education should be subsidized for everyone, but that for particular groups it should be subsidized at higher levels.

The final category of supportable goods to which Baumol refers are those that are both divisible and, arguably, nonpublic. These include the performing arts, restaurants, and automobile repair services. Here the distinction between rights and goods, in my opinion, breaks down. Although Baumol is correct to conclude that the price of all services will continue to increase, it is arguable that there are some services whose costs should be borne mostly by those who use them and other services whose costs must be borne by society as a whole.

To the extent that only the rich currently use some of these services, it makes sense to scrutinize what we mean by public goods (clean water and roads, perhaps—but what about airplanes and museums?) and what might be defined as rights that can be construed as in the public interest (education and health). What is left are those "unproductive services" for which costs will rise unless they are subsidized, such as restaurants and repair services, which are neither goods nor rights. The rich can move to the affluent suburbs and choose to pay (or free-ride) for good schools, clean streets, and the best medical care. My conclusion is that both public and group goods are increasingly contracting in the United States—both in terms of economic support and as social constructions. Inequalites in what I term *goods* and *rights* are beginning to mirror the inordinate inequalities of private income and wealth.

THE CIVICS OF COOPERATION

Of late, political and policy decisions have not especially enhanced the basis of a cooperative society. How does a civic society still maintain itself? It can be argued that there are social foundations that are fairly robust. The clue lies in a remark made to me by a Brooklyn taxi cab driver in New York. I quoted him at the beginning of this chapter, but it bears repeating:

> Where I live [Brooklyn] some Jews are black, and some blacks are Muslims; some whites are Italian and some whites are Muslims. So nobody cares. What's the big deal?

The expansion of the public sphere means that people participate in a web of overlapping social circles.[4] What does this mean in the daily rounds of one's life? It means, for example, that many American elementary schools are likely to have students who are native-born, African-American, Asian, and South American. It also means that in a medium-sized city it is possible to find Hungarian goulash, Tunisian couscous (eat in, take out), Greek dolmas, and a great variety of Chinese provincial cuisines. These examples are trivial, but they reflect in detail the extent to which we are a multicultural and multiethnic society, a society in which neighbors, friends, acquaintances, and in-laws come from different ethnic groups, work in different occupations, and have different life experiences.[5] Moreover, the expansion of education has simultaneously created a meeting ground on which collective interests can be defined.

According to Habermas, the expansion of the public sphere means the increasing power of organized interests and a decline in the autonomy of private interests.[6] But it is argued here that the public sphere is instead a complex set of overlapping groups in terms of which "mass social interests" can be defined on the basis of an understanding of the consequences of interdependence and reciprocity. Mass social interests counterbalance markets in which the consequences of collective social actions are at stake. A component of "massification" is the increasing inclusivity of what is "public" and a recognition of the differences on which social interests depend. Thus, a public presupposes equality, and a multiplicity of social roles presupposes differences. This is not, in fact, a contradiction, but an historical reality.

In the United States, we all originated from elsewhere, and it is generally ceded that most of us have fairly lowly origins, and relative to our origins we have not done so badly. Our social order rests on notions that opportunities have mattered historically and should continue to matter into the future.

The complexity of the social order also means that each individual is involved in multiple groups that intersect in unusual ways. We may have a neighbor who is a virtual hermit and quite eccentric, but is a well-known author. Another neighbor may be president of the local "right to bear arms club" and also founded the city's soup kitchen. The office janitor is an amateur and promising choreographer. A friend, the president of a chemical company, is president of the local Socialist Party. In fact, some Jews are black, and some blacks become Jews. The ramifications of this admixture are quite important. First of all, we suspend judgment and tend to assume a social equality in our day-to-day dealings with people, which is a recognition of the multiplicity of social positions that people have. Second, owing to the ambiguity of people's status, and therefore, ambiguity of vested interests, our initial encounters are based on trust, rather than suspicion. Because in interest politics and in moral debates we find ourselves squared off against people with whom we are allies on other issues, conflict tends to be muted. Third, in games of status, it does not work to play one-dimensional one-upmanship; cultural capital is not all that convertible into a single currency.

A component of this diversity must be the recognition that beyond mild proselytizing the imposition of personal beliefs (that is, moral beliefs) on others is not civil. For this reason, proselytizing has been ritualized historically and has its own local ecology—the college campus steps, the town square, the village commons. It would jeopardize the social order if that line, however vague, between in-group morality and broadly articulated ethical values was to be eradicated.

SUMMARY

In the real world, markets and social organization are confounded. Firms internalize labor markets, and within firms labor is sold and purchased, and yet, at the same time, cooperative arrangements evolve that transcend individual self-interests in their narrowest sense. Cooperation even develops outside firms in pure market situations when participants recognize that the rational pursuit of self-interest will undermine collective interests. And I have argued not only that, in our social arrangements, we are extraordinarily rational, but that people are locked into such a myriad of social relations that we act on the multiple ramifications of the consequences of the pursuit of self-interest and the recognition of interdependencies. Thus, social relations bear slight resemblance to economic markets. Civility is a consequence of social complexity, and, more precisely, of the ambiguities of social standing in a multiply differentiated social order.

I have tried to make a case that whereas markets and social life are empirically difficult to distinguish, the analytical difference is important for assessing the limits of economic principles to social realms. I have attempted to trace the following problems: (1) how the internalization of capital markets by firms leads to vicious competition; (2) that severe social dislocations occur when economic realities do not mesh with economic opportunities; (3) how the history of changes in economic opportunities has unfairly disadvantaged some groups; (4) how the public is increasingly vulnerable to producers' externalities in a deregulated economy; and (5) the possibilities of free-riding with the privatization of services. These problems illustrate that major social problems cannot be tackled without understanding their economic roots.

I have tried to distinguish between ethics and morals, which has bearing on distinguishing rights and goods at the individual, group, and collective levels. There are three objectives here. The first is to argue that complex social and economic arrangements affect distributions of rights. Likewise, the provision of goods must address issues of redress and special group needs; these are ethical problems that bear on public policy. The second is to suggest that there is a distinction between morals of homogeneous groups, and ethics, which are rooted in people's recognition of difference and interdependence. In microworlds of family and close friendships, our unpartialled commitment leads to demands for conformity and loyalty, and, indeed, moral codes provide a matrix of belonging and a symbol of allegiance.

In macroworlds in which there are complex interdependencies and partialled roles, the normative framework is defined in terms of positive externalities, for without this minimal criterion there would be no interdependence and, therefore, no society. Finally, a conception of society that depends for its well-being on complexity and interdependence must consider how public, indivisible rights, as well as group and individual rights, are all different in degree and in kind from the rights of individuals to pursue their own narrow self-interests.

Notes

1. Michael Freedan, *Rights*. Minneapolis: University of Minnesota Press, 1991.
2. William J. Baumol, "A Growing Economy Can Pay Its Bills," *The Wall Street Journal* (May 19, 1992).

3. See L. J. MacFarlane, *The Theory and Practice of Human Rights*. Hounslow: Temple Smith, 1985.
4. Georg Simmel, *Conflict and the Web of Group Affiliations*. Trans. Kurt H. Wolff and Reinhard Bendix. Foreword by Everett C. Hughes. Glencoe, IL: Free Press, 1955, pp. 140–141.
5. Peter M. Blau, *Inequality and Heterogeneity*. New York: Free Press, 1977, pp. 77–100.
6. Jürgen Habermas, *The Structural Transformation of the Public Sphere*. Trans. Thomas Burger with Frederick Lawrence. Cambridge: MIT Press, 1989.

Bibliographic Essay

Overview

In the last decade of the twentieth century, social scientists are attempting to take stock of how completely different the United States is now compared with itself at midcentury. Changes in the economy, the political culture, and core institutions—notably the family and work organizations—have profoundly altered people's ordinary lives and people's perceptions of what a good life is, and, indeed, what a good society is. A set of perspectives on this issue is provocatively developed in a book of essays that I had not read when I wrote this book: Alan Wolfe, *America at Century's End* (Berkeley: University of California Press, 1991). I highly recommend it.

The following books helped me to shape the arguments owing to their broad scope and provocative open-endedness: Ernest Gellner, *Plough, Sword, and Book* (London: Collins Harvil, 1988); David Harvey, *The Condition of Postmodernity* (Oxford: Basil Blackwood, 1989); Charles E. Lindblom, *Politics and Markets* (New York: Basic Books, 1977); Douglass C. North, *Institutions, Institutional Change and Economic Performance* (Cambridge: Cambridge University Press, 1990); and Karl Polanyi, *The Great Transformation* (New York: Rinehart, 1957).

My efforts to develop a microdynamic model of mapping and a contextual model of opportunity structures are influenced by Robert K. Merton's many works (e.g., *Social Theory and Social Structure* [New York: The Free Press, 1968]). If one is attempting to sort out issues about cooperation in complex societies, the following are helpful: Georg Simmel, *Conflict and the Web of Group Affiliations*, trans. by Kurt H. Wolff and Reinhard Bendix (New York: The Free Press, 1956); and Rose Laub

197

Coser, *In Defense of Modernity* (Stanford: Stanford University Press, 1991).

The underlying epistemological debates about the distinguishability of knower and known, reflexivity, explanation, and interpretation are widely scattered. Very different views are discussed in the following: E. P. Thompson (ed.), *The Poverty of Theory and Other Essays* (New York: Monthly Review Press, 1984); Margaret S. Archer, *Culture and Agency* (Cambridge: Cambridge University Press, 1988); Jeffrey C. Alexander, *Positivism, Presuppositions, and Current Controversies* (Berkeley: University of California Press, 1982); and Walter Wallace, *Principles of Scientific Sociology* (Chicago: Aldine, 1983).

I often refer to a tradition in sociology that is taken for granted by those who have had a basic course in social theory. For clear introductions to the works of classical sociological theorists, see Lewis Coser, *Masters of Sociological Thought* (New York: Harcourt Brace Jovanovich, 1971); T. B. Bottomore, *Karl Marx: Selected Writings in Sociology and Social Philosophy* (New York: McGraw-Hill, 1964); and Jonathan H. Turner, *The Structure of Sociological Theory* (Belmont, CA: Wadsworth, 1991).

The contemporary debates in the humanities and in literary theory are playing an increasingly important role in the social sciences. This is a vast and growing literature. A recent analysis is provided by Frederick Crews, *The Critics Bear It Away* (New York: Random House, 1992), and a collection that places these issues in the context of higher education is Darryl J. Gless and Barbara Hernstein Smith, *The Politics of Liberal Education* (Durham: Duke University Press, 1992).

As there is always a temptation to "fall into culture" in these debates and loose one's moorings as a sociologist, Raymond Williams's works always offer a useful reminder that there is an analytical distinction between society and culture (for example, *Problems in Materialism and Culture* [London: Verso, 1980]).

1. Reflexivity and Social Science

Of the vast collection of problems pertaining to the issue of rationality, perhaps the most interesting one deals with its locus. For some theorists, it is lodged in society and culture (for example, Max Weber, *The Theory of Social and Economic Organization* [New York: The Free Press, 1949]). For others it is a property of a system of interlocking groups and individuals who can provide incentives, rewards, and punishments (see Mancur Olsen, *The Logic of Collective Action* [Cambridge: Harvard University Press, 1965]). For others, the locus is the individual actor (for example, James S. Coleman, *Individual Interests and Collective Action* [New York: Cambridge University Press, 1986]). Alternatively, rationality is derived from institutions (see Émile Durkheim, *Rules of Sociological Method* [New York: The Free Press, 1953]). My own definition of rationality stresses the importance of individuals' multiple affiliations and the varieties of people's risk sets, opportunities, and rewards. I have benefited from the work of Jon Elster (*Nuts and Bolts for the Social Sciences* [Cambridge: Cambridge University Press, 1989]) and a book by Harold I. Brown (*Rationality* [London: Routledge, 1988]). An overview of functionalism in American sociology can be found in Arthur L. Stinchcombe, *Constructuring Social Theories* (New York: Harcourt, Brace & World, 1968). Talcott Parsons, the main theorist in this tradition, is difficult to read, but an important introduction can be found in Kingsley Davis, *Human Society* (New York: Macmillan, 1949). For an interesting contrasting view, an important sociological classic is C. Wright Mills, *The Sociological Imagination* (Oxford: Oxford University Press, 1959).

The current debate about postmodernism and what it means historically and in theory makes it difficult for anyone to definitely and concisely define it. Most of this literature is situated in cultural sociology and is influenced by French literary theory (for example, Jean-François Lyotard, *The Postmodern Condition* [Minneapolis: University of Minnesota Press, 1984] and Roland Barthes, *Criticism and Truth* [Minneapolis: University of Minnesota Press, 1987]).

I attempt to distinguish postmodern from postmodernism (or deconstructionism). By "postmodern conditions," I have relied on David Harvey, *The Condition of Postmodernity* (Oxford: Basil Blackwood, 1989). A useful discussion for sociologists that relates postmodernism to sociological theory can be found in Ben Agger, "Critical Theory, Poststructuralism, Postmodernism" (*Annual Review of Sociology* 17 [1991]: 105–131). A clear set of papers that deal with postmodernism in the arts and humanities is found in chapters in Stanley Trachtenberg (ed.), *The Postmodern Moment* (Westport, CT: Greenwood Press, 1985). More difficult materials are covered in Rosalind E. Krauss, *The Originality of the Avant-Garde and Other Modernist Myths* (Cambridge: MIT Press, 1986), and Andreas Huyssen, *After the Great Divide* (Bloomington: Indiana University Press, 1986). (The latter has an important discussion of identity and historical memory.) In sociology, the classic work is Daniel Bell, *The Coming of Post-Industrial Society* (New York: Basic Books, 1973), as he anticipated the subsequent changes in the labor force and communications technology.

2. TUMBLING TOWARD TWO THOUSAND

Irving Zeitlin's *Ideology and the Development of Sociological Theory* (Englewood Cliffs, NJ: Prentice-Hall, 1987) provides an overview of social thought from the Enlightenment through the early nineteenth century. Alfred Cobban's *In Search of Humanity* (New York: Braziller, 1960) and Tzvetan Tudobov, *The Deflection of the Enlightenment* (Stanford: Stanford Humanities Center, 1989) are cited in the text. A polemical and classical account of the self-destructiveness of the Enlightenment is Max Horkheimer and Theodor W. Adorno, *Dialectic of Enlightenment* (New York: Continuum [1944] 1991).

For an account of contract theory in the American context, see Alan Pendleton Grimes, *American Political Thought* (New York: Holt, 1955). Rousseau's arguments are not simple; whereas my argument stresses the importance of individual liberty and the sovereignty of the people, his works have also been interpreted as a justification of authoritarian rule. This is because Rousseau's political doctrines do not allow for a balance of power or multiple centers of power (see Robert Derathe, "Jean-Jacques Rousseau," *International Encyclopedia of the Social Sciences* 13: 563–578 (New York: Macmillan & The Free Press [1968]). Regardless of the problem for political theory, from a sociological perspective, Rousseau's work makes it possible to reconsider social exchange theory without a strong rationality assumption. Central to the social contract is an emphasis on equality and the intrinsic value of social relations. This is the connection between Marx's "use value" and the "social contract."

3. COMPETITION AND COOPERATION

New institutional economics has shifted the focus away from efficiency and competition to cooperation and, thus, allows the possibility of a normative context. Richard Sedberg and Mark Granovetter clarify why what is "economic" and what is "social" must not be separated (*The Sociology of Economic Life* [Boulder: Westview Press, 1992]). Another way in which a survival-competition model (Michael T. Hannan and John Freeman, *Organizational Sociology* [Cambridge: Harvard University Press, 1989]) is being joined with understanding of the institutionalization of political and religious ideologies can be found in Robert Wuthnow, *Meaning and Moral Order* (Berkeley: University of California Press, 1987).

Mass-society theory is briefly mentioned in this chapter, in which I refer to the works of LeBon, Michels, Mosca, and Pareto. Representative of mass-society theory in U.S. social sciences are Bernard Rosenberg and David Manning White (eds.), *Mass Culture* (Glencoe, IL: Free Press, 1957), and William Kornhauser, *The Politics of Mass Society* (Glencoe, IL: Free Press, 1959).

Supplementing the materials covered in this chapter would be literature on political movements and the social transmission of ideas, and the context of ideological formation. The following are illustrative: E. J. Hobsbawn, *Primitive Rebels* (New York: Norton, 1959); Doug McAdam, *Political Process and the Development of Black Insurgency, 1930–1970* (Chicago: University of Chicago Press, 1982); William A. Gamson, *The Strategy of Social Protest* (Homewood, IL: Dorsey, 1975); David Knoke, *Political Networks* (Cambridge: Cambridge University Press, 1990); and Charles Tilly, *From Mobilization to Revolution* (Reading: Addison-Wesley, 1978).

Informing the literature on social movements (and also social cooperation) is work on social networks. See Ronald S. Burt, *Toward a Structural Theory of Action* (New York: Academic Press, 1982). An earlier and more accessible book is Jeremy Boissevain, *Friends of Friends* (London: Basil Blackwell, 1974), and for substantive application of network methodologies, see Claude S. Fischer et al., *Networks and Places* (New York: Free Press, 1977).

My discussion of mapping recenters attention on agency and stresses the over-time and contemporaneous contexts of agency. This I want to contrast with "structuration" or routinized and recursive practices (Anthony Giddens, *Central Problems in Social Theory* [Berkeley: University of California Press, 1979]). Social exchange theory also informs my discussion of mapping. Representative works include George C. Homans, *Social Behavior* (New York: Harcourt Brace Jovanovich, 1961); Peter M. Blau, *Exchange and Power in Social Life* (New York: Wiley, 1964); and Karen S. Cook (ed.), *Social Exchange Theory* (Newbury Park, CA: Sage, 1987).

Interest in redesigning organizations to increase participation and cooperation among workers and managers began in the 1970s with Rosabeth Moss Kanter's *Men and Women of the Corporation* (New York: Basic Books, 1977). Other classics include Joyce Rothschild-Whitt, "The Collectivist Organization" (*American Sociological Review* 44 (1979): 509–527), and Paul Blumberg, *Industrial Democracy* (New York: Schocken Books, 1968). The subtle ways in which management is successful in domination strategies are explored in Michael Burawoy, *Manufacturing Consent* (Chicago: University of Chicago Press, 1979).

4. THE CIVILITY OF ORDINARY LIFE

An understanding of the development of microconventions and the way they shape participation is developed in symbolic interaction theory, ethnomethodology, and dramaturgical theory. I am drawing attention to the importance of conventions that individuals use and that help to sustain interaction. For a fine overview, see Jonathan Turner, *The Structure of Sociological Theory*, rev. ed. (Belmont, CA: Wadsworth, 1978, Part II). An early classic perspective on interactionism is George Herbert Mead, *Mind, Self, and Society*, edited by C. W. Morris (Chicago: University of Chicago Press, 1934). Herbert Blumer is considered to be Mead's successor (see Blumer, *Symbolic Interactionism* [Englewood Cliffs, NJ: Prentice-Hall, 1969]). Erving Goffman's works are especially helpful, as he draws attention to the role of signs, or semiotic codes, in interaction (see his *The Presentation of Self in Everyday Life* [Garden City, NY: Anchor Books, 1959]).

Although Suzanne K. Langer introduced symbolic analyses to American readers in 1942 (*Philosophy in a New Key*. Cambridge: Harvard University Press), anthropologists have been more influenced by this approach than sociologists. See, for example, Mary Douglas, *Natural Symbols* (New York: Pantheon, 1982). Imaginative papers by sociologists include Eviatar Zerubavel, "The French Republican Calendar" (*American Sociological Review* 42 [1977]: 868–877) and Stephen R. Barley, "Semiotics and the Study of Occupational and Organizational Cultures" (*Administrative Science Quarterly* 28 [1983]: 393–413).

There are a number of works that deal with efficiency in organizational settings. Two texts are W. Richard Scott, *Organizations: Rational, Natural and Open Systems* (Englewood Cliffs, NJ: Prentice-Hall, 1981) and Charles Perrow, *Complex Organizations* (New York: Random House, 1986). A more elementary introduction is Peter M. Blau and Marshall W. Meyer, *Bureaucracy in Modern Society* (New York: Random House, 1987). Controversies about authority are clearly reviewed in Jeffrey Pfeffer, *Power in Organizations* (Marshfield, MA: Pitman, 1981); a more critical analysis of efficiency and power is Dietrich Rueschemeyer, *Power and the Division of Labor* (Stanford: Stanford University Press, 1986).

5. WHENCE COME OPPORTUNITIES?

The idea of opportunities pervades the sociological literature. One emphasis is on how people acquire resources: John D. McCarthy and Mayer N. Zald, "Resource Mobilization and Social Movements" (*Ameri-*

can Journal of Sociology 82 [1977]: 1212–1241). Another emphasis is on how opportunities are structured independently of individuals: Peter M. Blau (*Structures of Opportunities*, forthcoming). Another is the idea that opportunities are the self-fulfilling prophecy of individuals' current places in society. This can be found in Pierre Bourdieu, *Distinction* (Cambridge: Harvard University Press, 1984). Social and cultural history sensitizes the sociologist to the changing context of opportunities. Among the very many enjoyable works I recommend are James Mac-Gregor Burns, *The Workshop of Democracy* (New York: Random House, 1985); Warren I. Susman, *Culture as History* (New York: Random House, 1973); and Lawrence A. Cremin, *American Education: The Metropolitan Experience* (New York: Harper & Row, 1988).

6. ECONOMY, PLACE, AND CULTURE

Supplementing Lefebvre, whom I cite in the text, a fine review of issues regarding space as it is implicated in changes in society, economy, demography, and politics is Janet L. Abu-Lughod, *Changing Cities* (New York: HarperCollins, 1991). An assessment of the world systems perspective that engages the core/periphery argument is Daniel Chirot and Thomas Hall, "World System Theory," *Annual Review of Sociology* 8 (1987): 81–106. A recent review of ecology theory in the context of changing spatial scale is W. Parker Frisbie and John D. Kasarda, "Spatial Process," pp. 629–666 in Neil J. Smelser (ed.), *Handbook of Sociology* (Newbury Park: Sage, 1988). Kevin Lynch's *What Time Is This Place?* (Cambridge: MIT Press, 1972) is a wonderful supplement to the literature on the declining significance of the meaning of space in a global economy; it is useful to read Lynch along with other literature in the planning field, such as Bill Hillier and Julienne Hanson, *The Social Logic of Space* (Cambridge: Cambridge University Press, 1984).

7. THE WHEREWITHAL OF SOCIAL CLASS

Class studies are central to sociology. Supplementing the references, the following provide an array of perspectives on class in American society: Erik Olin Wright, *Class, Crisis and the State* (London: New Left Books, 1978); John Goldthorpe et al., *The Affluent Worker* (Cambridge: Cambridge University Press, 1969); Peter M. Blau and Otis Dudley Duncan, *The American Occupational Structure* (New York: John Wiley, 1967); Melvin Kohn, *Class and Conformity* (Chicago: University of

Chicago Press, 1977); T. B. Bottomore, *Elites and Society* (Harmondsworth: Penguin, 1964); and Thorstein Veblen's classic, *The Theory of the Leisure Class* (New York: Mentor, [1899] 1912). Class and culture are joined in other important classics: E. P. Thompson, *The Making of the Working Class* (New York: Vintage, 1963); William H. Whyte, *The Organization Man* (New York: Simon & Schuster, 1965); and David Halle, *America's Working Man* (Chicago: University of Chicago Press, 1984).

It can be hoped and expected that in the coming year or so there there will be more research on poverty, minorities, and racism. I recommend a thoughtful essay by Bart Landry: "The Enduring Dilemma of Race," pp. 185–207 in Alan Wolfe (ed.), *America at Century's End* (Berkeley: University of California Press, 1991). A strident but scholarly book on the relevance of educational inequalities for understanding racial and class disparities in jobs is Samuel Bowles and Herbert Gintis, *Schooling in Capitalist America* (New York: Basic Books, 1976).

8. THE FIRM AND ITS CONTRADICTIONS

Besides references cited, other analyses of work are Joanne Miller, "Jobs and Work," pp. 327–359 in Neil Smelser (ed.), *Handbook of Sociology* (Newbury Park: Sage, 1988) and R. Hedley, *Making a Living* (New York: HarperCollins, 1992). Other books that center attention on organizations themselves are Richard H. Hall, *Organizations: Structures, Processes and Outcomes* (Englewood Cliffs, NJ: Prentice-Hall, 1987) and Howard E. Aldrich, *Organizations and Environments* (Englewood Cliffs, NJ: Prentice-Hall). A useful way of synthesizing an understanding of markets and structures is Arne L. Kalleberg and Ivar Berg, *Work and Industry* (New York: Plenum Press, 1987). Stewart R. Clegg provides a helpful summary of recent changes in organizations while summarizing various perspectives in organizational theory (*Modern Organizations*. London: Sage, 1990). The argument for cultural embeddedness of organizations can be traced to Paul DiMaggio and Walter Powell, "The Iron Cage Revisited," *American Sociological Review* 48 (1983): 147–160. An overview of interorganizational ties is Joseph Galaskiewicz, *Annual Review of Sociology* 11 (1985): 281–304.

9. WORLDS OF FASHION, LIVES OF LEISURE

Not cited, but essential, is Johan Huizinga, *Homo Ludens: A Study of the Play Element in Culture* (Boston: Beacon, 1955). Two good texts include John R. Kelly, *Leisure* (Englewood Cliffs, NJ: Prentice-Hall, 1982), and Thomas Kando, *Leisure and Popular Culture in Transition* (St. Louis: C.V. Mosby, 1975). An extremely good collection of readings and accompanying discussion is Chandra Mukerji and Michael Schudson, *Rethinking Popular Culture* (Berkeley: University of California Press, 1991). For class discussions, I have also used Ian Chambers, *Popular Culture* (London: Methuen, 1986); Dick Hebdige, *Subculture* (London: Methuen, 1979); and Hal Foster, *Recodings* (Port Townsend: Bay Press, 1985). *Aesthetics Today*, edited by Morris Philipson and Paul J. Gudel (New York: New American Library, 1980), has an offputting title, but is an exceptionally good collection of papers. A more recent compilation is Jeffrey C. Alexander and Steven Seidman, *Culture and Society* (Cambridge: Cambridge University Press, 1990). A literature review on research on art and culture is provided in Judith R. Blau, "Studies of the Arts," *Annual Review of Sociology* 14 (1988): 269–292.

10. The Micrometrics of Morals and the Macrometrics of Ethics

Sociologists attempt to interpret the moral frameworks of people and groups. Max Weber's *The Protestant Ethic and the Spirit of Capitalism* (New York: Scribner's, 1958) is essential reading. Another enduring classic is Alexis de Tocqueville, *Democracy in America* (New York: Vintage, 1954). Contemporary assessments include Robert N. Bellah et al., *Habits of the Heart* (Berkeley: University of California Press, 1985), and Herbert J. Gans, *Middle American Individualism* (New York: The Free Press, 1988).

The ethical premises of major theorists, including Georg Simmel, Karl Marx, and Émile Durkheim, are widely discussed in the literature. See, for example, Lewis A. Coser, *Masters of Sociological Thought* (New York: Harcourt Brace Jovanovich, 1981). My purpose is somewhat different, namely, to develop a critical analysis of ethics and to link ethics to considerations of public policy. One could begin such a project by reading the following: Herbert Marcuse, *One Dimensional Man* (Boston: Beacon, 1963); Antonio Gramsci, *Selections from the Prison Notebooks* (New York: International Publishers, 1971); Jürgen Habermas, *Legitimation Crisis*, trans. by Thomas McCarthy (Boston: Beacon, 1975); Vaclav Havel, *Disturbing the Peace* (New York: Knopf, 1988); T. B. Bottomore, *Sociology as Social Criticism* (London: George Allen & Unwin, 1974); Jean-Paul Sartre, *Existentialism and Humanism* (London: Methuen, 1948); and Barrington Moore, Jr., *Privacy* (Arnouk: M. E. Sharpe, 1984). Needless to say, this is but a smattering, and readers will think of others (for example, Arendt and Fromm).

The distinction I make between morals and ethics is drawn from an argument in theology about the difference between absolutist principles and contextual ethics. One's religious beliefs need not matter to appreciate the importance of H. Richard Niebuhr's discussion, *The Responsible Self* (New York: Harper & Row, 1963) and Nancy J. Duff, *Humanization and the Politics of God: The Kiononia Ethics of Paul Lehmann* (Grand Rapids, MI: William B. Eerdmans, 1992). Duff's book also helps to clarify the role of "difference" in religious communities and the controversies about black and feminist theologies. I should stress that one does not need to have religious commitments to appreciate the philosophical implications of these discussions.

11. Rights, Goods, and Welfare

Public-policy issues are increasingly the focus of American Sociological Association meetings. Some recent presidential addresses that directly engage public-policy issues include James S. Coleman, "The Rational Reconstruction of Society," *American Sociological Review* 58 (1993): 1–15; William Julius Wilson, "Studying Inner-City Social Dislocations," *American Sociological Review* 56 (1991): 1–14; Joan Huber, "Macro-Micro Links in Gender Stratification," *American Sociological Review* 55 (1990): 1–10; and Herbert J. Gans, "Sociology in America: The Discipline and the Public," *American Sociological Review* 54 (1989): 1–16.

In my opinion, further work along these lines must be more broadly informed by economics, law, and scholarship in ethics. When we were happy to be a value-free science, we left public-policy questions to economists, legal scholars, and political scientists, but now venturing into the policy domain, we have a new public responsibility to be more candid about our premises. The reader may not share mine, but I have attempted to be explicit about them.

Index